Star Trek as Myth

Star Trek *as Myth*
Essays on Symbol and Archetype at the Final Frontier

Edited by
MATTHEW WILHELM KAPELL

McFarland & Company, Inc., Publishers
Jefferson, North Carolina, and London

LIBRARY OF CONGRESS CATALOGUING-IN-PUBLICATION DATA

Star Trek as myth : essays on symbol and archetype at the final
   frontier / edited by Matthew Wilhelm Kapell.
       p.   cm.
   Includes bibliographical references and index.

   ISBN 978-0-7864-4724-4

   1. Star Trek television programs — History and criticism.
   2. Myth on television.   I. Kapell, Matthew.
   PN1992.8.S74S7275   2010
   791.45'75 — dc22   2010004827

British Library cataloguing data are available

©2010 Matthew Wilhelm Kapell. All rights reserved

*No part of this book may be reproduced or transmitted in any form
or by any means, electronic or mechanical, including photocopying
or recording, or by any information storage and retrieval system,
without permission in writing from the publisher.*

Cover images ©2010 Shutterstock

Manufactured in the United States of America

*McFarland & Company, Inc., Publishers
   Box 611, Jefferson, North Carolina 28640
       www.mcfarlandpub.com*

As is always the case,
this is for Zoe Blythe,
Starfleet Admiral *and* Jedi Knight,
and
for my sister Barbara,
who encouraged her little brother to read

Acknowledgments

No edited volume is possible without the support of a host of individuals. The contributors to this volume all worked under deadlines that would make Captain Kirk run scared. Nancy Greer acted as the editor's post office in North America. Amy Greer aided much, especially with the graphics (and thanks for the phaser!). This book would not exist without her aid. Thanks must also go to Amy Greer's firm, Closed Loop Marketing, for letting me have her services on those graphics *pro bono*. John Shelton Lawrence and Stephen McVeigh read the introduction and conclusion and made both immeasurably better. Stephen McVeigh also added his own chapter after the release of the newest *Star Trek* film, showing once again that he's both smart *and* fast. At the *Journal of Popular Culture*, Jen DeFore was a professional delight in helping with connections for reprint rights. Felicia Campbell, of the always wonderful journal *Popular Culture Review*, was exceedingly helpful in permission matters. The contributors who added an afterward to their previously published work did so with verve, style, great insight, and wit while also doing so on a strict time schedule, and each must be thanked.

Gratitude also goes to the Department of Political and Cultural Studies at Swansea University, Wales, and especially their programs in American Studies and War and Society for continued support.

Thanks are also due to those who have granted permission to have previously published work reprinted:

Tyrrell, Wm. Blake. "*Star Trek* as Myth and Television as Mythmaker." *Journal of Popular Culture* 10:4 (1977) 711–19. Copyright Wiley-Blackwell.
Claus, Peter J. "A Structuralist Appreciation of *Star Trek*." Copyright Peter J. Claus. Originally published in *American Deminsions: Cultural Myths and Social Reality*, William Arens and Susan Montague, eds. New York: Alfred, 1976, pp. 15–32.
Littleton, C. Scott. "Some Implications of the Mythology in *Star Trek*." *Keystone Folklore* 4 (1989): 33–42. Copyright The Center for Pennsylvania Culture Studies.
Pilkington, Ace G. "American Dream, Myth and Reality." *Encyclia: The Jour-*

nal of the Utah Academy of Sciences, Arts, and Letters 69 (1992): 65–76. Copyright Ace G. Pilkington.

Kapell, Matthew. "Speakers for the Dead: *Star Trek*, The Holocaust, and the Representation of Atrocity." *Extrapolation* 41.2 (2000): 104–114. Copyright, 2000 by The Kent State University Press.

Baker, Djoymi. "'Every Old Trick Is New Again': Myth in Quotations and the *Star Trek* Franchise." *Popular Culture Review* 12:1 (2001), 67–77. Copyright The Far West Popular Culture Association and American Culture Association.

Table of Contents

Acknowledgments vii

Introduction: The Significance of the Star Trek *Mythos*
    (Matthew Wilhelm Kapell) 1

PART ONE: A PARTIAL CANON OF *STAR TREK* MYTH CRITICISM

1. *Star Trek* as Myth and Television as Mythmaker
    (Wm. Blake Tyrell) 19

2. A Structuralist Appreciation of *Star Trek*
    (Peter J. Claus) 29

3. Some Implications of the Mythology in *Star Trek*
    (C. Scott Littleton) 44

4. *Star Trek*: American Dream, Myth and Reality
    (Ace G. Pilkington) 54

5. Speakers for the Dead: *Star Trek*, the Holocaust, and the Representation of Atrocity
    (Matthew Wilhelm Kapell) 67

6. "Every Old Trick Is New Again": Myth in Quotations and the *Star Trek* Franchise
    (Djoymi Baker) 80

PART TWO: BOLDLY GOING FORWARD: NEW FRONTIERS OF MYTHIC *STAR TREK* ANALYSIS

7. *Star Trek* as American Monomyth
    (John Shelton Lawrence) 93

8. The Sisko, the Christ: A Comparison of Messiah Figures in the *Star Trek* Universe and the New Testament
    (Jeffery S. Lamp) 112

9. Course in Federation Linguistics
	(Richard R. Jones) 129
10. Evocations and Evasions of Archetypal Lesbian Love in *Star Trek: Voyager*
	(Roger Kaufman) 144
11. The Protestant Ethic and the Spirit of Surak: *Star Trek: Enterprise*, Anti-Catholicism and the Vulcan Reformation
	(Jennifer E. Porter) 163
12. A Vision of a Time and Place: Spiritual Humanism and the Utopian Impulse
	(Bruce Isaacs) 182
13. The Kirk Doctrine: The Care and Repair of Archetypal Heroic Leadership in J.J Abrams' *Star Trek*
	(Stephen McVeigh) 197
14. Conclusion: The Hero with a Thousand Red Shirts
	(Matthew Wilhelm Kapell) 213

About the Contributors 221
Index 225

Introduction

The Significance of the *Star Trek Mythos*

MATTHEW WILHELM KAPELL

If USS *Enterprise* Captain James T. Kirk has any ancestors from our time it is likely that one of them would have been the British scholar of myth Geoffrey S. Kirk. Aside from having been a Cambridge professor of Greek myth and history, Geoffrey S. Kirk — much like his spiritual descendent James T. — was a naval officer (during World War Two) and, according to his 2003 obituary, once said of himself that he "liked, in one way or another, practically all girls" (Lloyd-Jones). Geoffrey S. Kirk also spent much of his career explaining how stories from individual imaginations could, over time, become the myths of entire cultures. As a result, he would understand both the creation of *Star Trek* and the reasons it continues to resonate with so many. Writing between the cancellation of the original *Star Trek* and its emergence as a cultural force (and sounding just a bit like Jean-Luc Picard) Kirk noted that "myths can possess significance through their structure, which may unconsciously represent structural elements in the society from which they originate or the typical behaviouristic attitudes of the myth-makers themselves" (252). It is the contention of this volume that Kirk's statement could apply to *Star Trek* as easily as to the Greek myths he was discussing. Why? Because within the narrative of *Star Trek* are found significant mythological traits of both the self-image of the American people and the specific attitudes of its creator, Gene Roddenberry.

In other words, *Star Trek* is a kind of contemporary mythological system that the various contributors to this volume examine through the "structural elements" of the "society from which they originate" and the "attitudes of the myth-maker" himself.

In addition to this, *Star Trek* has expanded greatly since its inception, increasing the size of its mythological system almost exponentially. There are now eleven feature films, five television series, countless novels, fan fiction, fan-based conventions, corporate conventions ... the list could (and does) go on. As of July 2009, Simon and Schuster, the U.S. publisher of *Star Trek*–based novels, lists over 750 in print. Of course, other popular culture artifacts have been developed through a similarly multiple set of mediums. Religious studies scholar William G. Doty, in a discussion of the films, comics, anime shorts and various books in *The Matrix* franchise, compared this multi-media production to a kind of total control of the narrative presentation similar to Richard Wagner's "all-embracing" *Gesamtkunstwerk* in his late nineteenth century operatic productions (9–10).

Wagner, in an attempt to control all aspects of his operas, from the very design of the theater, to the kinds of lighting, presentation of music and even the design of some of the instruments themselves, had created the first kind of artwork in which the artist tries to assert complete control. John Shelton Lawrence, who is a contributor to this volume, has applied the notion of *Gesamtkunstwerk* to George Lucas' *Star Wars* saga, too (3). There is no doubt that the idea fits such franchises, where the creators and producers of the art — such as in *The Matrix* and *Star Wars*— develop a kind of contemporary *Gesamtkunstwerk*. *Star Trek*, however, is an altogether different sort of artistic construct. Because it was the product, initially, of the mind of Gene Roddenberry there is a temptation to consider the full text of the entire franchise as Roddenberry's. However, besides the incredible number of different incarnations of *Star Trek*, there is also a tradition of a significantly decentralized process of creation and interpretation of the *Star Trek* narratives. This is not just the writers' and producers' creation, but fans have also been actively involved in the process of making *Star Trek*— through their own fiction, film productions, and conventions — almost since its beginning.

Such competing narratives as *Star Wars* and *The Matrix* might be both a kind of modern myth as well as a kind of modern *Gesamtkunstwerk*, but they remain a far different type of mythical narrative because of their centralized — and thus controlled — production. *Star Trek*, being the creation of literally thousands of people, both working together and separately, is a far more massive and varied mythologically polysemic construct. And because of this tremendous variety of sources in the creative process, the *mythos* that is *Star Trek* is open to a wider variety of interpretations.

A Pragmatic Definition of Myth

Of course, this raises an interesting question: under what definition of "myth" do the contributors to this book operate? As is appropriate for a volume on the myths found within and produced by *Star Trek*, each essay works from a definition of myth which pragmatically works for its own analysis. As much as these reprinted contributors have changed their opinions over time, and the new contributors offer their own working definitions either implicitly or explicitly, the situation would be far worse had I enforced a strict definition of "myth." Scholars of myth are notoriously incapable of defining the term. It is as slippery an idea as culture for anthropologists or truth for philosophers. This is because any attempt at a definition of the term must account for three things: the *structure* of myths, the *function* of myths, and, directly relating to the first two, the narrative organization *of* myths. This has, after countless attempts by many myth scholars, proven to be an impossible task, and usually fruitless as well. Each attempt at a rigorous universal definition of myth has proved to be a failure because such an attempt defies the very purpose of myths in the first place. Definitions which satisfy structural requirements tend to fail functionally, and vice versa. Definitions which tend to describe narrative universals of myths tend to fail either structurally or functionally — if not both. This introduction will suggest a number of different ways to approach myth and, through such definitions, *Star Trek*. Mark Schorer's well-known definition resonates with *Star Trek* nicely: "Myths are the instruments by which we continually struggle to make our experience intelligible to ourselves. A myth is a large, controlling image that gives philosophical meaning to the facts of ordinary life; that is, which has organizing value for experience" (355). As much as *Star Trek* provides insight into the experience of its many viewers — and its creators — it also offers a window into the cultural framework of its originary culture. To simplify Schorer's definition even more, this book accepts the very general definition of myth as proposed by myth scholar Bruce Lincoln — that *Star Trek* is an "ideology in narrative form" (207).

Lincoln's definition of myth is overly general, but it works — and it works because previous attempts to define the term more specifically have failed. A definition, by its very nature, cannot be part of a mythological view. Taking a hint again from Geoffrey S. Kirk, the various contributors to this volume collectively agree that "There is no one definition of myth, no Platonic form of a myth against which all actual instances can be measured. Myths, as we shall see, differ enormously in their morphology and their social function" (7). It is a central premise that forcing upon the contributors any requirement to offer a specific definition of myth consistent across the entire book would be, at best, folly. It is in such definitional requirements that the long-debated contest between *mythos* and *logos* in both academia and Western society are found. There is also a further contention that an attempt to force a definition upon mythological understandings is to use the requirements of *logos* to undermine the purpose of *mythos*. However, an examination of the emergence of the *Star Trek mythos* in the context of the *logos*-centrism of the late 1960s can explain one aspect of "myth" as used in this book and helps to explain *Star Trek*'s continuing success as well.

A *Context for* Star Trek: Mythos *and* Logos *in 1969*

The summer of 1969 was an eventful one for those interested in the exploration of space. On 3 June NBC broadcast the final original episode of the USS *Enterprise*'s mission into the "Final Frontier." "Turnabout Intruder" was far from the best of the original *Star Trek* television episodes, but it seemed at the time destined to be the last original *Trek* story. Then, just six weeks after the airing of that final *Trek* episode, on 20 July, Neil Armstrong and Buzz Aldrin completed John F. Kennedy's vision for the "New Frontier" and landed on the moon. An estimated 500 million people watched the Apollo 11 moon landing, far outstripping the viewership of the final episode of *Star Trek*, which came in a dismal third in its Tuesday night time-slot (Solow and Justman 414–415). In the hazy and tumultuous summer of 1969, if one were to bet on future success, the odds were very much against *Star Trek* and, it seemed, on the side of NASA. Indeed, as 1969 came to an end, the Final Frontier of *Star Trek* looked like a dismal failure compared to the New Frontier of NASA. However, quickly and perhaps not surprisingly, both *Star Trek* and NASA's Apollo program would be cancelled for the very same reasons: overly large budgets combined with poor television ratings. But very soon afterward it would be *Star Trek*'s journeys into the Final Frontier that became the ratings hits, not those of future NASA missions.

By 1972 the profound switch in popularity would be nearing warp speed. What has become recognized as the very first *Star Trek* convention would be mounted in a hotel in New York and the organizers, expecting at most a few hundred people, would have to turn away hundreds and, by some estimates, thousands (Lichtenberg). Blooper reels of *Trek* actors walking into doors that failed to swoosh out of their way and projected 16mm showings of the original episodes dominated the weekend. There was even a display in the dealer's room provided by NASA. And as we shall see, the publicity people at NASA had reason to tie their vision of the future with *Star Trek*. Unlike 1969 when *Star Trek* was being cancelled and hundreds of millions were watching Armstrong and Aldrin, by 1972's Apollo 17, still the last of the moon landings to date, NASA and *Star Trek* had switched places completely in popular culture. By the middle of the decade NASA would go so far as to name the first Space Shuttle *Enterprise*, after all!

The contrasting success of the two programs—Roddenberry's *Star Trek* and NASA's Apollo—can be best summed up by comparing the opening narration of *Star Trek* to the extemporaneous utterance of Buzz Aldrin as he stepped off the lunar module *Eagle* onto the surface of the moon. *Star Trek*'s Final Frontier found both "strange, new worlds," and "new life and new civilizations" in each of its 79 episodes. And while the lunar astronauts were certainly "boldly going" to the moon as well, on the harsh lunar surface all they found was, in Aldrin's words, "magnificent desolation."

Since 1972, the year of that first recognized *Star Trek* convention and the last lunar landing, much has changed that bears examination. NASA, for all its successes, has not sent another human being outside of low Earth orbit, while *Star Trek* has been the source material for an ever expanding mythic composition with a galactic frontier as the canvas. In short, the *mythos* of *Star Trek* dominates the popular imagination in ways NASA never has.

The ongoing success of *Star Trek*, when compared to NASA, also suggests the difference between the power of differing mythological structures when compared to the nitty-gritty of everyday life. *Star Trek*'s mythological purpose (Lincoln's "ideology in narrative form" again), allows the Final Frontier to carry far more cultural weight than the New Frontier of the 1960s ever did for NASA. *Star Trek* has one kind of *mythos*, while NASA another. Where *Star Trek*'s was a *mythos* based on the ongoing exploration of an ever expanding frontier, NASA's *mythos* was, although quite similar, bound by the technological and scientific requirements of real space exploration. In other words, NASA was forced to define its attempts at exploration of the frontier through the requirements of *logos*. Typically, *logos* should reign supreme in the modernist world of the late 1960s and early 1970s. The pragmatic reasoning, logical and willful planning, and scientific nature of NASA's lunar exploration is an almost case-and-point definition of *logos*—but the public lost interest in their *logos*-centrism faster than NASA's Saturn V boosters could leave the launch pad.

And while *Star Trek* retained some of the veneer of NASA's *logos*—there was supposed to be an internal logic to the concept of "warp speed" and the "transporter" after all—in reality it only needed to concern itself with its own, but far from unique, *mythos*.

Star Trek *as Myth-Making*

Yet, unlike the seemingly logical and rational *logos*, *mythos*, usually defined as a narrative or story carrying with it importance to a group or a culture, is what philosopher Mary Midgley has termed "networks of powerful symbols that suggest particular ways of interpreting the world" (1). And in that sense *Star Trek* is a product of the American cultural and mythological system. Jon Wagner and Jan Lundeen have explained that, "much of *Trek*'s phenomenal appeal has to do with its ability to confront and express, in a gratifying mythic way, some of the central concerns of American culture" (4). It is that ability to confront important and perennial issues in a new narrative fashion that makes *Star Trek* very mythological.

The *mythos* of *Star Trek* is the key to its success. When religious historian Karen Armstrong writes about *mythos* and *logos* she could quite easily be writing about the inherent differences between NASA's lunar landings and *Star Trek*'s voyages on the mythical Final Frontier. *Star Trek*'s narrative is about myth, and historically the subject of "myth" was considered far more important than the practical considerations of everyday life. As Karen Armstrong notes, "myth"

> was regarded as primary; it was concerned with what was thought to be timeless and constant in our existence. Myth looked back to the origins of life, to the foundations of culture, to the deepest levels of the human mind. Myth was not concerned with practical matters, but with meaning ... the *mythos* of a society provided people with a context that made sense of their day-to-day lives; it directed their attention to the eternal and the universal [*Battle*, xiii].

"These are the voyages of the Starship *Enterprise*," is not, nor was it meant to be, a statement about a logic-driven excursion. It is a statement about a mythic voyage as certainly as is "once upon a time." *Star Trek* concerned itself with the origins of culture, the relationship between the individual and the group, and other timeless questions of what it means to be human.

NASA in the 1960s, of course, did none of that. Where *Star Trek* was concerned with deep existential questions — the stuff of myth — NASA operated under the practical *logos* of landing a man on the moon. NASA is defined through its *logos*, which Karen Armstrong describes as something which

> must relate exactly to facts and correspond to external realities if it is to be effective. It must work efficiently in the mundane world. We use this logical, discursive reasoning when we have to make things happen [or] get something done.... *Logos* is practical. Unlike myth, which looks back to the beginnings and to the foundations, *logos* forges ahead and tries to find something new; to elaborate on old insights, achieve a greater control over our environment, discover something fresh, and invent something novel [*Battle*, xiv–xv].

The "logical, discursive reasoning" necessary for the Apollo moon landings was very practical. The Apollo astronauts were very much "making things happen" and getting "something done." Make no mistake, however: their efforts were, without question, heroic. They just were not, in the final analysis, mythically complex enough to watch more than a couple of times. As historian Gerard DeGroot puts it, Captain Kirk was far more interesting because he "didn't have to wear clumsy space suits or eat goop from tubes" (260). That means *Star Trek* differs markedly from NASA in that fans the world over have watched the various series and films, read the books and comics, and attended conventions in droves — and have done so repeatedly.

And the reason for this is *Star Trek*'s very specific kind of *mythos*.

Mythos is a more ephemeral term because it attempts to capture the meaning of something that is not at all ephemeral itself. But it is not particularly quantifiable either. The ideas captured in *mythos* are culturally timeless and unwavering. As a term, however, *mythos* is difficult to make hold still. It quickly jumps to warp, away from each attempt to specifically define it. This is why "myth" is used so freely today to mean so many different things. The real test for *Star Trek*, the real "ongoing mission" of the *Enterprise*, is to recreate and use myth in ways that are both internally consistent and relevant to its viewers. To do that meant using myth disguised as something altogether different. And that is where the power of *Star Trek*'s space opera setting allows it to "do" its mythological work in a very surreptitious fashion. By placing the narratives of each episode in the rational world of a science-fictional future Earth, *Star Trek*'s *mythos* is cleverly disguised as a kind of speculative *logos*. *Star Trek*'s *logos* of the future, in which the practical needs and pragmatic considerations of running a ship that travels faster than light and can move, conveniently, between worlds on a weekly basis is presented matter-of-factly and as the *logical* next step in human (and humanoid) cultural evolution. There is little about the premise of *Star Trek* that really is scientific, logical or, as the many, repeated incarnations would have the viewer believe, inevitable. But the contemporary world and its citizens need their myths presented to them as though they are facts. Karen Armstrong has noted that, "every time men and women took a major step forward, they reviewed their mythology and made it speak to the new conditions" (*Myth*, 11). Unlike NASA, *Star Trek* reviewed its mythology and allowed it to resonate with new conditions.

Star Trek's real insight then, is to present its *mythos*—its universal stories of adventure, trials, heroism, and apotheosis—as though they are the product of a logical and inevitable future. Again, for *Star Trek*, *mythos* is presented as though it were *logos*. For an American cultural artifact, pretending that myth is really scientific understanding is nothing new: indeed, Gene Roddenberry was not even the first to do this with his concept of the "frontier." The first mythical "frontier" packaged as a scientific truth—thus as *logos*—was that of the American historian Frederick Jackson Turner. His "frontier" was as much a myth as Gene Roddenberry's would be, 70 years later.

The Final "Frontier Thesis"

In 1893 Frederick Jackson Turner—a young historian from the University of Wisconsin—spoke to a meeting of historians in Chicago while the World's Fair went on just down the street. The meeting Turner was attending was the American Historical Association, which at the time was only nine years old, helping to make Turner one of the first generation of professional historians in the United States. His topic, which certainly sounded professional enough, was famously on "The Significance of the Frontier in American History." Few could have guessed the enormous ramifications this topic would generate for students of American history. Turner's work would define the field for generations, and still has repercussions today. But what became known as, variously, the Turner Thesis or the Frontier Thesis was, for the most part, not precisely a lecture on history. It was, instead, an American nationalistic manifesto that sought to explain American culture through the telling of an ideological narrative of Western expansion. As Vernon E. Mattson eloquently put it, what Turner did for Americans was invest in the "frontier" a powerful symbol for "an idealized version of their past as well as their aspirations for the future" (9). As we shall see, this is the same thing as saying what Turner presented in 1893 was a mythological system, not an historical analysis. Turner's Thesis, then, is also an American *mythos* presented, through social scientific language, as though it was *logos*.

Turner's thesis, in its simplest form, can be summed up through this famous quote from his essay: "the existence of an area of free land, its continuing recession, and the advance of American settlement westward, explain American development" (19). For Turner, then, it was an ever-expanding western frontier, continually opening before American Manifest Destiny, full of free land and opportunity that created the American way of life and allowed for the development of American individuality, freedom and democracy. No contemporary historian would argue that Turner was correct in this assertion, but at the same time an awful lot of them spend much of their time showing precisely how Turner got it wrong. Indeed, this sentence — which, if being quoted is an indicator, seems at times as if it is the only thing Turner ever wrote — draws the reader into a realm that has little to do with actual history and far more to do with myth. Turner's essay is, as the "New Western Historian" Patricia Nelson Limerick has noted, "an enchanted world ... [of] abstractions, conditions, forces, ideals, institutions, traits, types, elements, and processes" (697). Yet, as much as Turner happened to be a professional historian, what his work really accomplished was to take the abstraction of the frontier and through it, as Theodore Roosevelt noted, "put into definite shape a good deal of thought that has been floating around rather loosely" (Roosevelt, cited in Wrobel, 37). In other words, Turner put a social-scientific sheen on a mythological system of the frontier West — an invention not just of Turner's in 1893, but something that had been part of the zeitgeist for some time.

As historian Richard White has explored in detail, in Chicago as Turner gave his talk on the American frontier, another myth of that frontier was being perpetuated in William F. Cody's "Buffalo Bill's Wild West and Congress of Rough Riders of the World." Buffalo Bill's show — which was never actually referred to as a "show" by Cody — also told the story of the frontier. Where

Turner's story was of "free land" on an empty continent tamed by a farmer, Cody's was of "conquest" of the Indian Other by the "scout." Both, however, were about making the "Frontier" increasingly "American." White noted that Buffalo Bill Cody "produced a master narrative of the West as finished and as culturally significant as Turner's own" (202). According to White, Buffalo Bill and Turner were both "geniuses in their use of the iconography of the frontier ... the two men used all kinds of symbolic representations—from log cabins to stage coaches—that were reproduced over and over in American life, then and now. Turner incorporated such icons into his talk. Buffalo Bill set out to represent them" (205).

Both Cody and Turner were explaining a myth of the frontier in 1893—thus being mythographers—and expanding on that myth in their own ways—thus being myth-makers.

Had Turner and Cody been working a scant 70 years later, and in television, they would likely have been Gene Roddenberry. And Turner's "farmer" would have been a "Federation colonist" while Cody's "Scout" would have been named "Kirk."

Instead, it was Roddenberry who extrapolated Turner's Thesis of "free land" and Cody's show of "conquest" to their logical—and yet also mythological—conclusion, projecting the frontier experience into space during the heady decade of Kennedy's New Frontier. In 1964 Roddenberry spoke to a meeting of television producers and proposed an hour long drama that resonated with the landscape of Turner's and Cody's mythical American past, only projected into the twenty-third century and adding to it an assimilationist agenda. A former police officer and commercial pilot, Roddenberry turned to television writing because it was more lucrative. Cutting his teeth on shows such as the Western drama *Have Gun — Will Travel* (1957–63) and his own military-based 1963–4 series *The Lieutenant* (featuring, like his future James T. Kirk, a hero with the middle name of Tiberius), he was well suited to the task of bringing Western mythology together with a military scheme. The phrase that is most often cited from that meeting, claimed by Roddenberry to have been part of cinching the deal, was that he wanted to produce a "'Wagon Train' to the stars" (Whitfield and Roddenberry 23). Indeed, the Wagon Train cite is likely the most often quoted phrase from *The Making of Star Trek*, though there is no way to know if it was actually uttered in the pitch meeting. However, clearly, what Roddenberry was able to accomplish in that meeting was the idea that a science-fiction serial drama could be produced and be successful.

More importantly, though, what Roddenberry really accomplished was the projection of an American mythological system into the New Frontier headiness of the 1960s. With the sale of his show, he created a unique image of the American self that allowed him to channel an intellectual mythic history in the United States based on a concept of America's frontier. In other words, Roddenberry suggested that a television show, set in space, could be read as a mythic and idealized American past — an oft-used trope in written American science fiction. David Mogen has noted that the function of such literature has often been to create "visions of the future" that preserve "the myths of our past" (9). Roddenberry merely expanded this to its mythological conclusion and imagined a future where an entire region of the galaxy had been made part of a single culture — as Turner had suggested the frontier had done in the making of "Americans." As anthropologist Conrad Kottak put it, Roddenberry's *Star Trek* is very much about the process of Americanizing the frontier and turning different types of beings into members of the same culture. Kottak explains each of the characters in the original series as part of such an assimilationist project:

> Kirk is ... symbolic of the original Anglo-American ... McCoy's Irish (or at least Gaelic) name represents the next wave, the by now established immigrant. Sulu is the successfully assimilated Asian-American. The African-American female character, Uhura, whose name means "freedom," proclaims that blacks will eventually become full partners with all other Americans [103].

Thus, what Roddenberry did in 1964 as he pitched *Star Trek*, was stand in for two of the myth-makers of America: Frederick Jackson Turner and Buffalo Bill Cody. But, in extending the Turner Thesis and frontier myth into space he also added a version in which women, non–WASP males, and even non-humans could share the same cultural framework. As much as the most oft-quoted line of Roddenberry's was his "'Wagon Train' to the stars," for Turner it was his 1893 statement on the "existence of an area of free land [and] its continuing recession" (19). It would not be a stretch to say that Turner's famous quote mythically applies to Gene Roddenberry's *Star Trek* universe. Indeed, if one were to replace but a few words and write, "the existence of an area of free *space*, its continuing recession, and the advance of *Federation colonies* outward, explain Federation development," one would have a useful description of the "history" of the United Federation of Planets in *Star Trek*. It would also nicely describe both the "five year" and later "ongoing" scouting missions of the Starship *Enterprise*.

And while neither Turner's nor Cody's conception of the American "frontier" ever existed as historical reality, each provided a useful narrative for a nation losing its frontier: Cody's dramatic and violent and Turner's carefully "social scientific." Both provided a usable past — or, mythologically, an "organizing value"—for Americans. That "usable past" and "organizing value" was then, by Roddenberry, projected into a utopian future and made available to an entire planet. It is in examining that organizing value that the contributors to this volume offer their insights.

A Note on Organization: Some Ways to Read This Book

There are multiple axes for the organization of this book, but all center on the concept of *mythos* and, from that, extend through religion and archetypes. First, because of the historical nature of the reprinted essays, it is possible to see here an intellectual history of academic reactions to *Star Trek*. Secondly, as a result of the transition from Modernist to the many forms of postmodernism, both in the academy generally, and in myth studies particularly, there is an archeology of the emergence of postmodernity here as well. Because the study of myth finds itself—thankfully, many would say!—without a disciplinary home, there is also a hint of the broad way in which "myth" and "*mythos*" is studied from different disciplinary perspectives. There are scholars from anthropology, philosophy, American studies, history, classics, film studies, English, psychology, and religion in this volume and each of these disciplines approaches the academic study of "myth" in its own way. And, finally, *Star Trek*, too, has changed significantly since the time the first six essays appearing in this book were published. As a result, the reprinted essays in Part One are followed by short postscripts from each of the original authors. Reprinted essays are reproduced exactly as published with the exception that typographical errors have been corrected.

Since the serious academic study of *Star Trek* began in the 1970s literally hundreds of essays have appeared on one or another aspect of the franchise. In picking previously published work I have attempted to both include the most relevant essays centering on *Star Trek* and myth, as well as choose from essays that have been published in smaller journals. This is specifically designed to allow these essays to reach a larger audience—as they each richly deserve. Among essays published on *Star Trek*, however, none has been cited as frequently as "*Star Trek* as Myth and Television as Mythmaker." Thus, this volume must begin there.

That now seminal essay was published in 1977 by classics scholar Wm. Blake Tyrrell. The study of classics has always been the study of culture through language and Tyrell uses his knowledge of the "language" of *Star Trek* to try to understand the American culture that produced it. His essay examines how *Star Trek* attempts to clothe itself in a mythical structure of "the future" but is really a retelling of a mythical American past.

While Tyrrell was considering *Star Trek* as a classicist, many other academics from multiple disciplines in the mid to late 1970s also began considering *Trek*. While it was impossible to include them all here, Peter J. Claus' essay was selected because it remains important for two reasons. First, as with Tyrrell's essay, it is one of the very early significant looks at *Star Trek*. Secondly, it provides, in exquisite detail, a technically insightful structural analysis of the original series. While to a large extent the many "post-structural" and postmodern perspectives that have followed Claude Lévi-Strauss' work have tended to fully erase that perspective, there are more than a few social scientists—anthropologists, especially—who think that the structural model, for all its flaws, was abandoned a bit too soon.

Another anthropologist, C. Scott Littleton, specializes in myth and religion more generally. His work, which spans both medieval Europe and contemporary Japan, is brought forth in his essay which examines *Star Trek* as a representation of a class of myths from throughout the world containing a quest theme. Using examples from Greece, Mesopotamia, Eskimos, and contemporary NASA astronauts on a journey into space, Littleton reminds us that, from his perspective, the narrative of *Star Trek* is a universal one.

But as much as a universal quest theme is inherent in *Star Trek*, Ace G. Pilkington finds much of it to be distinctly American in its mythic pretensions. Pilkington, with a background in literature, history and film, works in a number of areas from Shakespeare to Slavic folktales. He is therefore able to take *Trek* both very seriously, with some amount of artistic reverence, and without belittling it for its popularity. For all its references to American Western mythology, Pilkington also sees two things that are universal in *Trek*: its ability to adapt itself to broader cultural changes over time, and its desire to promote an ever widening circle of humanism. For Pilkington, then, it is not necessarily a criticism to point to *Star Trek*'s particularly American brand of *mythos*.

My own essay, however, does find fault with that American aspect of *Trek*'s *mythos*. As both an anthropologist and historian, I am deeply suspicious of any representation of "race" or the misuse of "history." In *Deep Space Nine* the writers of *Star Trek* attempted to confront the reality of genocide through ways that specifically resonated with American Jewish stereotypes of the Holocaust but the end result was that the representation limited any significant impact. Djoymi Baker disagrees with that assessment, however. Trained in media and cultural studies, she notes that *Star Trek* presents a multitude of mythic connections and meanings. Baker's essay, which is based on a small part of her award-winning dissertation at Melbourne University in Australia, examines how *Star Trek* references both non–*Trek* mythological sources as well as itself. This broad web of interrelated mythological references combined with self-referential aspects allows *Star Trek* viewers to continually "find" textually complex meanings.

That textual complexity fuels the original essays in Part Two, beginning with philosopher John Shelton Lawrence's essay on *Trek*'s anti-democratic—but *very* American—narratives. An extension of his previous work with religious scholar Robert Jewett beginning with their 1977 book *The American Monomyth* and continued in *The Myth of the American Superhero*, their formulation of the "American Monomyth" looks to the anti-democratic and often violent tendencies in the *mythos* of American culture. Lawrence then employs that model in his essay on *Star Trek*—especially in its representations of the heroic but violent leader.

For the biblical scholar Jeffery S. Lamp, though, there is a very positive outcome in *Trek*'s heroic archetypes. Comparing the apotheosis of Benjamin Sisko in *Deep Space Nine* with Christ, Lamp's analysis considers many important questions about what the idea of a "Messiah" is to Christians, and how in a modern, secular world, the term remains significant. It is in significant terms, generally, that Richard R. Jones finds the main myth of all *Star Trek*: the idea that it is possible to translate ideas between ourselves and the Other, thus negating the very idea of the truly "alien." Jones is an anthropologist with training in linguistics *and* an ordained minister, and the concept of the translatability of differing world-views concerns him. Without the ability for stories of one group to translate—and resonate—with others, all of the *Star Trek* narrative would immediately collapse.

Where the *Star Trek* narrative has resonated quite strongly, however, is in the realm of same-sex relationships. The famous "slash" stories of *Star Trek* began almost as soon as the first episodes were aired in the 1960s, and Jungian psychoanalyst Roger Kaufman examines the lesbian archetypes found in the relationships of *Voyager*. The archetype is, of course, a staple of mythological analysis, but much like Djoymi Baker noting the richness of *Trek*'s textual tapestry, Kaufman is able to examine in great detail one example of the uses of such archetypes.

And it is with rich textual meanings that religious scholar Jennifer E. Porter concerns herself as well. No stranger to the religious implications of *Star Trek* as co-editor of *Star Trek and Sacred Ground*, Porter turns to *Star Trek: Enterprise* and examines it in light of the textual debates during the Reformation in the Christian West. As much as Luther's theses against Catholicism changed Christianity through an argument over their shared biblical text, Porter notes that this basic textual argument remains central to contemporary culture and to the world of *Star Trek*. Like Lamp's examination of the Messiah figure, Porter also works to treat both religious texts and *Star Trek* with equal respect, presenting images of a debate which still resonates.

Both sides in that debate—the Protestant Reformers and the Catholic Church—hoped to follow their text in a way that would lead to the return of Christ and a thousand year paradise. It is to a paradise that Australian film scholar Bruce Isaacs turns his attention as he wonders if the paradise envisioned in *Star Trek* is actually a Utopia. Drawing from his *Toward a New Film Aesthetic*, Isaacs sees in the *mythos* of *Star Trek* an idealized form of the present rather than a Utopian vision of the future.

And where *Trek* is, currently, according to American Studies scholar Stephen McVeigh, is trying to recapture an heroic archetype undermined by eight years of the presidency of George W. Bush. The brash gut-decisions and so-called "cowboy diplomacy" of the Bush years—through which McVeigh has previously framed his study of *The American Western*—has been critically attacked by many. Here, McVeigh examines how the newest film, which claims to fit a model of Obama-style leadership, optimism and "hope" actually presents an archetype of leadership that has more in common with the popular perception of President Bush. The newest *Star Trek* film quickly grossed over $250 million worldwide. It is therefore fitting that a book which examines the *mythos* of *Star Trek* because of its popularity should end with a statement about the most popular of all the incarnations of the franchise.

Star Trek *as a "Usable Mythology"*

The contributors to this book each take *Star Trek* as an integral part of an important and expanding contemporary *mythos*. What Gene Roddenberry and the *Star Trek* writers, producers and fans have done is take mythic journeys as old as *The Odyssey* and the *Epic of Gilgamesh*, combine them with newer mythic narratives of the American frontier and the very contemporary notion of cultural assimilation and make something at once both old and new. As a result, *Star Trek* both confirms a traditional *mythos* and adds to it.

As the contributors here each show, Gene Roddenberry's creation in the 1960s latched on to a mythic zeitgeist and quickly grew beyond itself. The tapestry of *mythos*, generally, and *Star Trek*'s specific contribution to that *mythos* evidences a significant cultural artifact. Once again we can turn to Geoffrey S. Kirk for insight into what this might mean. Trying to explain vast changes in Greek myth-making leading to the works we retain today, Geoffrey Kirk wrote that Hesiod and Homer (and perhaps even *Star Trek*) took age-old stories "and with new interests and techniques constructed out of [them] an erratic but vivid new world of myths in which the preoccupations of contemporary society were reflected against the background of traditional narrative situations" (251). *Star Trek*'s *mythos* remains, after more than 40 years, a valuable addition to our "ideologies in narrative form" that, for many, is a continually evolving way of making "our experience intelligible to ourselves." And, like all good myths, if we are lucky, *Star Trek* allows us to follow the mythic journey described by the omniscient Q in the final episode of *The Next Generation*, "All Good Things..." Describing the very mythical journey he has just forced upon Jean-Luc Picard, Q declares his motives, and perhaps also notes a key value of all myths:

> We wanted to see if you had the ability to expand your mind and your horizons. And for one brief moment, you did.... For that one fraction of a second, you were open to options you had never considered. That is the exploration that awaits you. Not mapping stars and studying nebulae, but charting the unknown possibilities of existence.

And that exploration is the journey charted by this book, for that is the *mythos* of *Star Trek*.

Works Cited

Armstrong, Karen. *The Battle for God*. New York: Alfred A. Knopf, 2000.
_____. *A Short History of Myth*. Edinburgh: Canongate, 2005.
De Groot, Gerard J. *Dark Side of the Moon: The Magnificent Madness of the American Lunar Quest*. New York: New York University Press, 2006.
Doty, William G. "Introduction: The Deeper We Go, the More Complex and Sophisticated the Franchise Seems, and the Dizzier We Feel." In *Jacking In to The Matrix Franchise: Cultural Reception and Interpretation*. New York: Continuum, 2004: 1–13.
Isaacs, Bruce. *Toward a New Film Aesthetic*. New York: Continuum, 2008.
Jewett, Robert, and John Shelton Lawrence. *The American Monomyth*. Garden City, NY: Anchor, 1977.
_____, and _____. *Captain America and the Crusade Against Evil: The Dilemma of Zealous Nationalism*. Grand Rapids, MI: W.B. Eerdmans, 2003.
Kirk, G. S. *Myth: Its Meaning and Functions in Ancient and Other Cultures*. Cambridge, UK: Cambridge University Press, 1970.
Kottak, Conrad Phillip. *Prime-Time Society: An Anthropological Analysis of Television and Culture*. Belmont, CA: Wadsworth, 1990.
Lawrence, John Shelton. "Introduction: Spectable, Merchandise, and Influence." In *Finding the Force of the Star Wars Franchise: Fans, Merchandise and Critics*. New York: Peter Lang, 2006:1–20.
_____ and Robert Jewett. *The Myth of the American Superhero*. Grand Rapids, MI: W.B. Eerdmans, 2002.
Lichtenberg, Jacqueline. *Star Trek Lives!* London: Corgi, 1975.
Limerick, Patricia Nelson. "Turnerians All: The Dream of a Helpful History in an Intelligible World." *American Historical Review* 100.3 (1995): 697–716.
Lincoln, Bruce. *Theorizing Myth: Narrative, Ideology, and Scholarship*. Chicago: University of Chicago Press, 1999.
Lloyd-Jones, Hugh. "Professor G.S. Kirk: Obituary." *The Independent*. 19 March 2003. www.independent.co.uk/news/obituaries/professor-g-s-kirk-730129.html. (Accessed 2 August 2009.)
Mattson, Vernon E. "West as Myth." *Journal of the History of the Behavioral Sciences* 24.1 (1988): 9–12.
McVeigh, Stephen. *The American Western*. Edinburgh: Edinburgh University Press, 2007.
Midgley, Mary. *The Myths We Live By*. London: Routledge, 2003.
Mogen, David. *Wilderness Visions: Science Fiction Westerns, Volume One*. San Bernardino, CA: Borgo, 1982.
Porter, Jennifer E., and Darcee L. McLaren, eds. *Star Trek and Sacred Ground: Explorations of Star Trek, Religion, and American Culture*. Albany: State University of New York Press, 1999.
Schorer, Mark. "Appendix: The Necessity of Myth." In *Myth and Mythmaking*. Ed. Henry Alexander Murray. Boston: Beacon, 1968: 354–358.
Solow, Herbert F., and Robert H. Justman. *Inside Star Trek: The Real Story*. New York: Pocket, 1996.
Turner, Frederick Jackson. "The Significance of the Frontier in American History." In *Does the Frontier Experience Make America Exceptional?* Ed. Richard W. Etulain. Boston: Bedford/St. Martin's, 1893: 17–43.
Wagner, Jon G., and Jan Lundeen. *Deep Space and Sacred Time: Star Trek in the American Mythos*. Westport, CT: Praeger, 1998.

White, Richard. "When Frederick Jackson Turner and Buffalo Bill Cody Both Played Chicago in 1893." In *Frontier and Region: Essays in Honor of Martin Ridge*. Ed. Robert C. Ritchie and Paul Andrew Hutton. Albuquerque: University of New Mexico Press, 1997: 201–212.

Whitfield, Stephen E., and Gene Roddenberry. *The Making of Star Trek*. New York: Ballantine, 1968.

Wroble, David M. Wroble. *The End of American Exceptionalism: Frontier Anxiety from the Old West to the New Deal*. Lawrence: University Press of Kansas, 1993.

Star Trek *Media Cited*

Star Trek: The Original Series

"Turnabout Intruder." Story by Gene Roddenberry. Teleplay by Arthur Singer. 3 June 1969.

Star Trek: The Next Generation

"All Good Things..." Written by Brannon Braga and Ronald D. Moore. 23 May 1994.

PART ONE

A Partial Canon of Star Trek *Myth Criticism*

1

Star Trek *as Myth and* Television *as Mythmaker*

WM. BLAKE TYRRELL*

The phenomenon of *Star Trek* is unique in television. More popular now than its first run in the late '60s, it has spawned books of adapted scripts and of fandom as well as countless fanzines. *Star Trek* regalia extend to complete blueprints of the *Enterprise* and code of conduct for its personnel. Fan clubs have led to conventions where attendance must limited. All this is the result of something beyond the dramatic spectacle. *Star Trek* is consistent but often childish science fiction, engaging but often belabored drama. I wish to propose a reason for the phenomenon of *Star Trek* as a contribution to our understanding of the power of television.

Star Trek never had high ratings; it did have in science fiction an intriguing format. By inventing a believable world, *Star Trek* provided the viewer with material for his own imagination. He could elaborate upon the sets and equipment, bandy arcane knowledge, even write his own scripts. That the format had the potential to involve the viewer beyond one hour each week is the initial basis for the phenomenon. *Star Trek*'s format created a world alive, turning viewer into fans.

Gene Roddenberry, creator of the series, referred to it, if only in jest, as "'Wagon Train' to the stars,"[1] and the similarity between groups journeying toward the unknown is evident. Movement is a prominent motif of both the Western and *Star Trek* where it is made visual in the flyby of the gliding starship. But the similarity goes deeper. The Western story is the only indigenous mythic narrative of the white American. "The isolation of a vast unexplored continent, the slow growth of social forms, the impact of an unremitting New England Puritanism obsessed with the cosmic struggle of good and evil, of the elect and the damned, the clash of allegiances to Mother Country and New

---

Originally published in the Journal of Popular Culture *10:4 (Spring 1977): 711–19.*

World, these factors," as Jim Kitses says in *Focus on the Western*, "are the crucible in which the American consciousness was formed."[2] Since the publication in 1893 of Frederick J. Turner's essay "The Significance of the Frontier in American History," the dominant symbol of the Western myth has been the frontier.[3] *Star Trek* views space as "the final frontier."[4] Despite its format *Star Trek* is not speculative fiction in the way of written science fiction or even of *Space: 1999* in its first season. It is American myths clothed in the garb of science fiction. "Space — the final frontier" is conceptualized through the same motifs and themes as the Western frontier. A brief example.

The heart of the Western myth is the encounter with the Indian. The myth-making imagination has contained the Indian's alienness in two types: Chingachgook, the noble warrior ever outside White Man's world, and Magua, sly, perfidious, fallen and by that fall, bound to the white world. Both types are found in *Star Trek*. The Romulans, whose name recalls the heroic founder of Rome, are aggressive, militaristic aliens. Nonetheless they are "hard to hate," *The Making of Star Trek* explains, "as they often display enormous courage." The Klingons, a name as low as Cooper's Magua, are ruled by the principle "that rules are made to be broken by shrewdness, deceit, or power."[5] There is nothing admirable about them and with them in time, one episode predicts,[6] the White Man of the *Enterprise* is destined to unite. Though apparently distinct figures in the series (and perhaps in their creator's imagination), their dark, satanic visages reveal Romulans and Klingons as aspects of a whole, the Indian reborn.

Yet *Star Trek* is more than the transposing of visuals and motifs, more than the shifting from one metaphor to another. Myths are narratives with the power to move our psychic energies toward integration of self and of self with the cosmos. Myths define an image of the world within and without and relate us to it emotionally. Myths put in narrative form the unconscious assumptions that constitute the spirit of a culture. They can inspire and direct those energies to monumental achievements of good or ill. During the '60s American myths and the values they supported, after a brief sojourn in Camelot, began coining apart, not to be replaced by those of the counter culture. *Star Trek* revitalizes American myths by displacing[7] them into a futuristic, quasi-scientific setting. In effect, *Star Trek* takes our roots and disguises them as branches for some of us to cling to. Moreover, *Star Trek* put them on television.

Television is the medium of immediate, personal communication. No willed suspension of disbelief occurs; television speaks not to be intelligence or to its pilot, the will, It works through the emotions on a non-reasoning level and is thus suited to the emotional word, *mythos*.[8] *Star Trek* exploits television's intimate communication. Things on *Star Trek* look right. The family of the *Enterprise* is closely knit, appealing and calmly efficient. The men are men, and the women are endowed. (Though set in the 23rd century, sexual roles are those of the '50s.) Kirk, broadly played by William Shatner, projects emotion, strength and unthreatening paternalism. Leonard Nimoy's Spock surpasses him by striving not to emote at all. The result was that *Star Trek*'s message of revitalized mythic narratives, brought directly to the emotional needs of the viewer, engendered the feeling that the shows were more than escapist entertainment. They had meaning. That feeling transformed the 48 minute episodes into rituals, and rituals, being group-creating, led to clubs and to the convention. This feeling and the power to generate it are, I believe, what is unique about *Star Trek* and the reason for the phenomenon.

Star Trek is a product of the dreams and nightmares of the '60s. It came to those who needed the confidence and triumph of the American past while fearing a present that foreboded the disappearance of the American way. The need has become stronger in the diffident '70s. *Star Trek*'s vision, as Roddenberry and the authors of *Star Trek Lives!* maintain, is "of a brighter future of man, of a world characterized by hope, achievement and understanding."[9] But *Star Trek*'s impact transcends simple optimism for a tomorrow we may never see. *Star Trek* creates a future world where the glories of the past are pristine and the failures and doubts of the present have been overcome. It gives us our past as our future, while making our present the past which, like any historical event for the future-oriented American, is safely over and forgotten. One way that myths function, particularly those of creation, is to anchor the present to the past and place the worshipper in the time of first beginnings.[10] Something similar is the source of *Star Trek*'s power. Myths no longer link us to the past, since we know the past is gone and is of historical, not immediate, relevance to the present. Bicentennialism recalls the past. On the other hand, any science fiction can link us to the future. But the future, even that imagined in books, is uncertain. *Star Trek*, by disguising our past as our future, puts us in it—not the historical past but the mythic past of our first beginnings. There ensues a feeling of permanence, stability and renewed confidence. This is what's different about *Star Trek*.

I wish now to illustrate this view by looking at one mythic theme of *Star Trek*—that of paradise, whose role in mythizing America began before the Puritans touched its shores.[11]

Paradise is a fundamental theme of the series, the subject of at least 13 of 79 episodes.[12] It is imagined as the lost Eden of Genesis or as the garden of the New World that lies just beyond the Western frontier. Paradise is destroyed, the victim of *Star Trek*'s unquestioned identification of tranquility with stagnation. In "The Apple," for instance, the crew of the *Enterprise* have happened upon a planet controlled in weather, food supply, everything by a computer named Vaal.[13] The inhabitants are humanoids living in a state of nature. Their single task is to feed Vaal with rocks. Watching the fueling process, McCoy, Spock and Kirk are speaking together:

McCoy: What's going on, Jim?
Kirk: Mess call.
Spock: In my view a splendid example of reciprocity.
McCoy: It would take a computerized Vulcan mind such as yours to make that kind of a statement.
Spock: Doctor, you insist on applying human standards to non-human cultures. I remind yon that humans are only a tiny minority in this galaxy.
McCoy: There are certain absolutes, Mr. Spock, and once of them is the right of humanoids to a free and unchained environment. The right to have conditions which permit growth.
Spock: Another is their right to choose a system which seems to work for them.
McCoy: Jim you're not just going to stand by and be blinded to what's going on here. These are humanoids. Intelligent. They need to advance and grow. Don't you understand what my readings indicate. There's been no change or progress here in at least ten thousand years. This isn't life. It's stagnation.
Spock: Doctor, these people are healthy, and they are happy. Whatever you choose to call it, this system works despite your emotional reaction to it.
McCoy: It might for you, Mr. Spock, but it doesn't work for me. Humanoids living so they can service a hunk of tin.
Kirk: Gentlemen, I think this philosophical argument can wait until our ship's out of danger.

For the men of *Star Trek* as for the pioneers paradise is to be exploited. Open land beckons the plow, way to the new beginning that brings rebirth. It is the dream our ancestors followed westward: it launches our descendants into space. Inseparable with rebirth is death: natives of paradise too contented to appreciate the virtues of progress and advancement are reeducated. Kirk violently inflicts Federation enterprise upon them by destroying Vaal. Despite the nagging of its conscience Spock, the series subscribes to McCoy's benevolent imperialism. At the time of "The Apple"'s first airing the belief in America as World Peacemaker and Liberator, a belief which is surely an aspect of the myth of the frontier, was coming apart in Vietnam and in Washington, D.C.[14] *Star Trek* assures us of its validity by showing it as the unquestioned truth of the 23rd century. Near propagandizing, to be sure, but *Star Trek* gives out the message to those who want to believe in a way that they can believe.

In one episode the theme of paradise is treated quite differently. The tensions inherent in the myth are relieved, not by the dogmatic destruction of one pole, but by the device of the mediator. Although not typical of the paradise-theme, "This Side of Paradise"[15] microcosm for the way the series generates its impact. The plot is as follows.

The *Enterprise* arrives on Omicron Ceti III expecting to find the members of an agricultural colony dead. The planet is bombarded by Berthold radiation that disintegrates human tissue. Yet they are greeted by the colonists. They have survived because of their symbiosis with spores that absorb the radiation. These spores are a group organism; they cause their hosts to lose the sense of self and of self-advancement. No progress has been made toward the goals of the colony. The crew succumbs to the spores and abandons the *Enterprise.* Included are McCoy and Spock, the latter experiencing the only painful conversion. While under the spores Spock falls in love with an old admirer who happens to be on the planet. Capt. Kirk is overcome by the spores while on the ship, but becomes so angered at the thought of leaving it, that he is released from their influence. He later discovers that violent emotions dissolve the spores. He provokes Spock to a fight in the Transporter Room,[16] and the ensuing violence dissolves his spores. Together they bring the crew to its senses and the *Enterprise* to order.

A mediator is a third between two opposites that shares something of the nature of each. Being anomalous, it may function to overcome the opposition. In *Genesis* the Serpent mediates between Man and God as well as between Man and Woman.[17] In the myth of the frontier the trapper, hunter or scout is the anomaly between White and Red. Fundamental to the psychology informing the myth is the tension between the longing for paradise and the knowledge of its passing. But both paradise myths, *Genesis* and the Frontier, link this tension with others—social, sexual and moral. Such is the way paradise is treated in *This Side of Paradise.* Paradise as an idea, desirable but manifestly impossible, is mediated by the alien Spock. Paradise as a place lost yet sought after is mediated by the *Enterprise.* These tensions are connected with those over drugs and the differences between generations which had become polarized because of drugs. The structure of the story may be diagrammed:

PARADISE	MEDIATION	PARADISE LOST
I. Paradise as an idea		
a. McCoy	Spock	Kirk
b. Spores	Spores then violent emotions	Violent emotions
c. Painless acceptance	Painful acceptance	
d. Abdication of duty	Return to duty	Unquestioned duty
e. Loss of self	Sacrifice of duty	self as all
f. Stagnation	Friendship	Ambition
II. Paradise as a place		
a. Omicron Ceti III	*Enterprise* with crew	*Enterprise* empty except for Kirk
b. down	Transporter Room	up

The *Star Trek* episode "This Side of Paradise" shows the mediation often seen in competing myth structures.

Reading down the columns ... McCoy accepts the spores painlessly. Forgetting his duty, he loses his self in the group induced by the spores. He gains peace and contentment, marked by the return of his Southern accent and evoking in the viewer's mind the opening scenes of *Gone with the Wind,* that is, the plantation as paradise.[18] Kirk, his opposite, is briefly affected. Because of his anger, he rejects the spores painlessly and without regret. Though he says he realizes their meaning, his sense of duty is too strong for them. Kirk is left by himself — literally, alone with his self. Spock, the middle ground between them, accepts the spores but painfully. For him as for Kirk they are unnatural: like McCoy, he experiences their effect, wants it and regrets its passing. Spock breaks continuity with the group by asserting his individuality; he fights back when Kirk insults his parentage and logical outlook. When he returns to duty, he does so knowing his loss. He sacrifices the happiness of the spores to his responsibility to others. The cost of the sacrifice is made real through the love affair with Leila. The spores suppress Spock's Vulcan side. Fully human, he can love. Once returned to normal, he can not even speak of his regard for her. Given the characterization of Spock as a constant struggle against emotions and the sexual feelings that lie has aroused in viewers, the affair expresses poignantly the pain of paradise lost.[19]

Star Trek is committed to technological progress as the answer to our problems. Roddenberry reiterated in a *Penthouse* interview (March 1976) his reasons for the series' popularity, one of which is:

> First of all, we live in a time in which everyone, and particularly young minds, are aware that we face huge troubles ahead. There are many people saying, "I doubt if we'll make it through the next twenty or thirty years." And indeed, if you read the newspapers it seems so. "*Star Trek*" was a rare show that said. "Hey, it's not all over. It hasn't all been invented. If we're wise, why the human adventure is just beginning." And this is a powerful statement to young minded people, to think that the explorations and discoveries and challenges ahead of us are greater than anything in the past.

For such an attitude as Roddenberry's paradise, a state of wholeness, of unity, can only be stagnation, for paradise denies the need for the quest. Sandoval, head of the colony, says after his release from the spores:

> We've done nothing here. No accomplishments. No progress. Three years wasted. We wanted to make this planet a garden.

Kirk pronounces the moral of the episode:

> Maybe we weren't meant for paradise. Maybe we were meant to fight our way through. Struggle. Claw our way up. Scratch for every inch of the way. Maybe we can't stroll to the music of the lute. We must march to the sound of drums.

Edifying but unpleasant. There is a third way, one suggested by the structure of the story: responsibility to others. Spock tells Leila:

> I have a responsibility. To this ship. To that man on the bridge. I am what I am, Leila. If there are self-made purgatories, then we all have to live in them. Mine can be no worse than someone else's.

Paradise is knowingly and willingly sacrificed for love of others and for duty.

Omicron Ceti III is depicted as rural America, and the *Enterprise* without its crew as a helpless hulk. The one place expresses the simplicity of the past. Kirk alone on the ship, whose vast technological capabilities are a repeated theme of the series, expresses the loneliness of those who have left the past for the uncertainty of the future. Between them is the *Enterprise* with crew. The struggle between Kirk and Spock that determines Spock's role as a mediator occurs in the Transporter Room, the intersecting point of the "down" of the planet and the "up" of the ship. Here the conflict over the idea of paradise is resolved, for here on the ship the sacrifice is ever made.

The authors intend for us to see the story in the context of the drug culture of the '60s. Their intended message is found in the pontifications of Kirk. But the meaning coming from the story's structure is very different: friendship and the self-sacrifice and responsibility it demands offer a middle way between the dropping out of the Flower Children and the rat race of their parents. The episode ends— the last thing we see — with the three friends reunited in the common mission of the *Enterprise*. This mission, stated after the teaser of every show, is never questioned (or questioned in order to be reaffirmed) in this or any episode. The bitter conflict over lifestyles of the '60s, as worked out through the mediator Spock, is relieved by a third: being with friends on a mission whose undoubted worth confers upon existence ready-made meaning and purpose.

In a similar fashion the series itself mediates the tension between the past and the present by establishing a third time, that of first beginnings, it is a time with the anticipation and wonder of the future without the anxieties of the present, with the glory and security of the past without its remoteness.[20] By transcending in an ultimately inexplicable way the sum of message and medium *Star Trek* puts the fan-become-believer in that time. As an indication of what I am saying I quote the following poem from a *Star Trek* fanzine[21]:

> Gliding swiftly through the dark,
> Sailing now in starry space.
> Silently and free you fly,
> Traveling midst time and place.
>
> Like a quiet thing, alive.
> Though your engines hum and roar,
> faster than the speed of light,
> High above the sky you soar.

> Oh! To he aboard you now
> As between the stars you roam,
> To he once move upon your decks.
> The *Enterprise* is my home.

For the believer "*Star Trek* Lives" is more than the slogan of a TV show that would not die. It is the ritual cry to a world where he belongs, where he has it all together. *Star Trek* offers the comfort of religion.

Notes

1. Stephen E. Whitfield and Gene Roddenberry, *The Making of Star Trek* (New York, 1968) 22. The context of Roddenberry's remark is one of throwing sand into the network's eyes in order to get the show on the air. But see Robert L. Shayon's comment in *Saturday Review* (June 17, 1967) 46: "*Star Trek* is a space version of *Wagon Train*. There's the crew, there's the encountered. The problems arise now from the in-group, now from the out. The future is not without its counterpart of violence in the past and present."

2. Jim Kitses, "The Western: Ideology and Archetype," In *Focus on the Western*, ed. Jack Nachbar (Englewood Cliffs, NJ, 1974) 66.

3. Frederick J. Turner, "The Significance of the Frontier in American History," *Annual Report of the American Historical Association for the Year 1893* (Washington D.C., 1894) 199–27. For a more convenient source see Ray A. Billington, *Frontier and Section: Selected Writings of Frederick Jackson Turner* (Englewood Cliffs, 1961).

4. Stated after the teaser of every episode is the series' continuing theme: "Space — the final frontier. These are the voyages of the Star Ship *Enterprise*. Its five year mission: to explore strange new worlds, to seek out new civilizations, to boldly go where no man has gone before."

5. Whitfield (above, note 1) 257 for both quotations.

6. Gene L. Coon, "Errand of Mercy," first shown on March 23, 1967. An adaptation of the script has been published by James Blish, *Star Trek 2* (New York, 1968) 41-54. Although many writers contributed to *Star Trek*, Coon along with D.C. Fontana (see below, note 15) and Roddenberry maintained consistency and provided the series with its best, most characteristic episodes.

7. The here term is Northrup Frye's *Anatomy of Criticism* (Princeton, 1957) 136–37: "Myth, then, is one extreme of literary design; naturalism is the other, and in between lies the whole area of romance, using that term to mean ... the tendency ... to displace myth in a human direction and yet, in contrast to "realism," to conventionalize content in an idealized direction. The central principle of displacement is that what can be metaphorically identified in a myth can only be linked in romance by some form of simile: analogy, significant association, incidental accompanying imagery, and the like."

8. For the intimate communication of television see Mawry Green, "The Mythology of Television," *Television Quarterly* 9 (1970) 5–13; Robert C. O'Hara, *Media for the Millions* (New York, 1961) 286–306; Horace Newcomb, *TV: The Most Popular Art* (Garden City, NY, 1974) 154–60; 243–64. Ernst Cassierer, *Essay on Man* (Cambridge, 1944; reprint: New York) 89) has suggested that myth has "not a substratum of thought but of feeling. Myth and primitive religion are by no means entirely incoherent, they are not bereft of sense or reason. But their coherence depends much more upon unity of felling than upon logical rules."

9. Jacqueline Lichtenberg, Sondra Marshak and Joan Winston, *Star Trek Lives!* (New York, 1975) 107–8. More revealing of *Star Trek*'s appeal, I believe, is the authors' comment (8) on what the reader may gain from their book: "Most of all, perhaps, we hope you will find that *you are not alone!*" [italics in original].

10. Mircea Eliade, *The Sacred and the Profane*, translated by Willard Trask (New York: 1961) 80–113.

11. Arthur K. Moore, *The Frontier Mind, A Cultural Analysis of the Kentucky Frontiersman* (Washington, 1957) 25–37. See also Henry Smith, *Virgin Land* (Cambridge, 1950).

12. The theme of paradise appears in order of airing in: "The Menagerie" (two-part episode), "Shore Leave," "This Side of Paradise," "Who Mourns for Adonais?," "The Apple, Metamorphosis," "Paradise Syndrome," "For the World Is Hollow and I Have Touched the Sky," "The Mark of Gideon," and "The Way to Eden."

13. Max Ehrlick, "The Apple." All quotations from the episodes are taken from the televised version of the script. There is an adaptation of "The Apple" by James Blish in *Star Trek 6* (New York, 1972) 49–68. Blish takes too many liberties with the scripts for his adaptations to be useful for the study of *Star Trek*.

14. "The Apple" was first shown on October 13, 1967. On October 21 and 22 demonstrations took place in Washington and in particular at the Pentagon, protesting the number of those killed in Vietnam.

15. Nathan Butler and D.C. Fontana, "This Side of Paradise," first shown on March 2, 1967, and adapted by James Blish in *Star Trek* 5 (New York, 1972) 58–72.

16. The transporter is a "device for converting matter temporarily into energy, beaming that energy to a predetermined point, and reconverting it back to its original pattern and structure" (Whitfield [above, note 1]) 192. It is the usual means of access to and from the ship.

17. Edmund R. Leach, "Genesis as Myth," *Myth and Cosmos*, edited by John Middleton (Garden City, 1967) 113.

18. Smith (above, note 11) 145–54.

19. See Lichtenberg *et al.*, (above, note 9) 71–105 for a discussion of Spock from the fan's point of view.

20. See above, note 4.

21. J. Clinkenbeard, "Love Poem to a Ship," *Warped Space*, fanzine of the *Star Trek* Club of Michigan State University, October 31, 1974.

2009 Postscript

409 Words on "*Star Trek* as Myth and Television as Mythmaker"

"Classic" *Star Trek*, as one of my students dubbed it, spun off five television series and ten movies with a eleventh as of this writing playing in a theater near you. My wife and I made a ritual of watching *The Next Generation*; dinner had to be ready by seven on Saturdays. We followed *Deep Space Nine* for a while but *Voyager* not much. Even so, these and the cartoon and *Enterprise*, none of which I saw, were television shows. They could carry on the defamiliarization and regeneration of American mythology and confront America's social problems, but they never would have spawned the movement that is *Star Trek*. That development belongs to the Trekkies/Trekkers who could move at a con between the actor Mark Lenard and the character Sarek with ease. Leonard Mlodinow (*Newsweek*, May 4, 2009) attributes the longevity of *Star Trek* to its "'corporate culture,' a culture of imagination" that put out new scientific ideas for scientists to "copy." Perhaps, but the two episodes written by science fiction writers were the least indicative of the series. America is deeply anti-intellectual, distrusting, even fearing, scientific advancements beyond a better iPod.

The science of the original series reflects the longing of its popular mentality for freedom from change, for security rather than enlightenment. *Star Trek* explains why machines can never replace men or research alter humankind. The defeat of the superman Kahn, for many fans the baddie quintessential, comes about by combat: Kirk knocks him unconscious. The series left the explanation of Kahn's failure to James Blish: "The man who cannot know fear is gravely handicapped," that is, genetic manipulation is bound to fail. (See my "*Star Trek*'s Myth of Science" in *Journal of American Culture* 2 [1979] 288–96.) J. J. Abrams, producer and director of the new *Star Trek*, while realizing his favorite *Star Wars* is "pure fantasy and disconnected from everything we knew," contends that "the universe Mr. Roddenberry created is all about us. Not only is his vision still relevant, I would argue that it's more relevant now than ever" (*TV Guide* May 6, 2009). Despite its theme of going boldly, *Star Trek* works best at easing the pain of longing for home, that time of first beginnings when the world was American. *Star Trek* gives us our mythological roots disguised as branches. It feels good and restores our collective soul to reach out to the future for what we used to be in the past.

–Wm. Blake Tyrrell, East Lansing, Michigan, May 2009

Postscript Works Cited

Logan, Michael. "Setting a New Course." *TV Guide* 6 May 2009.
Mlodinow, Leonard. "Vulcans Never, Ever Smile." *Newsweek* 4 May 2009.
Tyrrell, Wm. Blake. "*Star Trek*'s Myth of Science." *Journal of American Culture* 2 (1979): 288–96.

2

A Structuralist Appreciation of Star Trek

PETER J. CLAUS*

I ... want to emphasize the fact that anthropology should be not only the study of savage custom in the light of our mentality and our culture, but also the study of our own mentality in the distant perspective borrowed from Stone Age man.
— Bronislaw Malinowski, *"Myth in Primitive Psychology"*

The "Distant perspective" I bring to bear on television as our symbol of technological and cultural sophistication is that of the savage intellect revealed in myth by the theories and methods of Claude Lévi-Strauss. When Lévi-Strauss first used structural analysis in his study of the Oedipal myth (1955), his findings bewildered the academic world. He was variously accused of crediting myths with more and less than the savage mind was capable; by and large, though, his work was mistakenly considered to be a mere aberrancy. Not until Edmund Leach added a more pragmatic flavor to the theories and applied the methods to several classical Biblical and Hindu myths (Leach, 1961, 1962a, 1962b, 1966) did the English-speaking world become familiar with the technique.

Lévi-Strauss, meanwhile, was already conducting advanced exploration into the vast dimensions of the human mind as revealed by his methods (1963a). His work on myth— *Mythologiques,* as he calls it — has culminated in a tedious four volumes (1964, 1967, 1968, 1971). Tedious—his techniques reveal such complexity in even a simple story that the resultant labyrinth is again met with bewilderment and skepticism by even his close followers. However, his advocates are now legion and under his influence a variety of scholars have once more returned to seek the universal truths of human nature in myths of the ancient and the innocent.

Lévi-Strauss's structural analysis has been applied imaginatively and rewardingly to a wide variety of oral traditions over the last decade. In this

---

*Originally published in American Dimensions, Cultural Myths and Social Reality, *William Arens and Susan Montague, eds. New York: Alfred, 1976, 15–32.

paper I illustrate how a new medium, television, can be approached in a similar manner. My reasons for suggesting the application of structural analysis to this realm are not simply to add another study to the numerous ones already existing, nor to suggest that different methods are needed and different structures forthcoming, but rather to apply structural analysis to a tradition that we can all judge critically. A most surprising result of this approach is that it demonstrates that despite the enormous complexity afforded by an electronically transmitted visual dimension, the basic structural features of most television programs are virtually identical to the nonindustrial traditions analyzed by Lévi-Strauss and other structuralists. As a result, I shall be particularly concerned with demonstrating the similarities between television serials (using *Star Trek* as an example) and myth when compared in terms of Lévi-Strauss's formula ($f_x A : f_y B :: f_x B : f_{a-1} Y$); and discussing the nature of mediation and mediators in modern myth.

We need not concern ourselves with an elaboration of this cryptic formula or the use of the word "mediator" at the present time since these are discussed at length later. However, for those readers who hate to be left in the dark about the conclusion of a paper, the formula, briefly, states that the principal characters or imagery of a myth always stand in an initial relationship of opposition to one another; hence, the left-hand side of the formula. This opposition is resolved through the narrative of the myth by a series of mediating characters and processes in such a way that the characters partake in one another's character and function ("f"). This mediation is what the right-hand side "explains." This, Lévi-Strauss claims, is a structure (i.e., the formula or rule) common to all myth, which he views as many mental attempts at reconciling and transforming the basic contradictions between nature and culture, the real and the ideal.

Myth and Television Serials

Most structuralists would probably agree that it is not wise to define myth too rigorously. Although Lévi-Strauss places it at one extreme of verbal expression in opposition to poetry (1955), others have found it necessary to distinguish mythic structure from that of other oral traditions (Kongas-Maranda and Maranda, 1971). In this study I have taken inspiration from Lévi-Strauss's advice to "broaden one's perspective, seeking a more general point of view which will permit the integration of forms whose regularity has already been established ... but [are] incompletely analyzed or viewed in too narrow a fashion" (1963a: 46). Certainly television, like myth, is at the opposite end of the expressive spectrum from poetry.

From this perspective it could be argued that much of a weekly television schedule potentially qualifies as myth. Clearly, westerns, gangster shows, espionage thrillers, and others have a social function for our society similar to that of myths among many nonindustrial peoples. I shall choose *Star Trek*, strictly speaking a "prophecy tale," for my analysis and try to reveal the common internal, logical grounds it shares with myth. Each of the characteristics linking *Star Trek* to myth are internal ones. There is also an external correspondence, for as with myth in relation to religion, *Star Trek* has a cult-like following of believers whose association is perpetuated by some truths and values they distill from the program.

The features commented on are time, the logic of fantasy, narrative structure, and levels of reality represented and linked by myth.

Time

Though myth is placed in period long ago, in another sense it is also timeless. Lévi-Strauss has written: "[myth] explains the present and the past as well as the future" (1963c: 209). *Star Trek*, despite its futuristic time setting, is clearly meant to carry a message for the present. Given the fantastic machines and exotic forces of the universe that make up the scenarios, many of the episodes actually leap back into our own American past for their plots and settings. The promiscuous use of temporal settings achieves the same end as that achieved by using a temporal setting long ago in the past: ability to create an ideal model of existence bearing a "genetic" similarity to the present, but lacking all the annoying facts of the real world.

The Logic of Fantasy

The essence of myth is that it contradicts the elements and the logic of ordinary existence. Upon closer inspection, however, it is clear that myth is restrained by both physical and human nature. For those who adhere to its peculiar tradition, myth is enhanced by an extraordinary (though not exactly irrational) truth-value. *Star Trek*, while frankly acknowledged as fantasy, expresses fundamental values of American society precisely because they are seen to persist "victoriously" (to use Maranda's term) in what could have been an utterly imaginary future situation. From the perspective of a projected future, it is apparently reassuring to see that our present values have withstood time to confront the as yet unknown world of the future. The fantasy of television has a particularly powerful link to reality since there always persists the feeling that "seeing is believing."

Narrative Structure

Myth, as Lévi-Strauss has demonstrated, consists of meaningful units, mythemes, or gross constituent units that exist "at the sentence level" (1963c:

210–212). While myth is presented diachronically in narrative strings of such related units, the repetition of mythemes throughout the narrative creates bundles of related unit-relationships through which the meaning of the myth is expressed. Analysis consists of abstracting these sets of relationships and expressing them in a model that can be used for the purpose of comparing different versions of the same myth and for comparing different myths.

Since it is this aspect of Lévi-Strauss's technique that aroused so much skepticism when it was first presented, it is perhaps advisable to present a brief example of this style of analysis.

Hammel (1972) provides us with an excellent example of a structural analysis of the familiar tale of "The Three Bears." I abstract aspects of a synchronic analysis of one version and encourage the interested reader to consult Hammel's full analysis for a rewarding discussion and example of structural methodology. I quote in full:

> Papa Bear, Mama Bear, and Baby Bear were eating breakfast. Papa Bear said "My porridge is too hot." Mama Bear said, "My porridge is too hot, too." Baby Bear said, "My porridge is too hot, and I burned my tongue." So they went into the woods to look for some honey and to let the porridge cool. Meanwhile, Goldilocks had been walking in the woods and found their house. She went in and saw the porridge and tasted it. Papa Bear's porridge was too hot. Mama Bear's porridge was too cold. Baby Bear's porridge was just right and she ate it all up. Then Goldilocks sat in Papa Bear's chair, but it was too hard. Then she sat in Mama Bear's chair, but it was too soft. Then she sat in Baby Bear's chair, and it was just right, but she broke it. Then Goldilocks was tired and wanted to rest. She tried Papa Bear's bed, but it was too hard. She tried Mama Bear's bed, but it was too soft. Then she tried Baby Bear's bed, and it was just right, and she fell fast asleep. When the three bears came home with the golden honey, Papa Bear said, "Someone has been eating my porridge." Mama Bear said, "Someone has been eating *my* porridge." Baby Bear said, "Someone ate my porridge all up." Then Papa Bear said, "Someone has been sitting in my chair." Mama Bear said, "Someone has been sitting in *my* chair." And Baby Bear said, "Someone sat in my chair and broke it." Then Papa Bear said, "Someone has been sleeping in my bed." Mama Bear said, "Someone has been sleeping in *my* bed." And Baby Bear said, "Someone is sleeping in my bed." The three bears looked at Goldilocks. Goldilocks woke up and saw the bears and ran away home. The bears went back to their breakfast of porridge, milk and honey [Hammel, 1972: 8–9].

Mythemes, the meaningful unit Lévi-Strauss first identified in myth, is like a phoneme, the unit of meaning in ordinary speech. Just as semanticists talk of different types of meaning in ordinary speech (Leech, 1974), we may recognize different types of meaning in myths. At one level, we may analyze the equivalent of the semanticist's "conceptual meaning" by looking for contrastiveness and constituent structures:

Man =	+ human	Woman =	+ human	Boy =	+ human
	+ adult		+ adult		− adult
	+ male		− male		+ male

Gender differences which privilege the masculine are often found in myth structures as well as *Star Trek*.

At other levels we can look at "connotative meaning": woman implies a list of associative properties, such as housewife, mother, gregariousness, etc. "Collocative meaning" is implied by the words associated with the term: woman is pretty, man is handsome; and so on until every last aspect of meaning is accounted for. Detailed analysis of even a simple myth along these lines, using the Lévi-Straussian methods at each level and then for the whole has an effect similar to using a centrifuge to separate the constituents of a complex liquid such as milk. However, the whole process is extremely elaborate and complicated, so in analyzing this preliminary example, and even in dealing with *Star Trek*, we merely skim off the cream in a rather crude fashion.

The first step in a structural analysis is to identify the mythemes and arrange

Family of bears tries to eat breakfast of porridge: a) Papa Bear: "too hot" b) Mama Bear: "too hot" c) Baby Bear: burns tongue			Bears go into woods to gather honey
	Goldilocks walking through woods intrudes on bear's domain: a) Tries to eat porridge, twice unsuccessfully b) Tries to sit on chair, twice unsuccessfully c) Tries to sleep on bed, twice unsuccessfully	Goldilocks consumes or destroys the bears' property: a) Eats all of the baby Bear's porridge b) Comfortable on Baby Bear's chair but breaks it c) Falls asleep on Baby Bear's bed	
Family of bears return to home with honey to find their property tampered with: a) "Someone eating my porridge" b) "Someone sitting on my chair" c) "Someone sleeping on my bed"			Bears find their property consumed or destroyed: a) "Someone ate my porridge all up" b) "Someone sat on my chair and broke it" c) "Someone *is* sleeping in my bed"
	Goldilocks wakes up, runs from bears	Goldilocks returns to her home	
A$_{fx}$	Bfy	Bf$_x$	Y$_{a-1}$

The classic Structuralist example of "Goldilocks and the Three Bears" shows a common arrangement of mythemes.

them in groups, but try to preserve as much of the narrative sequence as possible.

The mythemes thus abstracted are grouped in columns. Throughout the narrative, abridged in the table but running from left to right, the mythemes are contrasted and repeated at another level of contrast to express their relationships. Myths are often cryptic; despite their repetitiveness, they often express different kinds of meaningful relationships simultaneously. Hence, the appreciation of a myth is usually at an "impressionistic," symbolic level, and the analysis is dependent upon scant clues and subtle nuances of usage. In my present analysis I shall deal only with the summary relationships expressed on the bottom of the table.

As Hammel notes, "Philosophically or interpretively speaking, Goldilocks' adventure consists of the introduction, playing out, and resolution of a conflict between Nature and Culture" (1972: 9). The summary logic of the narrative places the conflict in a well-defined metaphoric structure that dynamically reconciles the opposed elements by both interparticipation of their qualities or functions (e.g., B_{fx} becomes B_{fy}) and reduction of their opposed qualities or inversion of them (e.g., f_y becomes Y_{a-1}). This reconciliation of the conflict, then, is through a process of *mediation* in the terms and functions of the characters. Thus the culturalized Bear family is unable to partake in human activities (eating porridge, sitting in chairs, sleeping in beds) and goes to the woods to collect honey, activities associated with nature. The intruding girl, Goldilocks, succeeds where the bears fail; she ultimately returns to her home. The bears are left with a lifestyle less complete than before the intrusion: The Baby Bear's porridge, chair, and bed have been destroyed by her actions. Hammel carries the analysis to several other levels, which I shall let him summarize.

> The major dimensions of contrast are those of 1) Nature versus Culture, 2) object versus being, and 3) active/large versus active/small. The dimensions of similarity, which bridge and mediate the oppositions just stated, are 1) color and sweetness, which link Goldilocks and honey, 2) utilization, which places the bears and the honey in the same functional relationship as Goldilocks and the bed and the porridge, and 3) goodness to fit to an opposite, which unites the honey to the porridge and Goldilocks to the Baby Bear [Hammel, 1972: 14].

However, while I agree with his conclusion that the moral of the story is simply "people are not animals, Culture is not Nature," I would prefer to emphasize that the moral is expressed more exactly as:

Cultural bears : natural girl : : cultural girl : nature inverted

Or,

$$Af_x : Bfy : : Bf_x : Y_{a-1}$$

Comparisons of nature to culture are common mythological structures as exemplified by the Goldilocks tale.

The opposition of Nature and Culture, despite the recounter's attempts at reconciliation, is indeed irreconcilable. Although culture and nature are homologous in some ways, they are different in others. Even in the juxtaposition of cultural bears and natural girls we must recognize a lack in culture. So, "cultural bears are to natural girls as cultural girls are to Nature incompleted (less than whole, a-1)," says the myth.

In his expeditions through the mythological traditions of many cultures, Lévi-Strauss has come to the conclusion that mythic reality expresses a realization of man's place in the universe that is both hopeful and pathetic. It is hopeful in that it regards the achievements of man (culture) as superior to those of the universe around him (nature) — he is created in the image of God; it is pathetic in that it regards the achievements of man (culture) as a tenuous delusion — merely an artificial reality incapable of even self perpetuity and maintenance without the aid of nature. Human nature (culture) is a nature less than complete. Sex, eating, death, and so forth are facts of life no matter how nicely we dress them in cultural trappings (for a structural look at the cultural trappings of an American meal, see Douglas, 1971).

We will now return to our discussion of *Star Trek*. Careful recording and analysis of television serial episodes such as *Star Trek* reveal the same structural features and mythic logic as those found by Lévi-Strauss, Hammel, and others in diverse non–Western mythic traditions and children's fairy tales. Television, of course, has an additional visual dimension — a complex product of choreography, actors, and camera shots— but all this is governed by the same principles that underlie the verbal dimensions of oral myth. To the extent that a television serial is considered a single program, each episode may be treated as a different version of one myth with the same basic mythemic relationships— set in different external contexts. While a viewer can comprehend the meaning of a single episode in isolation, additional episodes elaborate on the basic relationships and add different dimensions. Thus a broader, yet more fundamental, understanding of the structures can be obtained by comparing the different episodes.

Levels of Reality Represented and Linked by Myth

Myth, as Lévi-Strauss has demonstrated over the years since his analysis of the Zuni material (1963c: 219–227), not only has a "horizontal" structure of relations between my theme bundles, but a "vertical" relation between different levels of reality (economic, ecological, cosmological, etc.). Further, myth stands in dialectical relationship to society, the "lived-in structure." Again, let me elaborate, for Lévi-Strauss is referring here not to the types of meaning discussed earlier but rather almost to their opposite, the kinds of deception in myth.

Myth somehow gets away with convincing one — even if only for the moment — that its message contains a truth in the face of a nonsensical circumstance. We accept its argument in part because a certain internal symmetry in its different levels of reality replaces that of the real world. For those who do not recognize this symmetry, the myth, no matter how well translated, is mere falsehood. In this sense we can say that one culture's bible is another culture's myth, for the dialectical relationship between mythic reality and the real world is not significant for the believer. Or, to be more accurate, the symmetry of the mythic reality could be said to be more perfect and more workable and therefore has instructional or inspirational value.

One of the major functions of myth is to resolve elementary dilemmas of existence. As E. R. Leach puts it, "Lévi-Strauss has argued that when we are considering the universalist aspect of primitive mythology we shall repeatedly discover that the hidden message is concerned with the resolution of unwelcome contradictions.... The repetitions and prevarications of mythology so fog the issue that irresolvable logical inconsistencies are lost sight of even when they are logically expressed" (1970: 58).

Myth represents those dilemmas in sets of imagery that are homologous to reality. In complex myths, or in myths represented in widely varying forms (as is often the case in non-Western traditions), many such sets occur in the same myth. The sets are arranged in an order to progressively reduce the initial opposites, sometimes through scenes that have no overt relationship but that still retain common structural properties. Often the dilemmas are pervasive enough in a culture's activities that the scene shifts (or is possibly simultaneously represented) from warfare to family life, from institutions of social control to those of daily livelihood, from the community to the individual, and so on. At each level, between each level, and through each level the major dimensions of the problems are posed, reduced, and resolved at what Lévi-Strauss has identified as a structural level.

In *Star Trek* the metaphor of the spaceship, its crew, and the various extraterrestrial phenomena they encounter constitute a highly complex and multidimensional reality subtly juxtaposed to the lived-in existence of American society.

Since *Star Trek* is shown as a series of episodes, to understand a given episode fully we must compare its structure to that of past ones. What in one episode is elaborate and exaggerated is tacitly presented in subsequent episodes. The development of the characters and their relationships to one another and to foreign beings is a process continued through the entire series.[2] The analytically active mind has no trouble seeing that the spaceship and its crew represent a number of contemporary organizations and institutions. That the metaphor has its origins in the common denominator of our culture's organizational categories and structures is clear. Transformations linking different episodes are simple and obvious. In one program, the organization is (1) *the military*, with a commander (Captain Kirk), lieutenants, corporals, and civilian advisors. In another, the metaphor is (2) *a nation*, with its president (Kirk) and a cabinet representing specialist functions such as scientific, technological, medical, sociological, etc. Equally obvious is (3) *a corporation* — the ship is named the *Enterprise* — with its chairman of the board, a scientific research division, industrial psychologist, public relations divisions, etc. A constant but only occasionally central metaphorical representation is that of (4) *humanity* — "spaceship Earth" — with each of the races and nationalities represented in stereotypic role relations. It is not hard to find the metaphor of (5) *the human body*, contained by an outer skin (the ship) and including counterparts to the various organs of food distribution, locomotion, emotions, intellect, and drives.

In any given episode, one or more of these metaphors, along with others, is overtly featured. The metaphorical representation, organized man, is presented in an adventurous situation, always in confrontation with that which seeks to destroy it. The confrontations take the form of clearcut dichotomies which are portrayed verbally and visually on many planes.

	Realm	vs.	*Opposition*
Nation:	The *Enterprise* crew is a good power protecting the weak and innocent		The evil Klingon Empire, which exploits the weak and innocent
Military:	The *Enterprise* crew of reasonable officers and devoted ranks		The Klingon crew of brutal officers and self-serving ranks
Military:	The *Enterprise* crew of orderly command		The primitive and rebellious band
Humanity:	Human free will and compassion		The computer being and the robot-populated worlds
Humanity:	Intellect combined with corporal desires		The mind-only beings and spiritual worlds
Ideology:	The man of action		Pacifists and idealists

The major dichotomies found in the mythological structures of many *Star Trek: The Original Series* episodes help explain how *Star Trek* attempts to define what is "human."

Inevitably, the *Enterprise* crew overcomes the adversary in a complex process of mediating the opposition and demonstrating the superiority of the *Enterprise* crew. The sequence involves a series of partial oppositions and partial mediators in a typically nonlineal progression. Each episode, for that matter, is clearly meant to be merely a part of a longer series of confrontations that serve to define human morality in the future.

To effect mediation, the program incorporates a wide variety of inherently medial beings, the most important of whom is Spock, the half-human, half-Vulcan being who is second in command of the ship. Others are encountered in different worlds; they vary from animated rocks to minimally materialized bundles of energy; from emotional robots to mechanized humans. But even Captain Kirk, the stereotyped ideal of American normalcy, can function as a mediator when the opposing ideals of our own society confront one another.

We have seen that the program is based on moral problems, stated in the form of conflict between opposites, and the resolution of these problems involves mediation. An altogether too brief synopsis and analysis of a single episode will help to establish the characteristic structure of the program and the role of the mediators in more detail. Again, I shall only have time to "skim the cream."

In this episode,[3] the *Enterprise* is engaged to bring a mineral from one planet (B) to save another planet (A) from an epidemic disease. One minute into the program we encounter multidimensional dialectic involving planet of disease (organic) — planet of medicine (mineral), *Enterprise* as mediator (technological). Rushing to planet B the crew discovers a revolution between the Dionysian miners who live on the surface of the planet and the planet's commercial rulers, who live an Apollonian existence in a cloud city. The social revolution is holding up the shipment of the mineral. When Captain Kirk forcibly and physically conquers the female (dark hair and complexion, ill-clad) leader of the miners and the intellectual Spock rejects the affections of the daughter (blonde, toga-clad) of the leader of the sky people, the classical dichotomy is partially mediated by the more extreme dichotomies inherent in the interstellar crew. Halfway through the program we see the sophisticated discipline of the sky people crumble and their aggressive tendencies surface. Meanwhile, the miners are shown to be capable of reason and feelings.

Together, Kirk and Spock reason that the apparently opposed races (or civilizations) are merely the result of the miners' continual exposure to the mineral-medicine, which accentuates their aggressive tendencies. After a sequence in which the miners are removed from the mineral's influence and the skyleader is exposed to it (thus each part fully takes on the character of the other) the two races recognize their common nature. In the end the *Enterprise* crew agrees to mediate a just settlement of reciprocal duties between the two peoples and finally leave to bring the medicine to avert the epidemic on planet A.

Interestingly, the internal dichotomy of the one planet (B) is not completely resolved, but is qualitatively altered from that of a natural one to a cultural one. The physical differences are the product of the invisible emissions of an inert environmental agent that is the backbone of the planet's economy. The physically based division of labor is changed qualitatively into a cultural one when the damaging effects of the mineral can be controlled by technology. The passage from nature to culture is apparently one of the concerns of our culture, and one of our methods of comprehending it (i.e., through myth) is the same as that in primitive societies.

The structure of *Star Trek* appears to adhere closely to the "law of myth" as expressed by Lévi-Strauss's formula ($f_x A : f_y B : : f_x B : f_{a-1} Y$). Dichotomies expressed as oppositions between the terms and functions of A and B are equated with a situation in which B is given the starting function of A and is opposed to the inverted character of A serving as a function of the earlier function of B. Hence, planet B is capable of providing the cure for planet A, but is itself diseased — socially — and the curative function of medicine is withheld because of internal opposition and conflict. The episode utilizes the formula again and again in relation to the oppositions inherent in planet B — repeatedly at various levels in the complex opposition between Apollonian and Dionysian imagery. Analytically this process may be treated somewhat like embedding in transformational linguistic analysis. Eventually the oppositions are mediated, though not eliminated, since a division of labor remains. Yet the transformation from nature to culture is complete.

Oppositions abound throughout the episode at all levels as expressed via ideology, materials, emotions, actions, and appearances.

Planet A		*Planet B*
Sickness, needs medicine		Has medicine
	sky people	earth people
	Apollonian rulers	Dionysian workers
	beauty	toil
	distribution	production

The classic formula of Claude Lévi-Strauss equating dichotomous poles can be mythically mediated through narrative.

The opposed elements undergo a series of operations that alter their oppositions. This process itself involves two types of mediators and mediating actions: (1) confrontation with a character (or character set) who shares the qualities of both poles, but is superior to each in its own way, and (2) the inversion of the characteristics of the opposed characters until their common nature is established.

The use of mediation and mediators is of fundamental importance to an understanding of the significance of *Star Trek* to its ardent followers. The initial and continual opposition of a planet in need of a curative mineral and a planet that possesses this mineral is mediated not only by the *Enterprise* but also by the entire play on contradiction, which occupies the body of the episode. The internal contradiction among the people of planet B is shifted from an irreconcilable natural one to an "understandable" cultural one based only on the arbitrary but necessary division of labor in a system of exchange.

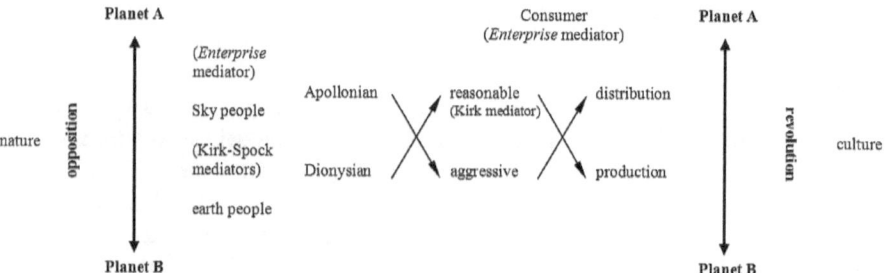

Mediation between culture and nature, as well as different types of culture, are common motifs in original *Star Trek* episodes.

Mediation, a logical process, may use medial beings, such as Spock, but need not. Actually, mediation is, in this episode at least, accomplished more frequently by balancing extremes with the "super-normal" hero Captain Kirk (he may be simply a "well-balanced" person), or by inversion of the characters' behavior as a reaction to the catalytic agent or element, the "medicine," which is not itself medial.

Thus the resolution of the conflict, felt to be a revelation or conquest of sorts, is transformed by the media into a logical encounter. What reason would the American public give for the popularity of such logical games? I suspect that the answer is analogous to the reply that any member of a nonliterate, nonindustrial society might give. Myth and *Star Trek* provide a model of real society in which the conflicts of life can reasonably be resolved precisely by adhering to values transcending nature, those same values that are so frail and elusive in the factual world.

Finding not only the same laws but the same significance in myth of television affirms Lévi-Strauss's expectations that "man has always been thinking equally well; the improvements lie not in the alleged progress of man's mind, but in the discovery of new areas to which it may apply its unchanged and unchanging powers" (1963c: 230).

Notes

This paper was first read in the symposium "Form and Formative in the Symbolic Process" held at the American Anthropological Association Annual Convention, 1974, Mexico City. I wish to thank the members of that symposium for their helpful suggestions and their critical comments.

1. Particularly noteworthy contributions available in English are: Leach, 1962a, 1966, and Kongas-Maranda and Maranda, 1971.
2. Although different episodes have different authors, a group of editors assures consistency from episode to episode. The overriding criterion, though, is public appeal — that the story encapsulate the collective fantasy of the audience. The potential objection (cf. Hammel, 1972) is that because each *Star Trek* episode has a known author, structural methodology, which is geared to collective representations does not apply. Even if it did, the question of authorship is, I think, a red herring.
3. I purposely omit the title and the details from the episode in order to divorce my analysis from a "literary" analysis of the episode. The analysis I give emphasizes the gross structural features. I expect that this type of analysis will draw criticism from certain elements of the large crowd of devoted fans, called "Trekkies," whose attention — as is true of Biblical scholars — is on the accuracy of the details.

Works Cited

Douglas, Mary. "Deciphering a Meal." In Clifford Geertz, ed. *Myth, Symbol, and Culture*. New York: Norton, 1971.
Hammel, Eugene. "The Myth of Structural Analysis: Lévi-Strauss and the Three Bears." Addison-Wesley Module in Anthropology, No. 25, 1972.
Kongas-Maranda, Elli, and Pierre Maranda. *Structural Models in Folklore and Transformational Essays*. The Hague: Mouton, 1971.
Leach, Edmund R. "Genesis as Myth." *Discovery*, May 1962: 30–35. Reprinted in John Middleton, ed., *Myth and Cosmos: Readings in Mythology and Symbolism* (New York: Natural History Press, 1967).
_____. "The Legitimacy of Solomon: Some Structural Aspects of Old Testament History." *Archives of European Sociology* 7 (1966). 58–101.
_____. "Lévi-Strauss in the Garden of Eden: An Examination of Some Recent Developments in the Analysis of Myth." *Transactions* of the New York Academy of Sciences, Ser. II, vol. 23, no. 4, 1961.
_____. "Pulleyar and Lord Buddha." *Psychoanalysis and Psychoanalytic Review* 49, no. 2 (1962): 81–102.
Leech, Geoffrey. *Semantics*. Baltimore: Penguin, 1974.
Lévi-Strauss, Claude. "Four Winnebago Myths: A Structural Sketch." In S. Diamond, ed. *Culture in History, Essays in Honor of Paul Radin*. Published for Brandeis University Press by Columbia University Press, New York, 1960.
_____. *Mythologiques I: Le Cru et le Cuit*. Paris: Pion, 1964. (English translation, *The Raw and the Cooked*. New York: Harper & Row, 1969.)
_____. *Mythologiques II: Du Mel aux Cendres*. Paris: Pion, 1967. (English translation, *From Honey to Ashes*. New York: Harper & Row.)
_____. *Mythologiques III: L'Origine des manières detable*. Paris: Pion, 1968.
_____. *Mythologiques IV: L'Homme Nu*. Paris: Pion, 1971.
_____. *La Pensée Sauvage*. (English translation, *The Savage Mind*. Chicago: University of Chicago Press, 1963.)
_____. *Structural Anthropology*. New York: Basic, 1963.

_____. "The Structural Study of Myth." In *Myth, a Symposium. Journal of American Folklore* 78, no. 270 (1955): 428–444.

_____. *Totemism*. London: Merlin, 1963. (English translation of *Le Totemisme aujourd'hui*, Paris.)

2009 Postscript

The Structure of Structuralism, or, Lévi-Strauss and the Use of Theory

One of the things an anthropologist has to do—for him or herself, if not for others—is to become convinced that the methods and tools he or she uses to analyze other peoples, their languages and cultures, is not of use because the anthropologist or the anthropologist's culture is presumed superior to the other, but because the tools themselves provide whatever insight is thought to be of value. A microscope or a telescope is such an instrument for physical scientists such as biologists and astrophysicists. Any human looking through a microscope at a drop of pond water has a new world revealed to them, whether or not they then wish to pursue that new world and explain its order and existence. But cultural anthropologists do not have these kinds of instruments to reveal culture in the same way physical scientists reveal nature.

When I wrote this article on *Star Trek* there was a nagging question on my mind. Claude Lévi-Strauss had proposed a method—a "tool"—for analyzing the world's myths derived from theoretical linguistics which looks at the units of sound which distinguish words in human languages. In linguistics, this method had long been a standard tool of proven worth. Lévi-Strauss's ingenious use of this tool to study longer stretches of narrative composition: "myths" was a big leap. Yet, just as the units of sounds that distinguish words in a language are not ordinarily perceived by the speakers of a language, so too, the units of myth—those elements that go into the composition of myths—are not apparent to the tellers of myth. Lévi-Strauss' leap was aided by his conviction that myth is rather more like philosophy (cosmology) than just fanciful stories. He took them far more seriously than most other anthropologists had. But there is one more feature to Lévi-Strauss' method, and that is that, like the units of sound in a language, the units of myth operate at a psychological level. Furthermore, the myth-teller's cosmological thoughts are more like a philosopher-poet's way of pursuing the nature of the universe than they are the government-funded scientist's. They explore with words and imaginative stories rather than with telescopes and space ships. But they, too, can go where "no man has gone before."

The tool used to reveal a fact need not even be understood by the user: it is still not clear how structuralism works. Lévi-Strauss himself resorted to enchanting metaphors in order to "explain" the workings of his method and the phenomena it revealed. But as a philosopher himself, he knew he was now talking with other philosophers and for the first time he felt he could understand them. It was for him, I think, something like finding a device, or a key, to understanding the language of other beings or entering the tower of babble.

Unfortunately, he was so far out there, that he lost most of his prosaic anthropological colleagues. So when I wrote this article, I only wanted to use an example familiar to my contemporaries to establish a communication link to Lévi-Strauss's craft. I think it helps, but there are still many more marvelous worlds of mythology for us to explore in Lévi-Strauss's logs.

— Peter J. Claus, Hayward, California, June 2009

3

Some Implications of the Mythology in Star Trek

C. SCOTT LITTLETON*

It is, I think, fair to say that *Star Trek* has long since become a veritable icon of American popular culture. Indeed, almost from its inception twenty-three years ago as a weekly television series, it has attracted a vast throng of loyal supporters, including that curious breed known variously as "Trekkies," "Trekkers," and simply "*Star Trek* freaks," who have remained faithful to the starship *Enterprise* and her crew through thick and thin. They agonized over its cancellation by NBC in 1969, have stayed up countless nights until the wee hours of the morning to watch re-runs, and have exulted in the resurrection that began with the first *Star Trek* film in 1979,[1] and which so far has witnessed three additional major motion pictures, with a fifth scheduled to appear in the summer of 1989.[2]

The reasons for this enduring popularity are many and varied, but surely not the least of them is the fact that, like all cultural icons, *Star Trek* reflects a number of fundamental mythic themes and motifs. To be sure, certain episodes, such as the celebrated "Who Mourns for Adonais?" (Episode #33), in which the crew of the *Enterprise* discovers a planet ruled by Apollo, are explicitly based on Greek mythology and make obvious use of its motifs.[3] And, in a recent critical essay, Sigmund Casey Fredericks has observed that *Star Trek* is a prime example of what he calls the "Odyssean" category of contemporary science fiction, a conclusion that is wholly consonant with what follows.[4] However, Fredericks is concerned with *Star Trek* only in passing, and his emphasis is upon the impact of classical mythology; as we shall see, the mythological dimension here is far more generalized. Indeed, a number of well-nigh universal mythical themes can be detected throughout the *Star Trek* canon, even in episodes that are not obviously "mythological."

*Originally published in Keystone Folklore 4 (1989): 33–42.

It should be emphasized, of course, that the remarkable television and film series in question is a conscious literary creation, and that the presence of these themes in the delineation of its characters and the unfolding of its plots is not altogether fortuitous. The makers of *Star Trek*—Gene Roddenberry, D. C. Fontana, Gene L. Coon, Marc Daniels, et al.[5]—are all thoroughly literate people who seem to have drawn intentionally on a wide variety of myths and legends, classical and otherwise, in the preparation of various episodes. Indeed, what ultimately emerges is a secularized mythology of the future that fuses the more or less rational attitudes and beliefs of the culture that spawned it with themes and motifs that pervade mankind's oldest and most sacred narratives. It is to this heretofore largely neglected aspect of the *Star Trek* phenomenon that this paper is addressed.

The Enterprise *and the* Argo

In a very real sense, the voyages of the *Enterprise* occur in as mythopoeic a context and time frame as that of Jason's *Argo*,[6] or the ship in which Odysseus embarked at the end of the Trojan War[7]; indeed, they are functional equivalents. Just as myths about a presumed "Golden Age" permitted the classical Greeks, who lacked the blessings of modern archaeology, to make sense out of their otherwise unknowable Bronze Age origins, so myths about the inherently unknowable future permit us to make sense out of the shape of things to come. What is more, in both cases, the narratives in question also serve to structure (and at the same time are structured by) the world-view of the myth makers. To the Greeks, the voyage of the *Argo* was at once an event that had happened far back in the mythopoeic age and a reflection of all the dangerous sea voyages ever embarked upon, or that ever will be embarked upon. In short, the adventures of Jason, Odysseus, et al., occurred outside of what may be called "real time": they had occurred, were occurring, and would continue to occur as long as Greeks ventured forth in frail boats to challenge the dangers of the "wine-dark" sea.

That *Star Trek* occurs in a similar dimension outside of real time is also clear. Captain Kirk is at once Captain Cook, as my late colleague Jim Kelly once suggested,[8] *and* every astronaut who has ever (or will ever) leave the surface of this planet—just as Jason was/is/will be the prototype of every Greek seafarer, including Odysseus. The example of the Jason legend was, of course, chosen advisedly, as both it and *Star Trek* seem to reflect the same fundamental mythic theme: that of the quest.

The Quest Theme

The quest theme is very ancient and well nigh universal in its distribution.[9] Indeed, the Eskimo story of the wanderings of Kiviok is an excellent example of a quest myth far removed from the sources of the Western tradition.[10] But the immediate roots of *Star Trek* lie in the ancient Near Eastern and Aegean quest stories, some of which date from the third millennium B.C. A good example is the story of Gilgamesh, whose quest for the secret of immortality is perhaps the prototype of all subsequent Western quest stories.[11] Another very ancient manifestation of this theme can be found in the Egyptian accounts of Sinuhe the Wanderer, which date at least from the Middle Kingdom, and are the immediate forerunners of the well-known tales of Sinbad the Sailor in the Arabian Nights.[12] In addition, of course, there is the aforementioned account of Jason and the Argonauts, as well as Homer's *Odyssey* and the more recent, but still respectably ancient, tales of the Wandering Jew and the Flying Dutchman.[13] The theme in question also crops up in medieval European folklore the most famous example, of course, being the quest for the Holy Grail.[14]

In India, the quest theme can be found in the *Ramayana*, wherein Rama and his "sidekick" Hanuman engage in a quest for the former's abducted bride, Sita, a story that is closely paralleled by the account of the abduction and subsequent rescue of Kudrun in medieval Germanic folklore.[15]

To be sure, most of these quest stories involve a fairly specific goal or object: to find the secret of everlasting life, to recover a lost bride, to return to one's home, to find the Grail, etc. But the object of the quest in *Star Trek* is much less definitive. In the television series, it was a "five-year voyage ... to boldly go where no man has gone before," that is, presumably, to explore the galaxy. Nevertheless, the quest theme is very evident in the overall *structure* of the original television series, as well as the subsequent films. Indeed, many of the episodes themselves closely parallel episodes in the *Odyssey*, the *Argonautica* and other quest stories just mentioned. For example, in at least one episode there is a close parallel to the Siren motif, as found in the *Odyssey*. Believing himself to be possessed by some alien being, Kirk tells his crew to restrain him and disregard any orders he might give to the contrary (e.g., "The Naked Time" [Episode #71]).[16] In other episodes, a Circe-like female figure gains psychic (or, indeed, physical) control over one or more members of the crew. Like Odysseus, Kirk (or Spock) finally figures out a way to release them, and the quest continues (e.g., "Catspaw" [Episode #30],[17] "Spock's Brain" [Episode #61],[18] "Turn-about Intruder" [Episode #79],[19] "Wink of an Eye" [Episode #68][20]). Indeed, in one such episode, "By Any Other Name" (Episode #50),[21] the crew of the *Enterprise* are temporarily transformed into another state of being, in this case small tetrahedronal blocks, which recalls the fate of Odysseus's crew at the hands of Circe.

Still other episodes broadly resemble the visit of the Grail Knight to the Castle of the Fisher King. While exploring the surface of a hitherto uncharted planet, Kirk (or Spock) ventures into a fantastic building, wanders from room to room, and eventually discovers a mysterious figure, perhaps the last survivor of some calamity, who is guarding a unique power or secret (e.g., "Miri"

[Episode #12],[22] The Squire of Gothos" [Episode #18][23]). Moreover, in at least two episodes, "Requiem for Methuselah" (Episode #76)[24] and "Plato's Stepchildren" (Episode #67),[25] the figure in question is described as afflicted with a debilitating infirmity, a trait reminiscent of the festering wound that debilitates the Fisher King in the Grail Romances.[26]

From a structural standpoint, then, *Star Trek*, like the quest stories of Western antiquity, has some important implications for the ways in which we Westerners have tried to come to terms with the universe we find ourselves in. Underlying all such tales, ancient or futuristic, is a structural opposition not primarily between "good" and "evil," in its pure Zoroastrian and/or Manichaean sense, but rather between "cosmos" and "chaos," as Eliade puts it,[27] between order and entropy, between rationality and the irrational realm "out there." The quest story, then, is necessarily a primer on how to navigate the treacherous seas of chaos-entropy-irrationality, or whatever label one might wish to use.

At an even deeper level, it is a metaphor for the individual journey from cradle to grave, a journey in which the human psyche is continually called upon to impose some sort of order on an inherently hostile and at the sane time inchoate universe, As I see it, the ultimate goal of any quest is survival itself, and the significance of the voyage of the *Enterprise* is best understood in this context.

Kirk as Trickster

The protagonists of most quest stories, *Star Trek* included, are "tricksters": figures who gain their ends primarily by recourse to their cognitive abilities rather than their physical prowess.[28] Both Jason and Odysseus are tricksters; so is Gilgamesh; even the Grail Knight Galahad relies not so much on his sword, miraculous though it may be, but upon his purity and superior psyche. That Kirk represents such a figure, at least in a great many contexts, is clear. It is Kirk, more than any other member of the crew, who survives by his wits — not his intellect, for Spock certainly has him beaten on that score, but rather by what is sometimes today called "street smarts." Like all successful tricksters, he is what Lévi-Strauss calls a *bricoleur*, that is, a person who "makes do" with what is at hand by integrating otherwise disparate elements and ideas, and, by doing so, is able to achieve a desired end.[29] A good example can be seen in "The Arena" (Episode #19), in which an unarmed Kirk must use all of his wits and ability to improvise in order to overcome a physically superior (and intellectually equivalent) lizard-like adversary.[30] Indeed, from a Lévi-Straussian standpoint, Kirk's persona emerges as the mediation of the contrast between the hyper-rational Spock, who is most certainly not a *bricoleur*, and the hyper-emotional Doctor McCoy.[31] In essence, then, the figure represented by Kirk is composed of the essential ingredients of a true trickster: rationality plus imagination.

The appeal of the trickster, especially a benevolent trickster like Kirk, lies in his essential humanness. Even the malevolent ones, such as the Norse Loki and, indeed, the Judeo-Christian conception of Lucifer, are sympathetic characters in that they are projections of the inherently human drive to survive despite great odds. That Lucifer could defy God and get away with it is one of his most attractive features, as George Bernard Shaw so eloquently demonstrates in *Don Juan in Hell*. I do not, of course, mean to suggest that the character of Kirk is in any way specifically modeled on that of Lucifer (to say nothing of Satan); I simply wish to call attention to his trickster-like capacity for endurance, for beating the odds against his own survival and that of his crew. And the fact that Kirk's adventures, like those of Jason and Odysseus, occur in a thoroughly mythopoeic context serves to underscore the extent to which he may be classed with other timeless tricksters/*bricoleurs*.

Death and Resurrection: Spock as Osiris?

In the course of the second and third *Star Trek* films, yet another major mythological theme made its appearance. At the end of the second film (*The Wrath of Khan*), the Vulcan figure dies heroically of radiation burns suffered while saving the *Enterprise* from certain destruction, and his corpse is ejected from the ship. However, the final scenes show the casket gently falling to the surface of the "Genesis planet," where, thanks to an experimental "seeding" operation, we (the audience) know that regeneration is possible. In the third film (*The Search for Spock*) Spock is indeed recovered as a small child who rapidly ages, and is eventually returned to his native planet, where we are given to believe that the restoration of his lost personality will eventually be complete. We thus have here a "death and resurrection" theme that broadly parallels the death and rebirth of the ancient Egyptian god, Osiris.[32] To be sure, unlike his Egyptian counterpart, Spock is not assassinated, nor is he specifically mutilated, although the effects of the radiation are clearly degenerative. However, the search for his reborn (if not exactly stitched together) body by Kirk and the rest of the crew, accomplished in the face of great odds, does broadly parallel the Egyptian myth. Moreover, the role played in that search by Saavik, a female Vulcan officer, and, by implication, Spock's would-be consort (thanks to the unique Vulcan mating cycle[33]), can perhaps be compared to the crucial part played by Osiris's loyal wife, Isis, in his resurrection.[34]

Star Trek *as a Mirror of Contemporary Society*

Finally, it should be emphasized that *Star Trek* like myths generally, is a projection of both the society which created it and the mythopoeic context in which it is supposed to unfold. Just as Homer's *Iliad* is at once a fusion of early eighth century Ionia (that is, Homer's own society) and the half-remembered glories of the late Mycenaean era, so the milieu of Kirk and his crew reflects both contemporary American society as well as what its creators believe will be the future shape of that society. It would be impossible to explore all of the dimensions of this relationship in an article of this scope, so I will confine my remarks to one important aspect of *Star Trek* that both anticipated the future and reflected the tenor of the times, that is, the late sixties, when the series first appeared: the casting of women and/or minorities as highly trained technicians, the best examples, of course, being the characters of the Asian navigator, Mr. Sulu, and the black female communications officer, Lt. Uhura.

As Whitfield and Roddenberry point out, such casting was considered rather daring in 1966:

> The decision to have an obvious mixing of races in the cast caused a lot of raised eyebrows. Integration was not commonplace in television at that time.[35]

Indeed, in retrospect, the decision to integrate the bridge of the *Enterprise* was something of a breakthrough. Yet neither Sulu nor Uhura are true decision makers. Even the half-human, half–Vulcan figure of the Executive Officer, Mr. Spock, reflects this pattern to some degree, for it is abundantly clear that he is not the Captain, and his celebrated intellect is ultimately at the disposal of Kirk.[36] Moreover, as an alien (or half-breed, if you will) serving among human beings, Spock is visibly different from the rest of the crew, and is a member of a projected minority group. This mythopoeic image of "high-tech," albeit "child-like" minorities and women who are subservient to white, male "father-figures," such as Kirk in his official role as Captain, reflects both the current American ambivalence about how to deal with such people and a presumed future when their expertise will be taken for granted by all concerned.

Conclusions

In sum, these are some of the implications of the mythology in *Star Trek*: the presence of a mythopoeic time frame, in which can be detected the quest theme, the trickster figure, and the "Osiris theme," all of which are couched in images reflecting, among other things, the ambivalent attitudes toward women and minorities characteristic of contemporary American culture. There are, of course, a great many more such themes and images that remain to be detected, especially if the growing corpus of *Star Trek* fiction, fan-produced and otherwise, is taken into consideration. But I do hope that the foregoing, which is admittedly a preliminary analysis, will inspire other folklorists to undertake a more comprehensive assessment of the mythical and folkloristic underpinnings of this and other manifestations of that endlessly fascinating and remarkably durable genre known as science fiction, Indeed, as Fredericks aptly concludes in his brief but trenchant discussion of *Star Trek*:

> Like every other mythology, SF asks those ultimate questions about the limits of man and all his imaginative extensions of himself to the very ends of time and space which demand the full resources of his intuitional capacities, from dream and nightmare and wish fulfillment, as well as their formal extrapolations in myth, religion, and theology.[37]

Notes

This article is dedicated to the memory of my late colleague, James F. Kelly, who organized and chaired the symposium in which the earliest version of it was presented: "Anthropology and Science Fiction: The *Star Trek* Case," Southwestern Anthropological Association, Santa Monica, CA, April 13, 1974. I should like to thank the members of that symposium, Elliott Oring, John Baughman, Anthony Lord and, of course, Jim Kelly, for their thoughtful comments and suggestions. The current version also owes a debt of gratitude to Camille Bacon-Smith, Luanne B. Hudson, and Bernard K. Means for their willingness to read and comment on a draft. I should emphasize, however, that my interpretations are wholly my own, and that I take full responsibility for them.

1. *Star Trek: The Motion Picture*; see Gene Roddenberry and Susan Sackett, *Star Trek: The Making of the Motion Picture* (New York: Pocket, 1980).

2. *Star Trek* followers have also greeted with mixed emotions the debut in 1987 of a syndicated weekly series, *Star Trek: The Next Generation*, which is set eighty to a hundred years later than the time period of the original series and subsequent motion pictures and therefore involves a wholly different cast of characters. This article will not attempt an assessment of this new series, and will restrict itself to the original characters and context.

3. Allan Asherman, *The* Star Trek *Compendium* (NewYork: Simon & Shuster, 1981), pp. 110–111.

4. Sigmund Casey Fredericks, "Greek Mythology in Modern Science Fiction: Vision and Cognition." In Classical Mythology in 20th Century Thought and Literature, ed. Wendell M. Aycock and Theodore M. Klein (Lubbock, TX: Texas Tech Press, 1980), pp. 89–106.

5. For a detailed account of the people who made *Star Trek*, see Stephen E. Whitfield and Gene Roddenberry, *The Making of Star Trek* (New York: Ballantine, 1968). See also Asherman, op. cit., pp. 23–62.

6. See Appolonius Rodius, *The Argonautica*. Translated by R. C. Seaton (Cambridge, MA: Harvard University Press, 1961).

7. The definitive English translation of the *Odyssey* is Richmond Lattimore, *The Odyssey of Homer* (New York: Harper and Row, 1965).

8. Personal communication (March 1974).

9. For a discussion of the quest theme, see Stith Thompson, *The Folktale* (New York: Holt, Rinehart and Winston, 1946), pp. 105–108.

10. For a discussion of the Kiviok legend and its parallels with the story of Odysseus and other Western wanderers, see Andreas Lommel, *Shamanism: The Beginnings of Art*. Translated from the German by Michael Bullock (New York: McGraw-Hill, 1967), p. 105.

11. See E. A. Speiser, "Akkadian Myths and Epics." In *Ancient Near Eastern Texts Relating to the Old Testament*, ed. James B. Pritchard (Princeton, NJ: Princeton University Press, 1955), pp. 72–100.

12. For the Sinuhe story, see John A. Wilson, "Egyptian Myths, Tales, and Mortuary Texts." In *Ancient Near Eastern Texts Relating to the Old Testament*, ed. James B. Pritchard

(Princeton, NJ: Princeton University Press, 1955), pp. 18–22. For Sinbad, see *Sinbad the Sailor, and Other Stories from the Arabian Nights* (London: Hodden and Stoughton, 1914).

13. For the Wandering Jew, see Joseph Gaer, *The Legend of the Wandering Jew* (New York: Mentor Books, 1961). For the Flying Dutchman, see Gerndt Helge, *Fliegender Hollander und Klaubautermann* (Gottingen: O. Schwartz, 1971); Catherine Jolicoeur, *Le vaisscau fantome: legende etiologique*. Québec: Presses de Université Laval, 1970.

14. See Jesse L. Weston, *From Ritual to Romance* (New York: Doubleday Anchor Books, 1957), p. 113 ff. See also C. Scott Littleton, "The Holy Grail, the Cauldron of Annwn, and the Nartyamonga: A Further Note on the Sarmatian Connection," *Journal of American Folklore* (Vol. 92, 1979), pp. 327–333.

15. See Donald Ward, *The Divine Twins: An Indo-European Myth in Germanic Tradition* (Folklore Studies 19; Berkeley: University of California Press, 1968), pp. 70–80.

16. Asherman, op. cit., pp. 71–73.
17. Ibid., pp. 107–108.
18. Ibid., pp. 152–153.
19. Ibid., pp. 173–175.
20. Ibid., pp. 160–161.
21. Ibid., pp. 134–135.
22. Ibid., p. 79.
23. Ibid., pp. 87–88.
24. Ibid., pp. 168–170.
25. Ibid., pp. 159–160.
26. See, for example, Weston, op. cit., pp. 20–22.
27. Mircea Eliade, *Cosmos and History: The Myth of the Eternal Return* (New York: Pantheon, 1954), pp. 10–11.
28. See, for example, M. L. Ricketts, "The North American Indian Trickster," *History of Religions* (Vol. 5, 1966), pp. 327–350.
29. Asherman, op. cit., pp. 88–89.
30. Claude Lévi-Strauss, *The Savage Mind* (Chicago: University of Chicago Press, 1966), pp. 16–20.
31. Cf. Claude Lévi-Strauss, "The Structural Study of Myth," in *Reader in Comparative Religion*, eds. William A. Lessa and Evlon Z. Vogt (New York: Harper and Row, 4th ed.,1979), pp. 185–197.
32. For a summary of the Osiris story, see Rudolf Anthes, "Mythology in Ancient Egypt." In *Mythologies of the Ancient World*, ed. Samuel Noah Kramer (New York: Doubleday Anchor, 1961), pp.33–50.
33. That is, the so-called *pon far*, or "mating frenzy," which occurs every seven years and which, if not alleviated by his return to the planet Vulcan for participation in a marriage ritual, will culminate in Spock's death. See "Amok Time" (Episode #34); Asherman, op. cit., pp. 111–113.
34. This theme was not carried forward in the fourth film ("The Return"), which was something of a departure from the usual format in that it focused on a visit to 20th century San Francisco. Whether it will be picked up again in the next film ("The Final Frontier") remains to be seen.
35. Whitfield and Roddenberry, op. cit., p.111.
36. At the outset, Roddenberry proposed casting a woman in the role of Executive Officer of the *Enterprise*, and indeed did so in the first pilot, "The Menagerie" (originally entitled "The Cage"); cf. Asherman, op, cit., pp. 27–30. But the studio later vetoed the idea. As Whitfield and Roddenberry, op. cit., p. 128, put it: "Although *Star Trek* was a show about the 23rd century, it was being viewed by a 20th century audience — who resented the idea of a tough, strong-willed woman ... as second-in-command."
37. Fredericks, op. cit., p. 103.

2009 Postscript

The Mythology Continues: An Afterword

Much has happened in the *Star Trek* universe since this article first appeared in 1989. Four additional television series—*Star Trek: The Next Generation* (1987–1994; it is mentioned in passing in the foregoing essay), *Star Trek: Deep Space Nine* (1993–2000), *Star Trek: Voyager* (1995–2001), and *Star Trek: Enterprise* (2001–2005)—have come and gone, at least as first-run series, although most of them can still be seen, along with the original series, as reruns on TV screens around the planet. Moreover, there have so far been a grand total of eleven *Star Trek* movies. In addition to the four discussed in the essay, these include *Star Trek V: The Final Frontier* (1989), *Star Trek VI: The Undiscovered Country* (1991), *Star Trek: Generations* (1994), *Star Trek: First Contact* (1996), *Star Trek: Insurrection* (1998), *Star Trek: Nemesis* (2002); and the most recent, *Star Trek* (2009), a prequel of sorts, which plays fast and loose with the *Star Trek* canon under the thin veneer of an alternate-universe plot. In this latest addition to the big-screen series, a young Jim Kirk, straight out of the Academy, assumes command of the Starship *Enterprise*—that is, the one featured in the original TV series, as opposed to its precursor and namesake captained by John Archer in the most recent spin-off series, *Star Trek: Enterprise*—during an emergency and must come to grips with, among other things, the total destruction of the plant Vulcan, as well as two incarnations of Spock, one of them close to his own age and the other (played by Leonard Nimoy) a grizzled elder.

And, of course, *Star Trek*'s beloved creator, Gene Roddenberry, passed away in 1991; most appropriately, in 1992, his ashes were carried into space by the Space Shuttle *Columbia*.

Nevertheless, despite this remarkable array of *Star Trek* TV series and films, to say nothing of a plethora of *Star Trek*–themed books, I'm happy to report that most of the mythic elements I identified in the original series and first few films are still very much present. For example, in *The Next Generation*, the binary opposition between McCoy and Spock reappears in that between the thoroughly human First Officer William Riker and the supremely intelligent android, Lieutenant Data, who, like Spock before him, is incapable of human emotions. There is, however, an added dimension here in that this latter opposition is usually mediated by the all-wise father-figure, Captain Jean-Luc Picard, who is less of a trickster/*bricoleur* than Kirk. One can see here, perhaps, an omniscient Odinic figure mediating between the hyper-emotional war god Thor and the clever, albeit malicious Loki. To be sure, Data is neither evil, malicious, nor a trickster, and is Riker is *not* portrayed as a chest-thumping, blood-thirsty warrior. Far from it. Still and all, the basic opposition is the same: emotion vs. logic. What's more, the fact that Picard manifests both human emotions and, where necessary, cold logic, is reminiscent of the role played by the supreme god Odin in Norse mythology, perhaps even more so than that played by the more ambivalent Zeus among his fellow Olympians.

And, of course, the quest theme continues to resonate in almost every episode and film. Perhaps the most striking example can be seen in *Voyager*, in which, like Odysseus and his companions, the goal is simply to overcome seemingly insurmountable obstacles and return home.

It is also evident that the impact of changing cultural mores has not been lost in the crafting of the more recent avatars of *Star Trek*. A good example is the fact that Captain Kathryn Janeway, of the Starship *Voyager*, is a woman. How different this is from Paramount's reluctance even to cast a woman as second in command in 1967! An analogous example can be seen in *Deep Space Nine*, where Benjamin Sisko, the station commandant, is an African-American. Indeed, one might go so far as to suggest that it presaged the American presidential election of 2008.

It would be impossible here even to begin to trace out all of the mythological manifestations in the post–1989 *Star Trek* series and films. Indeed, the most recent film adds a decidedly post-modern — and often confusing — dimension to the ongoing narrative. But one can say with certainty that, as of 2009, the franchise remains committed to portraying a space-time that lies well beyond what I've called "real time." It is a universe in which Captains Kirk, Picard, Janeway, Sisko, and Archer are still one with Jason, Odysseus, Sinbad, Columbus, Cook, Ahab, Armstrong, and every other sea- or spacefarer, real or fictional, that has ever left (or will ever leave) the comfort and safety of home port in search of what's lurking "out there" and waiting to be discovered.

— C. Scott Littleton, Los Angeles, California, June 2009

Postscript Works Cited

Star Trek. Directed by J.J. Abrams. Screenplay Roberto Orci and Alex Kurtzman. Paramount Pictures, 2009.
Star Trek V: The Final Frontier. Directed by William Shatner. Screenplay by David Loughry. Paramount Pictures, 1989.
Star Trek VI: The Undiscovered Country. Directed by Nicholas Meyer. Screenplay by Nicholas Meyer and Denny Martin Flynn. Paramount Pictures, 1991.
Star Trek: First Contact. Directed by Jonathan Frakes. Screenplay by Brannon Braga and Ronald D. Moore. Paramount Pictures, 1996.
Star Trek: Generations. Directed by David Carson. Screenplay by Ronald D. Moore and Brannon Braga. Paramount Pictures, 1994.
Star Trek: Insurrection. Directed by Jonathan Frakes. Screenplay by Michael Piller. Paramount Pictures, 1998.
Star Trek: Nemesis. Directed by Stuart Baird. Screenplay by John Logan. Paramount Pictures, 2002.

4

Star Trek

American Dream, Myth and Reality

ACE G. PILKINGTON*

William Shatner says, "*Star Trek* is like a modern Ulysses, a myth that has been passed down over a period of 25 years and through a number of generations" ("*Star Trek*: The Third Season" 55). In *The World of Star Trek*, David Gerrold writes from a similar perspective, "Science Fiction is the contemporary fairy tale, it's the twentieth century morality play ... at its best, it is the postulation of an alternate reality with which to comment on this one" (7).

For more than a quarter of a century *Star Trek* has been an American dream machine, shaping the present and predicting the future of the American experience. Like most myths, its stories are at once didactic and aesthetic, politically powerful and psychologically satisfying. It has simultaneously shown Americans as they wanted to see themselves and promised that the future would be better than they knew their troubled past or uncertain present to be. As a result, the most potent of *Star Trek*'s messages has always been hope. However, part of the success of the series and the films has come from the multiplicity of mythic messages and the many mirrors they have provided for America. *Star Trek* has shown us everything from unity to alienation, from prejudice to acceptance, from passivity to predation, and from logic to emotion.

Gene Roddenberry initially sold the concept of *Star Trek* to NBC as "Hornblower in Space" (Gerrold 5) or a "Wagon Train to the Stars" (Whitfield and Roddenberry 23). Both the military ambience of a naval vessel and the frontier ethos of the American West are clearly part of the mythic furniture of the series and of its continuing appeal. Captain Kirk as the center of the films is a

---

*Originally published in Encyclia: The Journal of the Utah Academy of Sciences, Arts, and Letters 69 (1992): 65–76.

military leader, invested with the power that such a position implies. He has the authority to give orders in any circumstances. In "The Devil in the Dark," for instance, Doctor McCoy, who, as a physician, has his own air of authority, objects to treating a monstrous creature which is, as he says, "virtually made out of stone." He complains, "I'm a doctor, not a bricklayer," and Kirk responds, "You're a healer. There's a patient. That's an order."

William Shatner's role has taken on some of the aura of invincibility that Spock in "The Enemy Within" says must invest the leader, "You're the captain of this ship. You haven't the right to be vulnerable in the eyes of the crew. You can't afford the luxury of being anything less than perfect. If you do, they lose faith, and you lose command." *Star Trek*'s producers and directors have never allowed the helm, figurative or literal, to slip from Kirk's grip. When Steve Meerson and Peter Krikes were brought in to work on the screenplay for *Star Trek IV*, they were told, "make sure that the character of Admiral Kirk is the driving force behind every aspect of the story" (Gross 100).

And the writers, directors and producers have made full use of the issues and emotions which war in its many forms can raise. Perhaps this is because war as metaphor, as art commenting on reality, has had a particular relevance for America. As Geoffrey Perret argues in *A Country Made by War*, "America's wars have been like the rungs on a ladder by which it rose to greatness. No other nation has triumphed so long, so consistently or on such a vast scale, through force of arms" (558). The *Enterprise* and her crew have been involved in almost every kind of warfare, much of it a filmic commentary on American foreign policy.

In "Balance of Terror," a single Romulan vessel tests Federation defenses by attacking its "Neutral Zone" outposts. Kirk and company respond by pursuing and destroying the ship in a chase sequence drawn largely from the World War II submarine film *The Enemy Below*, with occasional borrowings from *Run Silent, Run Deep* (Asherman 40). Although the *Enterprise*'s ostensible rationale is to "fight to prevent a fight," the comparisons between Kirk and the Romulan commander throughout the episode make clear the similarities of the two professional soldiers and the admiration the series creators have for the breed.[1] All of this is summed up in the Romulan Commander's last speech, delivered, of course, to Kirk, "I regret that we meet in this way. You and I are of a kind. In a different reality, I could have called you friend." In another Romulan adventure, Kirk and Spock engage in espionage, going behind enemy lines to steal a new piece of technology in "The *Enterprise* Incident."

If the Romulans were given the militaristic philosophy and military virtues of Nazi Germany, the Klingons became obvious stand-ins for the Soviets. This is clearest in *Star Trek VI*, where the Klingon Empire is falling apart, and Spock volunteers his comrades to help in easing the peace process. During the series, however, there was little doubt of the Klingons' real origins and no suggestion of friendship. In "A Private Little War," the Klingons and the Federation arm two opposing sides on a primitive planet in a ritual of one-upsmanship which Kirk specifically compares to "the twentieth century brush wars on the Asian continent." Though the episode contains much passionate argument between McCoy and Kirk and both of them feel defeated by the conclusion they reach, they ultimately endorse the policy which the United States was even then pursuing. Kirk says, "The only solution is what happened back then — balance of power."[2]

The Federation and the Klingons engage in an economic competition to develop a planet in "The Trouble with Tribbles"; in a violent variety of diplomacy designed to impress a primitive tribe in "Friday's Child"; and in total war (stopped by the Organians, a group of aliens who have evolved beyond bodies to a state of pure mental energy) in "Errand of Mercy." But perhaps the clearest example of the aggressive nature of the Federation comes in the non–Klingon episode "A Taste of Armageddon." There, Captain Kirk, held hostage on the planet Eminiar 7, gives "General Order 24," which means in Montgomery Scott's words, the destruction of a planet's "entire inhabited surface." The surprise is not that the Federation would use such force in an extreme situation but that the destruction of planets is part of the *Enterprise*'s everyday codebook. The series looked at an even darker side to the Federation in "Mirror, Mirror," a parallel universe where the benevolent coalition of planets has become an evil empire.

There was, however, hope to be found among the battlefields. Human beings had survived the twentieth century, the brush wars had not become a nuclear holocaust, and the little victories of rationality continued to accumulate in the future chronicled by *Star Trek*. In "Day of the Dove," Kirk and his crew are trapped aboard the *Enterprise* with an equal number of Klingons by an entity which feeds on their savage emotions, increasing those emotions by mental manipulation to increase its nourishment. The two warring groups are forced to make peace in order to survive. In "A Taste of Armageddon," Kirk provides a plan for survival and a rationale for hope; he says, "We're human beings with the blood of a million savage years on our hands, but we can stop it. We can admit that we're killers, but we're not going to kill today. That's all it takes."

Star Trek's emphasis on hierarchy and military bureaucracy was counterbalanced by its connections to the Western and its vision of space as "the final frontier." In fact, the series boasts two episodes which might be considered Westerns, one containing a science fiction version of the gunfight at the OK Corral and the other an Indian tribe.[3] In "Spectre of the Gun" the Melkotians, a reclusive alien species, attempt to execute Kirk and his crew for intruding on their space by forcing them to act the roles of the Clantons in the famous showdown. Kirk himself is specifically linked to the American West because the aliens employ his "frontier-family history as the template" (Weinstein 48).[4] In

"The Paradise Syndrome," a Captain Kirk who has lost his memory becomes Kirok, medicine man for an Indian tribe transplanted to the stars by a mysterious race called "the Preservers." Interestingly, Kirk comes closest to happiness in this episode, where he marries an Indian princess.

More than anything else *Star Trek* took the Western's sense of freedom, of unlimited horizons and untrammeled action. The science fiction series also borrowed the Western hero's sense of isolation. As David Gerrold says of Kirk, "He would be explorer, ambassador, soldier, and peacekeeper. He would be the sole arbiter of Federation law wherever he traveled—he would be a law unto himself" (6). Of course, this unfettered "space marshall" sometimes comes into conflict with the military hierarchy he represents, the Federation which provides his ship and recruits his crew, but that too is very much a "Western" response. As Malone and Etulain note in *The American West*, after pointing out the dependence of the Western states on the Federal government, "Such reliance ... bred more antagonism than affection" (220).

Indeed virtually every representative of Federation upper echelons in the series was a bureaucratic bungler incapable of understanding the "frontier." In "A Taste of Armageddon," Ambassador Fox nearly gets the *Enterprise* destroyed and himself disintegrated as a result of separate blunders. Other official (and officious) fools whom Kirk does not suffer gladly include Commissioner Nancy Hedford in "Metamorphosis," cultural observer John Gill in "Patterns of Force,"[5] Federation Undersecretary of Agricultural Affairs Nilz Barris in "The Trouble with Tribbles," and virtually all of the ambassadors in the pointedly named "Journey to Babel."

Kirk finds his superior officers equally annoying. In "The Doomsday Machine," Commodore Decker, driven by guilt over the destruction of his own ship and crew, attempts to use the *Enterprise* to commit suicide; in "Amok Time," Spock's life is endangered by an Admiralty more interested in a diplomatic show of force than in the quirky realities of space exploration. And in *Star Trek III* Kirk is denied the chance to save Spock's soul (and possibly his body) by the Commander of Starfleet who states he has "never understood Vulcan mysticism." Kirk's response in this situation is typical: "The word is 'no'; I am therefore going anyway." He steals the *Enterprise* and sails off to do what a hero (or a friend) has to do. In reuniting Spock's disparate halves, Kirk loses his rank of admiral, his son, and his ship, but when Sarek, Spock's father, points out the high cost, Kirk responds, "If I hadn't tried, the cost would've been my soul."

Gene Roddenberry declares that "Star Trek basically presents old-fashioned heroes who believe in integrity and personal responsibility and in taking stands against intolerance" ("*Star Trek*: The Third Season" 51). Here, *Star Trek*'s creator links the old fashioned heroism of the Western with a more modern concern for integration. The freer, "frontier" environment supposedly allowed for greater tolerance, for a society that soared beyond all planetary boundaries and narrow ethnic jealousies. The settings on strange, unrealistic worlds also allowed Roddenberry to, in his words, "get the ideas past the studio, the network, and the censors" (McDonnell 6).

The interracial crew, nevertheless, led to early conflict with television decision makers. "A number of people expressed concern that the viewer might reject the concept of different races, particularly Negro and white, working side by side" (Whitfield and Roddenberry 111).[6] There was additional concern that segregationist elements might work to have the show taken off the air in certain markets, and there were also those who were troubled by "the vessel's designation *United Space Ship Enterprise* ... suggesting that this 'one world' concept would be unpopular" (Whitfield and Roddenberry 112).

However, *Star Trek* went boldly where no television show had gone before with such episodes as "Let That Be Your Last Battlefield," in which two humanoids, each half black and half white but with the white and black halves reversed seek to destroy each other. "Plato's Stepchildren" "is best remembered for the kiss between Captain Kirk and Lieutenant Uhura — the first interracial kiss on network television" (Asherman 120). It got past the censors since the two characters were forced into it by evil aliens. According to Ken Taylor on *E! Features Star Trek VI: The Undiscovered Country*, "Nichelle Nichols' character of Uhura proved so distinctive that none other than Dr. Martin Luther King convinced her to remain on the television series as a positive role model for African Americans." He goes on to quote Whoopi Goldberg's assertion "that in the 1960's, Uhura represented the fact that there was a future for black folks." Sulu and Chekov were also important to *Star Trek*'s message. Sulu, an Asian-American, was chief helmsman and fourth in command on the *Enterprise* at a time when the United States was fighting yet another Asian war. And Chekov, with his thick Russian accent, was a visible and audible prediction that former enemies would eventually become fast friends, a prediction which history is even now validating.

One of Roddenberry's main devices for fooling the studio was the creation of the alien first officer, Mr. Spock. In fact, the studio was uneasy about the character, ordering that Spock be eliminated from the cast in the second pilot, but Roddenberry insisted he could not do a science fiction show without an extraterrestrial, and NBC reluctantly went along (Whitfield and Roddenberry 126).

Spock may well have been devised not only as a case study of the alien but also of alienation, and it is, in part, his struggle with and his success in resolving these problems that have fascinated his viewers and, again, given them hope. He is, throughout the series and most of the movies, a man without a planet. On Vulcan, he suffers rejection because of his human emotions, and on earth he is criticized for his Vulcan lack of passion. As his mother, Amanda, says in "Journey to Babel," "It hasn't been easy on Spock, neither human nor Vulcan, at home nowhere except Starfleet."[7] Alone with Spock later in the same episode, she reminds him and makes clear to the audience just how hard it was for him to grow up on Vulcan, "When you were five years old and came home, stiff-lipped, anguished because the other boys tormented you, saying that you weren't really Vulcan, I watched you, knowing that, inside, the human part of you was crying, and I cried too."[8]

In the course of the series, he became a sentient and therefore sensitive lightning rod who caught the discharges of discrimination, illuminating the issue while preventing the sort of direct confrontation that might have offended the audience and the network censors. Spock also became a representation and a representative of another kind of "alien" in America, the intellectual. As Richard Hofstadter writes in his Pulitzer-Prize winning *Anti-intellectualism in American Life*, "The background of alienation in America made an uncompromising position of alienation seem orthodox, axiomatic, and traditional for twentieth-century intellectuals" (399).

Spock — who is a scientist, mathematician, computer expert, chess master, and musician — comes in for some of the name calling which often attaches to American intellectuals. In "A Private Little War," McCoy, relieved to find that his Vulcan friend has recovered from an illness but covering up his emotion says, "Well, I don't know why I was worried; you can't kill a computer." In "This Side of Paradise," Kirk and his crew are infected by spores which cause them to abandon ship and join a utopian commune. When the Captain's strong emotion at the thought of leaving his ship destroys the spores, he sets out to produce an equally strong reaction in his first officer with insults, including, "What can you expect from a simpering, devil-eared freak, whose father was a computer and his mother an encyclopedia?"

However, unlike many of his American counterparts, Spock's journey through the vicissitudes of alienation ends in the beatitudes of fulfillment in the fictional film world because of his friends and crewmates and in the real fan world because *Star Trek* found a way to make superior intellect less threatening.[9] Spock not only has the tremendous intellectual sophistication of a cerebral alien, but also the innocence and naivete of the outsider, the man who gets it wrong, not because he is stupid but because he is excluded from the shared culture. In "Patterns of Force," for example, Kirk says to Spock, "I don't care if you hit the broad side of a barn. Just hurry, please." And the response is, "Captain, why should I aim at such a structure?" In *Star Trek IV*, when Gillian Taylor asks Spock, "Sure you won't change your mind?" he answers, "Is there something wrong with the one I have?"

There is certainly nothing wrong with that mind. Spock is the brainiest modern hero (with the possible exception of Sherlock Holmes) to be accepted and loved by his audience, and he is accepted in large part because, in his intense struggle to integrate his conflicting halves, human and Vulcan, logical and emotional, as he says himself in "The Enemy Within," his "intelligence wins out over both, [and] makes them live together." He becomes a symbol for the hope that the mind can find a path of reconciliation in a labyrinth of conflict. He is also symbolic of the intellectual who finds a place to stand, a platform for action and a refuge for rest, in short, a home. For Spock, the *Enterprise* is that place.

In *Star Trek V*, Spock's half-brother, Sybok, attempts to recruit him to the cause of religious terrorism by playing on his internal inconsistencies and inadequacies. But Sybok is singularly unsuccessful. Spock subjects himself to his half-brother's psychodrama, a performance that includes a vision of Spock's birth with his father saying disapprovingly, "So human." But Spock refuses to abandon Starfleet and Captain Kirk: "Sybok, you are my brother, but you do not know me. I am not the outcast boy you left behind those many years ago. Since that time I have found myself and my place. I know who I am, and I cannot go with you."[10] Spock's refusal is particularly interesting because he does not cite duty but identity as his justification and because it is such a clear indication of his successful reconciliation of his two halves and further of his successful integration into the life he has chosen.[11]

By the end of the film, it is clear that Spock has not only transcended his alienation to find himself, he has also found a home and a family among aliens. In discussing Spock's grief over the death of Sybok, Captain Kirk says, "I lost a brother once. But I was lucky. I got him back." He is referring, of course, to Spock's death and resurrection, but there is an additional undercurrent. In the television episode "Operation: Annihilate!" Kirk's brother, Sam, was killed, and many members of the film audience (as well as McCoy and Spock) will have thought first of Captain Kirk's biological brother.[12] One message that Kirk's statement therefore sends is of the primacy of the chosen family, the possibility of voluntarily extending loyalties and empathies. That message is reinforced immediately when McCoy remarks, "I thought you said men like us don't have families," and Kirk responds, "I was wrong."

In a very real sense *Star Trek* provided (and provides) a chosen family for its audience, a dream machine and a home, a haven from the alienations of daily life and a hope for the future of humans and humanness. It is the great strength of *Star Trek* that while it provides a means of escape it also points a road to go forward, while it comments on the frictions and issues of the day, it also depicts the frontier of the future as a place rich with possibilities. Ultimately, *Star Trek*'s vision is mythical because of the luminous and numinous world it presents, but it never completely abandons the real world where its audience lives, thinks, and suffers.

Notes

1. This is hardly surprising when one remembers that one of Gene Roddenberry's earlier careers was that of combat pilot in World War II and that in a later incarnation he was a Los Angeles police officer.

2. Allan Asherman points out that the script's "earliest version contains more specific references to the Vietnam conflict" (90). Interestingly, William Shatner (in a film specifically made for the Smithsonian Exhibition) tells of a Vietnam veteran's account of a group of American soldiers who kept themselves sane during imprisonment and torture by playing the "*Star Trek* game." This involved taking turns playing different parts in the series episodes, all of which they had memorized.

3. There is also a sample of the urban equivalent of the Western, the gangster film, called "A Piece of the Action."

4. *Star Trek*'s "big three" had all appeared in Westerns; most appositely, "DeForest Kelley appeared as an Earp in the 1955 movie classic *Gunfight at the OK Corral*" (Weinstein 48). Kelley's own favorite is *Warlock*, about which he says, "I liked [my role] because he was a complex kind of guy" (Drennan 93)." On 8 December 1991, the TNT network ran an evening of Shatner, Nimoy, and DeForest Kelley Westerns which it called "The First Frontier."

5. Gill is a historian who remakes an alien planet in the image of Nazi Germany.

6. Pauline Kael provides evidence that not all such attitudes have disappeared. She calls Kirk's "crew an ethnic joke" and says "the Oriental, Sulu, is smiling, willing and obliging; the black woman, Uhura, is sensual ... the Russian, Chekov, never seems to have got past the language barrier" (*Taking It All In* 356). In this case the stereotypes are in the eye of the reviewer, not surprising when one remembers that Kael also wrote that Olivier could *play* a Negro better than a Negro could "at this stage in the world's history." Indeed she seems to equate blackness and hatefulness, saying "I saw Paul Robeson and he was not black as Olivier is; Finlay can hate Olivier in a way Jose Ferrer did not dare—indeed did not have the provocation—to hate Robeson" (*Kiss Kiss Bang Bang* 173–74).

7. In the *Star Trek* novel *The Vulcan Academy Murders*, Spock tells his father, "I would have ended up in Star Fleet anyway. For there I can be myself ... whatever that may be" (Lorrah 197).

8. The animated *Star Trek* episode "Yesteryear" actually showed such an encounter with a group of Vulcan boys taunting Spock, shouting such things as, "Earther! Barbarian! Emotional Earther! ... You could never be a true Vulcan.... Your father brought shame to Vulcan: he married a human." At the end of the encounter, Sarek apologizes for his son's display of emotion but says nothing about the behavior of the other boys.

9. As Isaac Asimov points out, "To the average man there is danger in intelligence. The strong man, being stupid, can be bent to one's will, even to the will of the average man, for the strong man is *very* stupid. The clever man, however, cannot be relied on. He can always turn on you for reasons of his own" (188).

10. Spock's sense of self is particularly important (and satisfying) because as Harvey R. Greenberg points out, "His noble, flawed figure recapitulates in outer space many a Terran youngster's search for a viable identity" (54).

11. Initially, the writers and director (William Shatner) of *Star Trek V* had planned to have Spock desert his Captain and follow Sybok, but Leonard Nimoy "adamantly opposed the story," arguing "that Spock had already reconciled the pain of his half-breed status in prior movies" (Lisabeth Shatner 67).

12. J. M. Dillard's novelization of *Star Trek V: The Final Frontier*, which was based on the shooting script and her own long study of the series and films, has "'I lost a brother once,' Jim said, knowing they would think he referred to Sam" (186).

Works Cited

"Amok Time." Writ. Theodore Sturgeon. *Star Trek*. Dir. Joseph Pevney. 1967–68 Season (9/15/67).

Asherman, Allan. *The Star Trek Compendium*. Rev. ed. New York: Pocket-Simon & Schuster, 1989.

Asimov, Isaac. "The Immortal Sherlock Holmes." *Past, Present, and Future.* Buffalo, NY: Prometheus, 1987. 185–90.
"Balance of Terror." Writ. Paul Schneider. *Star Trek.* Dir. Vincent McEveety. 1966–67 Season (12/15/66).
"The Day of the Dove." Writ. Jerome Bixby. *Star Trek.* Dir. Marvin Chomsky. 1968–69 Season (11/1/68).
"The Devil in the Dark." Writ. Gene L. Coon. *Star Trek.* Dir. Joseph Pevney. 1966–67 Season (3/9/67).
Dillard, J. M. *Star Trek V: The Final Frontier.* New York: Pocket-Simon & Schuster, 1989.
"The Doomsday Machine." Writ. Norman Spinrad. *Star Trek.* Dir. Marc Daniels. 1967–68 Season (10/20/67).
Drennan, Kathryn M. "DeForest Kelley's Western Days." *Starlog* July 1989: 93.
E! Features Star Trek VI: The Undiscovered Country. With Ken Taylor. Entertainment Channel. December 1991.
"The Enemy Within." Writ. Richard Matheson. *Star Trek.* Dir. Leo Penn. 1966–67 Season (10/6/66).
"The *Enterprise* Incident." Writ. D.C. Fontana. *Star Trek.* Dir. John Meredyth Lucas. 1968–69 Season (9/27/68).
"Errand of Mercy." Writ. Gene L. Coon. *Star Trek.* Dir. John Newland. 1966–67 Season (3/23/67).
"Friday's Child." Writ. D.C. Fontana. *Star Trek.* Dir. Joseph Pevney. 1967–68 Season (12/1/67).
Gerrold, David. *The World of Star Trek.* New York: Ballantine, 1973.
Greenberg, Harvey R. "In Search of Spock: A Psycholoanalytic Inquiry." *Journal of Popular Film and Television* 12.2 (Spring 1984): 53–65.
Gross, Edward, Kay Anderson, Wendy Rathbone, Rone Magid, and Sheldon Teitelbaum. *The Making of the Trek Films.* New York: Image, 1991.
Hofstadter, Richard. *Anti-intellectualism in American Life.* New York: Alfred A. Knopf, 1969.
"Journey to Babel." Writ. D.C. Fontana. *Star Trek.* Dir. Joseph Pevney. 1967–68 Season (11/17/67).
Kael, Pauline. *Kiss Kiss Bang Bang.* London: Calder & Boyars, 1970.
———. *Taking It All In.* New York: Holt, Rinehart and Winston, 1984.
"Let That Be Your Last Battlefield." Writ. Oliver Crawford (story by Lee Cronin [Gene L. Coon]). *Star Trek.* Dir. Jud Taylor. 1968–69 Season (1/10/69).
Lorrah, Jean. *The Vulcan Academy Murders.* New York: Pocket, 1984.
Malone, Michael, P., and Richard W. Etulian. *The American West.* Lincoln: University of Nebraska, 1989.
McDonnell, David. "Gene Roddenberry." "*Star Trek*: The Third Season." *Star Trek 25th Anniversary Special.* Ed. David McDonnell. New York: Starlog Communications, 1991. 6, 8.
"Metamorphosis." Writ. Gene L. Coon. *Star Trek.* Dir. Ralph Senensky. 1967–68 Season (11/10/67).
"Mirror, Mirror." Writ. Jerome Bixby. *Star Trek.* Dir. Marc Daniels. 1967–68 Season (10/6/67).
"Operation: Annihilate!" Writ. Stephen W. Carabotsos. *Star Trek.* Dir. Herschel Daugherty. 1966–67 Season (4/13/67).
"The Paradise Syndrome." Writ. Margaret Armen. *Star Trek.* Dir. Jud Taylor. 1968–69 Season (10/4/68).
"Patterns of Force." Writ. John Meredyth Lucas. *Star Trek.* Dir. Vincent McEveety. 1967–68 Season (2/16/68).
Perret, Geoffrey. *A Country Made By War: From the Revolution to Vietnam—The Story of America's Rise to Power.* New York: Random House, 1989.
"A Piece of the Action." Writ. David P. Harmon, Gene L. Coon (story by David P. Harmon). *Star Trek.* Dir. James Komack. 1967–68 Season (1/12/68).
"Plato's Stepchildren." Writ. Meyer Dolinsky. *Star Trek.* Dir. David Alexander. 1968–69 Season (11/22/68).

"A Private Little War." Writ. Gene Roddenberry. *Star Trek*. Dir. Marc Daniels. 1967–68 Season (2/2/68).
Shatner, Lisabeth. *Captain's Log: William Shatner's Personal Account of the Making of Star Trek V: The Final Frontier*. New York: Pocket, 1989.
"Spectre of the Gun." Writ. Lee Cronin (Gene Coon). *Star Trek*. Dir. Vincent McEveety. 1968–69 Season (10/25/68).
Star Trek III: The Search for Spock. Dir. Leonard Nimoy. Paramount. 1984.
Star Trek IV: The Voyage Home. Dir. Leonard Nimoy. Paramount. 1986.
Star Trek V: The Final Frontier. Dir. William Shatner. Paramount. 1989.
"*Star Trek*: The Third Season." *Star Trek 25th Anniversary Special*. Ed. David McDonnell. New York: Starlog Communications, 1991. 48–59.
"A Taste of Armageddon." Writ. Robert Hamner, Gene L. Coon (story by Robert Hamner). *Star Trek*. Dir. Joseph Pevney. 1966–67 Season (2/23/67).
"This Side of Paradise." Writ. D.C. Fontana. *Star Trek*. Dir. Ralph Senensky. 1966–67 Season (3/2/67).
"The Trouble with Tribbles." Writ. David Gerrold. *Star Trek*. Dir. Joseph Pevney. 1967–68 Season (12/29/67).
Weinstein, Howard. "Spectre of the Gun." "*Star Trek*: The Third Season." *Star Trek 25th Anniversary Special*. Ed. David McDonnell. New York: Starlog Communications, 1991. 48.
Whitfield, Stephen E., and Gene Roddenberry. *The Making of Star Trek*. New York: Ballantine, 1968.
"Yesteryear." Writ. D.C. Fontana. *Star Trek* (Animated). 9/15/73.

2009 Postscript

Star Trek's Myths to Live By

Seventeen years later, *Star Trek* is still alive, and its myths and their comments on our realities still resonate. Perhaps the most sustained mythical journey in that time was the Starship *Voyager*'s seven-year struggle to get home. And perhaps the most startling correlation between *Star Trek* and the real world, the most interesting connection between predicting the future and helping to shape it, is the link between *Star Trek* and the new American President, who said during his campaign last year, "I grew up on 'Star Trek'—I believe in the final frontier" (Daly).

Voyager was one place in Federation space where women truly had equal rights. The captain (Janeway), the chief engineer (B'Elanna Torres), the de-facto science officer (Seven of Nine), the crewmember who evolves into a higher life form (Kes), the precocious child who will grow up to be a Starfleet officer (Naomi Wildman), the main villain (Borg Queen), and the most important traitor (Seska) were female. It would take all the other *Trek* series combined to equal that number of major female roles. And Janeway more than holds her own among *Trek* captains. She operates on a farther frontier than the others faced, and on this seven-year odyssey, she becomes Odysseus, wily and violent but bound by her own rules.

If Picard is cautious and Kirk is dangerous, Janeway, who sometimes seems to be an authentic maniac, has left such conservative strategies far behind. In "Scientific Method," after plunging her ship between the suns of a binary pulsar, Janeway says to her blindly loyal Vulcan security officer, "I never realized you thought of me as reckless, Tuvok." He responds, "It was clearly an understatement." In the two-part episode "Year of Hell," Janeway struggles with Annorax, captain of a time ship. Tom Paris, *Voyager*'s irreverent helmsman, labels him "Captain Nemo" and says of his behavior, "That's called paranoia ... with a hint of megalomania." But Janeway is equally unyielding. She states, "We're going through their space whether they like it or not." She fights her ship for the year of the title until it is not much more than wreckage, and then, alone on *Voyager*, she destroys Annorax, kills herself, and restores the timeline by ramming the time ship.

In the long arc of *Star Trek*'s storylines, the partly mechanical, partly biological Borg are the Federation's most terrifying enemies. Only Janeway regards their powerful ships as good places from which to take technology by force. She makes deals with the Borg, steals Seven of Nine from them, and comes back from the future as Admiral Janeway to crush the Borg Queen one last time. In *The Farther Shore*, a *Voyager* novel set after the end of the series, Christie Golden has Janeway say, "The Borg are so familiar to us, they're like old friends" (31).

But *Star Trek* is never about one gender or one person, however indomitable. *Voyager*'s journey is, as all *Trek* journeys are (and Odysseus's was), a quest for humanness. Seven of Nine, a human assimilated by the Borg when she was six and forcibly rescued by *Voyager* eighteen years later, reluctantly abandons her Borg nature and struggles to rediscover and reinvent her humanity. Or as the title of *Star Trek Scriptbooks Book Two* puts it *Becoming Human: The Seven of Nine Saga*. In "The Gift" Janeway says of the appeal of the Borg, "You were part of a vast consciousness, billions of minds working together, a harmony of purpose and thought, no indecision, no doubts, the security and strength of a unified will." In this description the Borg seem to be more than unity; they are approaching divinity.

Seven complains, "This drone is small now, alone, one voice, one mind, the silence is unacceptable." But she fights her way from nonentity to identity, from despair to hope. In the process of finding herself she questions the assumptions and values of her crewmates. Though Janeway is her mentor, Seven finds the strength to question and even defy her, no mean feat where Janeway is concerned. In "Prey," Seven, who has just disobeyed the Captain's orders and saved the ship, complains, "You made me into an individual.... You encouraged ... my independence and my humanity, but when I try to assert that independence, I am punished."

Janeway responds, "Individuality has its limits. Especially on a starship where there's a command structure." But Seven is not easily silenced, "I believe that you are punishing me because I do not think the way that you do, because I am not becoming more like you." It is a continuing argument, an engagement with the self who is also the other, that leads to enlightenment for them both, just as Seven's journey to humanness and hope illuminates the transformations of the other crewmembers and their joint struggle to get home.

Hope has always been a primary ingredient in *Star Trek*. The new film (and earlier *Trek*) is connected to President Obama and his message of hope in many ways. Zachary Quinto, the new Spock, predicted in October of 2008, "The new sci-fi blockbuster will be more successful at the U.S. box office if Barack Obama is president" ("Zachary Quinto Says '*Star Trek*' Will Be Big If Obama Is Elected"). In Mark Simpson's words, "There was always a very close relationship between the American Dream — not to mention American imperialism — and *Star Trek*, with its liberal, secular, multiracial, technophiliac vision of the future. But the two seem almost to have mind-melded with the election of an optimistic, liberal, multiracial President." Steve Daly also paid tribute to the power of *Star Trek*'s images, "Spock's cool, analytical nature feels more fascinating and topical than ever now that we've put a sort of Vulcan in the White House. All through the election campaign, columnists compared President Obama's unflappably logical demeanor and prominent ears with Mr. Spock's."

And as for Barack Obama himself? Asked about the last movie he saw, the President said, "We got this nice theater on the ground floor of my house.... So *Star Trek*, we saw this weekend, which I thought was good. Everybody was saying I was Spock, so I figured I should check it out and — [the president makes the Vulcan salute with his hand]" (Meacham). Of course, that was not President Obama's first *Trek* experience. He said, "I used to love *Star Trek*. You know, *Star Trek* was ahead of its time.... The storylines were always evocative ... there was a little commentary and a little pop philosophy for a 10-year-old to absorb" (Meacham). Pop philosophy is one way to say it or as Joseph Campbell put it, "myths to live by."

— Ace G. Pilkington, St. George, Utah, June 2009

Postscript Works Cited

Campbell, Joseph. *Myths to Live By*. New York: Bantam, 1972.
Daly, Steve. "We Are All Trekkies Now." *Newsweek* 4 May 2009. http://www.newsweek.com/id/195082/output/print.
"The Gift." Writ. Joe Menosky. *Star Trek: Voyager*. Dir. Anson Williams. Season 4. 10 September 1997.
Golden, Christie. *The Farther Shore*. New York: Pocket, 2003.
Meacham, Jon. "A Highly Logical Approach." *Newsweek* 25 May 2009. http://www.newsweek.com/id/197891/output/print.
"Prey." Writ. Brannon Braga. *Star Trek: Voyager*. Dir. Allan Eastman. Season 4. 18 February 1998.

"Scientific Method." Writ. Sherry Klein, Harry Kloor, Lisa Klink. *Star Trek: Voyager*. Dir. David Livingston. Season 4. 29 October 1997.

Simpson, Mark. "*Star Trek* Boldly Goes into the Obama Era." *The Times* April 16 2009. *http://entertainment.timesonline.co.uk/tol/arts_and_entertainment/film/article6099278.ece*.

The Star Trek Scriptbooks: Book Two: Becoming Human: The Seven of Nine Saga. New York: Pocket, 1998.

"Year of Hell." Part I. Writ. Brannon Braga, Joe Menosky. *Star Trek: Voyager*. Dir. Allan Kroeker. Season 4. 5 November 1997.

"Year of Hell." Part II. Writ. Brannon Braga, Joe Menosky. *Star Trek: Voyager*. Dir. Mike Vejar. Season 4. 12 November 1997.

"Zachary Quinto Says '*Star Trek*' Will Be Big If Obama Is Elected." *Starpulse.com*. 17 October, 2008. 8 June 2009. *http://www.starpulse.com/news/index.php/2008/10/17/zachary_quinto_says_star_trek_will_be_bi*.

5

Speakers for the Dead

Star Trek, the Holocaust, and the Representation of Atrocity

MATTHEW WILHELM KAPELL*

> *And one would like to have us believe that TV will lift the weight of Auschwitz by making a collective awareness radiate, whereas television is its perpetuation in another guise, this time no longer under the auspices of a site of annihilation, but of a medium of deterrence.*
> — Jean Baudrillard

A while ago in the editor's pad of this journal (Winter 1998) Mack Hassler called for some work and insight into the way science fiction deals with things like the Holocaust. Frankly, the last thing I want to write about is the Holocaust; I find it too wrenching. But for the last seven years I had been watching one of the most popular forms of science fiction in this country — a television program — play with notions of death and atrocity all the while slipping its Holocaustal connotations in under the radar so to speak. The show, of course, is *Star Trek: Deep Space Nine* (*DS9*) and its allusions to the Holocaust, Jewish history, and the era of World War Two are central to its unique position in the *Trek* canon. Instead of focusing on the adventures of the crew of a single starship as the previous shows did, we now are shown the trials and tribulations of a single alien planet and the Starfleet and alien people who live there. As Mack Hassler and Clyde Wilcox have shown in their recent edited volume, *Political Science Fiction*, maybe all science fiction is political. However, this backstory makes *DS9* by far the most political of the *Trek* shows. The planet in question is called Bajor and the inhabitants are the Bajorans, but in significant ways they evoke the Hebrew people of Earth.

The Bajorans differ in that their Diaspora and their Holocaust are both placed within a sixty-year span of time and are both caused by the same species, the Cardassians. This event, which the Bajorans call the Occupation, saw the

*Originally published in Extrapolation 41:2 (Summer 2000): 104–114.

death of over 10 million people, often in camps. Yet, with struggle and the help of a United Nations of a sort (read: The United Federation of Planets), the Bajorans are able to regain their homeland, and establish a fragile self-government. All this begs a rather difficult question, though. *Star Trek* has been seen, usually, as a rather Utopian future-as-progress narrative depicting liberal-humanist values that on the face of things are wholly antithetical to any possible representation of the Holocaust. How the creators and producers of *DS9* manage to pull together the appropriate allusions and tropes of such atrocity and place them in Gene Roddenberry's Utopian future is the first theme of this essay. Secondly, I concentrate on how the representation of such an event in a fiction like *Star Trek* distorts the event being represented and in this specific case both lessens the dramatic impact of the spectacle and harms the memory of the event.

The representation of the Bajoran Holocaust, the Occupation, and the people who inflicted it as well as those who suffered it is a central theme to *DS9* and one of many major allusions drawn from the period of World War Two. Michael Piller and Rick Berman, the original creators of the series, as well as the host of producers and writers who worked on the series managed to fit this horrific historical incident into *Star Trek*'s value system is at once ingenious and dangerous. They have ultimately transformed the images of the Holocaust they present by making them over in the American fashion which *Star Trek*, by its very nature, cannot avoid. As a result of this Americanization, *Star Trek*'s Holocaust cannot quite manage to capture all that it is reaching for and in the end must fall back on kitsch and happy endings rather than stare into the black abyss of evil that is the Holocaust. Rather than allude to the actual Holocaust, *DS9* nods instead to the American representation of the Holocaust found in films such as *Schindler's List*. Because of its inherent American tropes, *DS9* becomes a simulacrum of history, rather than a representation of it.

In one of the first critical photon torpedoes across the bow of the USS *Enterprise*, William Blake Tyrrell accepts Gene Roddenberry's original claim that in essence *Star Trek* is a "*Wagon Train* to the Stars" (Whitfield and Roddenberry, cited in Tyrrell). Indeed, this analysis is useful, as *Star Trek* does tend to traffic in the political tropes of American frontier ideology. *Star Trek*, then, can be read as an extension of the western frontier archetype into space, making the Federation officers carriers of "culture" to the barbarian and savage "others." A host of critics have made this connection to many of the televised *Trek* series. Valerie Fulton makes one of the most cogent statements on the topic, writing, "the Federation's goals are both 'to seek out new civilizations' and 'to boldly go where no one has gone before'—missions that clearly contradict each other unless read through the lens of frontier ideology, which grants new civilizations existence only to the extent that the originary culture has 'found' them" (6).

Indeed, like the myths and legends of the American West, *Star Trek* has passed through a host of media formats so that when Kent Steckmesser notes that Western legends pass, "through a typical cycle which includes dime novels, biographies, histories, novels, juveniles, movies, and television plays" (247) he could easily be referring to the success of *Trek*. This is because *Star Trek* has obviously approached this mythological (cf. Tyrrell) status through a similar multitude of media outlets; five television series, one animated series, eleven films, novels, fanzines of many sorts, computer games, conventions, and that's just so far! And while the West has become associated with the search for a better life in the future, *Star Trek*'s frontier is that better life (Mattson 10). While the newer series maintain a similarity to the frontier tropes found in the original series (*TOS*) (see Worland, Clyde Wilcox), *Star Trek: The Next Generation* (*TNG*) and *DS9* present a Federation surrounded by other cultures which are considered different, but equal, a departure from the previous formula. The newer series are less like the Odyssey (as was *TOS*) and more like, as Richards has noted, a space Iliad (ii). This difference is a reflection of changes in contemporary society since *TOS*. The newer shows are less about confronting the other and going home to tell about it (the Odyssey) and more about maintaining a balance of powers between known, equal others (the Iliad). While *DS9* turns away from these frontier images in many ways, it does still traffic in the tropes of the West. Where *TOS* was *Wagon Train* to the stars, *DS9* is more *The Rifleman*, the frontier town on the very edge of civilization, where a constable and a single father keep order and the local tavern is a place of gambling and fighting.

In a certain sense, *Star Trek* represents a transference of the frontier myth to outer space through technology, implying an important relationship between technological innovation and the extension of the [western] myth life-cycles (Pfitzer 51). By extending the Western genre into outer space, *Star Trek* becomes an ideologically American, technological Utopia in all meanings of the word. Also, this stress placed on technology is another major aspect of *Star Trek* that is distinctly American in function. F.S. Braine places the origin of the American idea of a technological fix for all of society's ills (5) in the late nineteenth century (where most Westerns are set, as well!) through an examination of the works of Mark Twain and Edward Bellamy, among others. To Braine, *Star Trek* presents a future built on the old values of human wisdom, good government, and the proper use of technology (8). Further, In *Star Trek*'s comforting vision, the United Federation of Planets and Starfleet (also known as Big Government, Big Science, and Big Military) are benevolent and honorable institutions, not authoritarian or duplicitous regimes. Science has even liberated humans from their earthly constraints, and made them calmer, wiser, even braver (8). As a result, of course, it seems perfectly reasonable that *Trek* characters are forever interfering with other cultures they encounter, even though such behavior is against their own Prime Directive (See Logan, for example). Katrina Boyd suggests the same trope, saying that *TNG* (though her statement is applicable to all of *Star Trek*), "Constructs its Utopian future by drawing on nineteenth-century faith in progress, human perfectibility, and expanding frontiers" (95). Obviously, this notion is drawn from Karl Marx's concept that human nature is bound to the mode of production (and, by eliminating want and need, future generations [will] become more civilized and humane (Fulton 3).

The American notion that science and technology will help eradicate human wants and human needs, allowing individuals and society to progress toward a Utopian future, is central to the *mythos* of *Star Trek*. It is technology that allowed twenty-third- and twenty-fourth-century humans and their allies to evolve beyond the petty wants and needs of their ancestors. Of course, as an anthropologist who teaches human evolution and human paleontology courses every year, I must take note with the notion that evolution is in any way progressive. This one major error in the *Trek* philosophy has been a major thorn in the side of viewers with backgrounds in biology. And, regardless of technology, such progressive evolution remains unlikely.

This progressive history through technology is even somewhat of an in-joke among fans who both glorify and gripe about the technobabble of the many series. Indeed, in many episodes the dramatic conclusion comes about through the intervention of the *deus ex machina* of unreal technological fixes. As one fan, anthropologist Richard Jones, told me, "Sometimes, there's five minutes left in the episode and someone says, 'Maybe if we reverse the energy flow through the negative power couplings we can generate an inertial dampening field and create a low-level proteon beam which will allow the ship to extend it's warp field and should free us.' Then, after the commercial the ship flies away and you think, 'What the heck was that?'" While occasionally awkward for viewers of the shows, these solutions are perfectly reasonable to the characters in them. Technology is there to aid them, and whoever has the better technology almost invariably wins. To paraphrase Dow Chemicals old slogan, this is better living through technology.

Star Trek's emphasis on technology as a solution to problems and it's representation of a multiethnic culture, avowing notions of liberal democracy and benevolent imperialism, are the essence of the American tropes which underlie all the series and films. For *Star Trek* the future is better than the present, because technology will solve our material problems and we will all get along together as a result. Yet how can an event like the Holocaust become part of a narrative of the dialectical process of moral ascent (Ezrahi 189). How can the Holocaust be represented in a fiction that holds these ideals? The Holocaust, after all, is the direct refutation of all *Star Trek* seems to argue for. Where *Trek* suggests that increased technological know-how will improve lives, in the Holocaust it only made the killing easier, swifter, and surer. *Trek* promotes (at least on the surface) acceptance of diversity, yet those who died in the camps and elsewhere were murdered because they were seen as different, inferior both biologically and culturally. There was no strength in holding a different perspective or being a different ethnicity: being different meant death. The creators, producers, and writers of *DS9* have succeeded in this accomplishment only because the show isn't really a representation of Holocaust; it is a representation of the American representation of the Holocaust. As an historical simulacrum, then, it is also a misappropriation of atrocity (Rosenfeld, *Double Dying* 181).

Lawrence Langer, now Emeritus Professor of English at Simmons College in Boston, has written extensively on the Holocaust and its representation. "We bring to the imaginative experience of the Holocaust," he has written, "a foreknowledge of man's doom. Not his fate, but his doom.... We feel alien, not akin. The drama of fate reminds us that man, should he so choose, can die for something; the drama of doom, the history of the Holocaust, reveals that whether they chose or not, men died for nothing" (157). This is the central "problem" of the Holocaust for the dramatist; there is no sense to it. Millions perished without a hero to save the day, without even any level of reasonableness. In the end there can be no hope, there can be only silence. The process of rendering an artistically interesting and viewable narrative from the blackness that is the Holocaust while maintaining a level of truth to the subject is, at best, difficult. This is especially true of American popular culture that dotes of stereotypic heroes and heroines. As Langer writes, "the American mind itself is not yet ready to end in such silence. The heroic gesture still seizes us with its glamor, tempering the doom of men and women who have lost control of their fate" (176).

In any realistic rendering of the Jewish catastrophe that is the Holocaust, senseless death must take a central position. Yet this is a difficult idea to face, especially for a dramatic writer. The historian Raul Hilberg has seen the representation of the Holocaust a tendency toward typological understanding, showing not individual human beings but instead, "a variety of perpetrators, a multitude of victims, and a host of bystanders" (ix). Most would suggest that in a representation of this atrocity the victims should take center stage. It is upon them that these crimes were committed. Yet in recent renderings of the story of the Holocaust the victims are rarely noticed, while new types find themselves thrust forward as dramatic leads. These new groups include, according to Alvin Rosenfeld[1] such types as "survivor," "rescuer," "liberator," and "resistor" (1997, 135). Somehow the dramatic spectacle turns to them and away from the victims who remain faceless and, as a whole, not central to the drama.

While many plays, television miniseries, novels and other media forms are available for an understanding of the Americanization of the Holocaust, none is so well positioned as the Steven Spielberg film *Schindler's List*. Preceded by works like the television miniseries Holocaust and various stage plays, *Schindler's List* outmatches all in popularity and the degree to which it Americanizes the Holocaust. Here, at last, is a film by a "good" director that deals with this most horrific of times. Finally we will see a film about the Holocaust. And the two main characters are, strangely enough, a German Nazi and a German Catholic. One is a perpetrator, it is true, and the other a "rescuer." As Miriam Bratu Hansen has written, *Schindler's List*, "narrates the history of 1,100 rescued Jews from the perspective of the perpetrators while the Jewish characters are reduced to pasteboard figures" (299–300). This lack of emphasis in the narrative for the victims, which leaves them, "weakly imagined figures, either passive victims of random atrocity or venal collaborators with their persecutors" (Rosenfeld 1995, 39) is fundamental to the Americanization process. Indeed, *Schindler's List* is a film about the Holocaust in which most of the Jews the viewers know are saved by a German, the "bad guy" Nazi is punished, and we can all leave the theater with a sense of renewed hope.

Schindler's List fundamentally transforms the Holocaust into a dramatic work in which each character can be easily placed. From the start, writes Sarah Howowitz, "the viewer recognizes Goeth as the villain, Schindler as the hero. The dichotomy places the audience outside the film ... never implicated in the moral economy of the film, never prodded to examine its own social and political ethics" (138). All one need do is look at the characters to find out what side they're on (much like *Star Trek*, actually).

This process of transformation of narrative emphasis from the senseless and brutal deaths of millions to the more understandable and acceptable saving of hundreds is what I mean by the "Americanization of the Holocaust." Rather than deal with the true victims, the real tragedy of millions dead, in an Americanized Holocaust "'rescuers' like Schindler [are moved] from the margins to the precise center of events" (Rosenfeld 1997, 139). As a result, "the impact of the dramatic spectacle is to affirm the heroic fate of the few, and to mute the unmanageable doom of the wretched rest" (Langer 163). By transforming the narrative, changing the focus, ignoring the most difficult areas, the "American [preference] for 'heroes' and 'happy endings' is satisfied" (Rosenfeld 1997, 140).

This description of *Schindler's List* also quite adequately describes the representation of the Bajoran people and their Holocaust, the Occupation. In contrast to other films, plays or television shows, however, *DS9* dispenses with the very notion that a Holocaust needs Jews and instead presents us with the Bajorans. By the time *DS9* began its seven-year run in syndication the backstory of the Bajoran people had been already shown to *Trek* viewers in a number of episodes of *TNG*. And the presentation of the Bajoran people and their nemesis, the fascist Cardassians, is ripe with the tropes of European Jewish history and an Americanized Holocaust. When first we meet the Bajoran people it is in the fifth-season *TNG* episode, "Ensign Ro." In that episode Captain Jean-Luc Picard (Patrick Stewert) converses with Admiral Kennelly (Cliff Potts) about the Bajoran people, their lot in life, and their recent Diaspora. Kennelly tells Picard, "I'm the first to say the [Bajorans] deserve attention. Chased off their own planet by the Cardassians, forced to wander the galaxy, settling wherever they can find room. Its tragic." Picard replies, firmly placing the stereotypes of Jewish history on Bajoran shoulders, saying, "On many worlds we've been to they're isolated, treated as pariahs." Later, in a voiced-over "Captain's Log," Picard further adds to the stereotypes, saying, "I read about the achievements of the ancient Bajoran civilization in my fifth-grade reader. They were architects, artists, builders and philosophers when humans were not yet standing erect. Now I see how history has rewarded them." While the age of the Bajoran civilization was later changed to be somewhat less than the 4 million years or so implied in that statement, they are still ancient and have been forced into a Diaspora, suffered attempted genocide and generally are held together as a culture by their religion.

The Cardassians, the perpetrators of this Occupation, are also initially presented in episodes of *TNG*. It is in the two-part sixth-season episode, "Chain of Command [parts 1 and 2]" that the fascist and militarist pretensions of the Cardassians are rendered with great skill. Capt. Jean-Luc Picard is sent on a covert mission against the Cardassians and is captured and tortured in an attempt to learn military secrets. His torturer is Gul Madred (David Warner), who during the torture discusses with Picard some of the history of the Cardassian people, and in doing this sounds not unlike Adolf Hitler skewering the Weimar Republic. Madred tells Picard that prior to military rule more liberal leaders had spent Cardassia into bankruptcy. Thus they were forced into wars of conquest for, like Germany, they were land-poor and needed "agricultural land" (See Manuel 188–89). This situation closely mirrors the rise of power of Adolf Hitler whose Nazi Party began gaining popularity after the hyperinflation of the 1920s which bankrupted Germany and an agricultural crisis between 1927 and 1929 (Brustein 41; Abraham 85–86). Finally, after Picard argues with his logic Madred falls back on the old fascist stand-by for proving the worth of this fascist state of the *Star Trek* universe declaring, "We are feeding the people." One may safely assume that the trains run on time as well.

Holding with the typological analysis of Freidlander and Rosenfeld, we can turn to the first Bajoran victim of *Star Trek*, Ensign Ro Laren (Michelle Forbes). First seen in the episode "Ensign Ro," Ro Laren is typologically a victim before she is a survivor as her backstory makes clear. In "Ensign Ro" we learn that at the age of seven she watched as Cardassians tortured and killed her father. As with many victims of genocidal violence she sums up her feelings about this event, saying, "I was ashamed of being Bajoran." In many ways Ro represents a non–Americanized view of the Holocaust. A victim, she never fully recovers emotionally from her experiences during the Occupation. Because of her experiences, she (like many Holocaust survivors) has lost her faith in her religion ("The Next Phase").

Faced with Michelle Forbes's decision not to continue the Ro Laren character on *DS9*, creators Michael Piller and Rick Berman replace her with a character who typologically is almost diametrically opposed to Ro. The character, Kira Nyrese (Nana Visitor), has had a far different experience with the Occupation, in ways that Americanize this Holocaust even further. Kira Nyrese is no victim; instead she is a resistor and even liberator. She joined the Bajoran underground at the age of twelve ("Emissary, parts 1 and 2"), fighting for freedom for her people. As a member of that underground she helped liberate one of the most notorious camps, Gallitep ("Duet"). In the first few seasons of *DS9* she remains actively involved with former members of that resistance ("Duet," "Past Prologue") and, most importantly for my purposes here, unlike Ensign Ro Laren, she maintains an active belief in the Bajoran religion. It appears that the Occupation was not so horrible, so without sense, as to be a test of her faith. Actual survivors of the Holocaust, especially those who experienced that event during childhood, usually find maintaining religious faith difficult (see Hass 93–105). Maj. Kira Nyrese, however, doesn't seem to have experienced anything so horrible as to wreck permanent emotional distress. Faced with genocide, she did not acquiesce and become another faceless victim. Instead she resisted and fought and became heroic. This transition in character type may be among the most important changes in allowing *DS9* to represent an Americanized Holocaust. With this new character who was not broken by her experiences, not forever harmed, the viewer is presented with a new paradigm of understanding of the Occupation. No longer is it the central event of the life of the character Ro Laren that is responsible for so much pain and anguish and victimhood from which there could be no fighting back. Instead it was a glorious fight for freedom, full of heroes bent on throwing the Cardassian perpetrators of their planet. And, lo and behold, they succeeded heroic to the end.

The Holocaust is one of the most horrible events of modern history, and *DS9* remains true to that topic throughout the run of the series. In the final two years of the series, the Federation even gets to have war much like the Second World War and save two enemies from genocide as well. In the penultimate episode of the series, "Extreme Measures," Dr. Julian Bashir (Alexander Siddig) and Chief Miles O'Brien (Colm Meany) uncover a plot by a rogue organization of the Federation to commit genocide against the Founders, a species the Federation is currently at war against. They respond by infiltrating that rogue group (called Section-31), recovering a cure, and saving their enemies. This response suggests the moral underpinning *DS9* attempts to bring to the subject of genocide. This moral fundament is reaffirmed in the series finale,

"What You Leave Behind." In that episode the leader of the Founders, known only as The Female Shapeshifter (Salome Jens) learns that her one-time allied Cardassians have rebelled and joined forces with the Federation. Her response is to order genocide of her own, saying, "I want the Cardassians exterminated." She uses the word "exterminate" (over, say, "eliminate"), and it is a word better applied to cockroaches or other vermin, serving to once again allude to the Holocaust. Ironically, this called for genocide is against the very species that perpetrated a genocide of their own and thus made the entire series possible. And, through the intervention of the intrepid heroes of *DS9*, the Cardassians are saved, but at the cost of 800 million faceless lives.

And it is because the victims remain faceless that the images of the Holocaust in *DS9* are so American. The series begins after the Occupation has ended, so every Bajoran seen is, by definition, now a survivor. There are no victims left, because even those victimized that lived, by virtue of the time frame, are now survivors. Where earlier *Treks* accepted historical tropes of the nineteenth century, *DS9* accepts the period of World War Two and the Holocaust as its chronotope but turns it instead into a chrono*trope*. While the creators, producers, and writers of the series are to be commended for attempting to use their narrative to examine such a bleak and monumental tragedy, their narrative, by virtue of its unique American status was simply not quite up to the task. It is difficult to lay too much blame at the feet of the creators and producers, though, because seeing such an atrocity in our past, who would wish to place it in our future as well?

In one of the final scenes of the final episode of *DS9*, "What You Leave Behind," Admiral Ross (Barry Jenner) accepts the surrender of the Founders and puts to end the great war of *Star Trek*. As he accepts the surrender, he quotes from a "great general" of another "great war." True to form, the general quoted is Douglas MacArthur. "Today the guns are silent. [The] great tragedy has ended.... We have known the bitterness of defeat and the exultation of triumph, and from both we have learned there can be no turning back" (Wittner 33). But indeed, *DS9* has turned back to the last good war and they may have learned enough of history not to repeat its genocidal mistakes, but they do repeat the mistakes of those Americans who have represented the Holocaust before them. Like Holocaust or *Schindler's List*, *DS9* is a historical simulacrum. Perhaps Ira Stephen Behr and Hans Beimler, who wrote "What We Leave Behind," should have included another line from Gen. Douglas MacArthur's speech of September 2, 1945, in Tokyo Bay. For as MacArthur presumed to do that day on board the Battleship Missouri so have the creators and writers of *DS9* presumed to do as well, they, "speak for the thousands of lips, forever stilled." And that is always a difficult thing to attempt without doing injustice to those dead. But it is even harder when they have never lived in the first place, but are only a dramatic bit of backstory.

Notes

A special thanks must go to Anca Vlasopolos, who seemed more than happy to have an anthropology graduate student in her English class writing about *Star Trek* and encouraged me to develop this paper for publication. Thanks also to Alvin Rosenfeld for permission to use his work on the Americanization of the Holocaust prior to publication and to Sid Bolkosky for suggesting many useful sources. Amy Hawkins read and critiqued multiple drafts of this paper, and her help cannot be undervalued. And thanks to Erin Holman, for thoughtful editorial advice.

1. I refer to two papers by Alvin Rosenfeld, both with the title "Americanization of the Holocaust." Both present similar themes but offer slightly different insights. I chose to include both because of this and in hopes that interested parties would more easily find at least one of them.

Works Cited

Abraham, David. *The Collapse of the Weimar Republic: Political Economy and Crisis.* Princeton, NJ: Princeton University Press, 1981.
Baudrillard, Jean. *Simulacra and Simulation.* Trans. Sheila Faria Glaser. Ann Arbor: University of Michigan Press, 1994.
Boyd, Katrina. "Cyborgs in Utopia: The Problem of Radical Difference in *Star Trek: The Next Generation.*" Ed. Taylor Harrison, et al. *Enterprise Zones: Critical Positions on* Star Trek. Boulder, CO: Westview, 1996. 95–114.
Braine, F.S. "Technological Utopias: The Future of *The Next Generation.*" *Film and History* 24:1–2 (1994): 2–18.
Brustein, William. *The Logic of Evil: The Social Origins of the Nazi Party, 1925–1933.* New Haven, CT: Yale University Press, 1996.
Fulton, Valarie. "Another Frontier: Voyaging West with Mark Twain and *Star Trek*'s Imperial Subject." *Postmodern Culture* 4.3 (1994): 1–24. http://jefferson.village.virginia.edu/pmc/text-only/issue.594/fulton-v.594.
Hassler, Donald M. "Editor's Pad." Extrapolation 39.4 (1998): 285–86.
_____ and Clyde Wilcox, eds. *Political Science Fiction.* Columbia: University of South Carolina Press, 1997.
Hilberg, Raul. *Perpetrators, Victims, Bystanders: The Jewish Catastrophe 1933–1945.* New York: HarperCollins, 1992.
Horowitz, Sarah R. "But Is It Good for the Jews? Speilberg's Schindler and the Aesthetics of Atrocity." *Spielberg's Holocaust: Critical Perspectives on* Schindler's List. Ed. Yosefa Loshitzky. Bloomington: Indiana University Press, 1997.
Jones, Richard. Personal communication, 1996.
Lagon, Mark P. "We Owe It to Them to Interfere: *Star Trek* and U.S. Statecraft in the 1960s and 1990s." In Hassler and Wilcox. eds. *Political Science Fiction.* Columbia: University of South Carolina Press, 1997. 234–50.
Langer, Lawrence. "The Americanization of the Holocaust on Stage and Screen." Ed. Susan Blacher. *From Hester Street to Hollywood: The Jewish-American Stage and Screen.* Bloomington: Indiana University Press, 1983. 157–76.
Manuel, Paul Christopher. "In Every Revolution, There Is One Man with a Vision: The Governments of the Future in Comparative Perspective." Hassler and Wilcox eds. *Political Science Fiction.* Columbia: University of South Carolina Press, 1997. 183–95.
Mattson, Vernon. "West as Myth." *Journal of the History of the Behavioral Sciences* 24.1 (1988): 9–12.
Pfitzer, Gregory M. "The Only Good Alien Is a Dead Alien: Science Fiction and the Meta-

physics of Indian-Hating on the High Frontier." *Journal of American Culture* 18:1 (1995): 51–66.
Richards, Thomas. *The Meaning of Star Trek*. New York: Doubleday, 1997.
Rosenfeld, Alvin H. "The Americanization of the Holocaust." *Commentary* 99.6 (1995): 35–40.
____. "The Americanization of the Holocaust." *Thinking About the Holocaust After Half a Century*. Ed. Alvin H. Rosenfeld. Bloomington: Indiana University Press, 1997. 119–50.
____. *A Double Dying: Reflections on Holocaust Literature*. Bloomington: Indiana University Press, 1980.
Steckmasser, Kent Ladd. *The Western Hero in History and Legend*. Norman: University of Oklahoma Press, 1965.
Tyrrell, Wm. Blake. "*Star Trek* as Myth and Television as Mythmaker." *Journal of Popular Culture* 10.4 (1977): 711–19. [Reprinted this volume.]
Whitfield, Stephen E., and Roddenberry, Gene. *The Making of Star Trek*. New York: Ballantine, 1968.
Wilcox, Clyde. "To Boldly Return to Where Others Have Gone Before: Cultural Change in the Old and New *Star Treks*." *Extrapolation* 33.1 (1992): 89–100.
Wittner, Lawrence S., ed. "MacArthur: Great Lives Observed." Englewood Cliffs, NJ: Prentice-Hall, 1971.
Worland, Rick. "From the New Frontier to the Final Frontier: *Star Trek* from Kennedy to Gorbachev." *Film and History* 24.1–2 (1994): 19–35.

2009 Postscript

Victims and Perpetrators, with Movie Producers Standing By

In the "reboot" of the *Star Trek* franchise (2009) the plot of the early adventures of the original crew of the USS *Enterprise* is furthered through the destruction of two planetary populations. One, the planet Romulus, is not genocide as it happens as a tragic accident. However, it provides convenient character motivation for the movie's villain, Nero (Eric Bana), to commit near genocide against the planet Vulcan and its six billion inhabitants—a number that seems conveniently selected to match the current population of our own home planet. While fans of the franchise now have an extensive fictional history of the inhabitants of Vulcan, in the newest film they are mostly unknown other than as convenient, but significantly non-human victims.

They are a people whose destruction is a plot device used to provide proof of the villainous intent and heroic mettle of the film's characters and nothing more.

True to the American *mythos* of *Star Trek*, by the end of the film the main characters don't seem particularly upset by this genocide. Spock, as played by Zachary Quinto, is moved to forgo command through his emotional outburst at the death of his human mother as much as the genocide of his entire home planet. The other main characters find themselves on the bridge of the *Enterprise*, happily ready to boldly go into *Star Trek*'s rebooted future. The deaths of six billion individuals are safely put behind them. The true center of the Federation's hegemony, Earth, has been saved after all. The heroic mettle of the newly minted Captain, James T. Kirk, has been proven. The suddenly subaltern Vulcans may be gone, but so is the villain who destroyed them. Thus, all is well.

Indeed, when I first wrote this essay I was far more interested in the way the "Americanization of the Holocaust" functioned to deaden the impact of narratives about genocide in general. I felt then, and still do, that the process of "Americanization" (or, perhaps more correctly today, globalization), is a process in which the cultural *mythos* of hegemonic powers are foisted off onto others—and usually not for a good reason.

Watching the newest *Star Trek* with a packed audience in Swansea, Wales, I was not surprised that no one seemed all that upset by the fictional destruction of an entire planet. In fact, mostly they seemed to think the special effect was "cool." We audience members have watched this before, after all. The first *Star Wars* (1977) film proved the evil of the Empire to us all in exactly the same manner. The voiceless many are destroyed to provide narrative momentum, and their deaths affect us little.

Of course, *Star Trek* had used genocide as a plot device from the *TOS* episode, "The Doomsday Machine" through the "Xindi" sequence of *Star Trek: Enterprise* beginning with "The Expanse" in which, a conveniently large number of humans—seven million (one million more than the generally accepted number for the Holocaust)—have been killed as a prelude to an attempt at genocide. However, from *TOS*, through the genocidal possibilities of the "Genesis Device" in *Wrath of Kahn*, and, finally, in *Star Trek: Enterprise*, the intent was usually a narrative about avoiding or preventing such tragedy. In the newest film, much like *Star Wars* before it, the destruction of a planet is simply a way to show the truly evil nature of the villain.

A decade after writing this essay and with the newest film behind me as well, I'm given to be more kind toward the narrative of *Deep Space Nine*. As a series it tried, in its own way, to move the fictional population of Bajor from the subaltern margins of Federation culture and history to the hegemonic center. It was, at the very least, trying to give them a *voice*. *DS9* attempted, in ways that too few narratives of genocide attempt, to show characters come to grips with both the physical and emotional consequences of genocide. Indeed, using the measure provided by Jeffrey Shandler in his work on television representations of the Holocaust, *DS9* stands up rather well. Representations of the Holocaust, according to Shandler, would not be "proper" (a word he puts in quotes, underlining the irony of the idea) if it does not "consider its larger implications for Holocaust remembrance" and "include an engagement with this [tragic] disquietude" (259). I would say that, with the view of a few years, *DS9*—for all its other failings on the issue of genocide—can be seen as an attempt to do precisely that: engage with the disquietude.

The new film, in rewriting the *mythos* of the entire franchise in its reboot, does the precise opposite: it takes the main fictional non-human and non-villainous species that had been allowed to be front and center in *Star Trek*, the Vulcans, and removes them almost totally. The one significant alien species—and thus friendly "other"—voice of the entire franchise becomes a plot point of the heroic narrative of the mostly human *Enterprise*.

Director and producer J.J. Abrams has been often quoted in the marketing of his version of *Star Trek* that he hoped to make "optimism cool again." I hope he does. But I remain unconvinced that the fictional genocide of six billion souls as a simple way of furthering the plot of a major motion picture is in any way optimistic. In the above essay I quote Holocaust scholar Lawrence Langer on the Americanization of the Holocaust in general. What he writes about that process remains, unfortunately, applicable to the newest *Star Trek*:

> The impact of the dramatic spectacle is to affirm the heroic fate of the few, and to mute the unmanageable doom of the wretched rest.

That remains a *very* American mythological process. It is not, however, optimistic at all.

— Matthew Wilhelm Kapell, Swansea, Wales, June 2009

Postscript Works Cited

"The Doomsday Machine." *Star Trek: The Original Series*. Written by Norman Spinrad. 20 October 1967.

"The Expanse." *Star Trek: Enterprise*. Written by Rick Berman and Brannon Braga. 21 May 2003.

Shandler, Jeffery. *While America Watches: Televising the Holocaust*. New York: Oxford University Press, 1999.

Star Trek. Directed by J.J. Abrams. Screenplay Roberto Orci and Alex Kurtzman. Paramount Pictures, 2009.

Star Trek II: The Wrath of Khan. Directed by Nicholas Meyer. Screenplay by Jack B. Sowards. Paramount Pictures, 1982.

Star Wars: Episode IV — A New Hope. Directed by George Lucas. Twentieth Century–Fox, 1977.

6

"*Every Old Trick Is New Again*"

Myth in Quotations and the *Star Trek* Franchise

DJOYMI BAKER*

The original series of *Star Trek* first aired on U.S. television in 1966 and was cancelled by NBC in 1969. Despite the program's low official Nielsen ratings, a large and dedicated fan following of the series developed during, but mostly after, it's initial broadcast run (Asherman 31–32, 67–9, 103, 139, 141). Syndication of re-runs allowed the series to reach a broader audience, as well as an opportunity to re-watch the series before the advent of home video machines. Sequels to the series emerged in the form of an animation series (broadcast in the U.S. in 1973–4), feature films (the first being *Star Trek: The Motion Picture*, Wise 1979), live-action series, and an increasing range of related merchandise and cross-media forms. Perhaps due to this relative longevity, *Star Trek* as a "franchise,"[1] beyond its individual manifestations, has been described as "mythic" and "classic."[2] Linda Johnston notes that whether a work is a "classic" tends to be a matter of "faith because it has stood the test of time [...]. But is *Star Trek* a classic because it has survived since 1966?" (65). The "classic" status of *Star Trek*, therefore, is relative to its position within a specifically twentieth century communication technology. *Star Trek*'s sequel series of the 1980s and beyond have increasingly played upon this status in its narrative strategies, positioning itself as a form of contemporary myth through an interplay with its own textual past and appropriated myths.[3]

While myth comes from the Greek *mythos*, originally meaning simply words or a speech (*Iliad* 6.381–2, 9.431, 9.443), the definition of myth has been much contested.[4] Traditional explanations tend to focus upon supernatural and heroic subject matter, oral composition, and archaic setting. More broadly

Originally published in Popular Culture Review, *12:1 (2001): 67–77.*

defined, myths are narratives that embody communal ideas about the natural and social world. Conceptualized in this broader sense, myths can be seen to articulate universal themes of human life (such as birth and death) as well as reflecting and mediating specific cultural shifts. The concept of a "modern myth" has been anathema to many scholars working with more traditionally defined myths, and for whom distinctions between myth, legend and folklore are themselves much debated.

In popular use, myth has also come to stand for a fictitious story, or a widely believed falsehood. Myth has become conceptualized in terms of an ever-broadening field of narrative and belief systems (Brockway 2). In particular, the characterization of film and television as contemporary myth has been the focus of heated debates in cinema studies, most notably in the short-lived appropriation of Claude Lévi-Strauss' structuralism in the 1960s and 1970s, as well as in the context of genre theory from the 1970s. Myth has also been understood as one possible communication system that may be incorporated into specific contemporary texts, rather than applying to an entire medium (Chesebro 21-2, 37-41).

Myth has not only continually broadened in popular and academic use, but has also become the subject of a deliberate narrative strategy. The traditional myths of various cultures and time periods have become subject matter for writers of television programs—programs which span ostensibly ancient settings, such as *Xena* and *Hercules*; present-day settings, such as *The X-Files*; as well as futuristic settings such as *Red Dwarf* and the various *Star Trek* series. Whether or not television programs function as myths, the conscious manipulation of mythic material at the very least produces texts which are *about* myth.

Plundering the Past: Quoting Myth Within the Layers

The intentional play upon the notion of myth mobilizes different potential interpretative strategies, including the interaction between the text and its appropriated myth, and the degree to which the process of appropriation is highlighted within the text. Myth becomes one or more nodes in an interconnecting array of texts; a narrative strand as well as a possible interpretive vantage point.[5] While myth can be seen to function as part of an intertextual array in the case of *Star Trek*, its position becomes more complex as the *Star Trek* franchise develops over time.

In the original *Star Trek* series episode "Who Mourns for Adonais?" (*sic*) (Daniels 1967), the Greek god Apollo is found living on an alien planet, and is revealed to be the member of a space-faring alien race. The humans of the twenty-third century *Star Trek* world are accustomed to dealing with alien beings, and refuse to become Apollo's new worshippers. Apollo eventually accepts the change in human belief systems, and proclaims that his "time has passed. There is no room for gods," upon which he fades into a non-corporeal form. While the ancient Greeks are shown to have mistaken powerful aliens for gods, their mythology is nonetheless given a basis in fact. When Apollo compares Captain Kirk and his away team with the Greek epic heroes Agamemnon, Hector and Odysseus, it suggests not only that these heroes actually lived, but also that the *Enterprise* crew have taken up the heroic role of these figures. In this respect "Who Mourns for Adonais?" retells its mythic subject matter to both renounce the past and yet embody its heroic nature.

While Kirk acknowledges the contribution of ancient Greek culture to Earth, he nonetheless rejects its remaining "god." Greco-Roman myth and culture form part of a number of non–*Star Trek* sources that are reworked in the original series. Thus "Elaan of Troyius" (Lucas 1968) takes its name from classical inspiration (Helen of Troy from the *Iliad*) but little, if any, of its plot or scenario—indeed it is loosely based upon Shakespeare's play *The Taming of the Shrew* (Asherman 106). In this case, references to non–*Star Trek* sources are layered together and reworked within a *Star Trek* narrative. Other sources brought into the original series include the horror genre, a retelling of Jack the Ripper, the gangster genre, the western genre, and Shakespeare. Further, the original series also engages with various periods of Earth history, both directly through time travel and through the analogy of alien cultures. The discovery of a living Apollo in the original series of *Star Trek* must, therefore, be viewed within the broader context of multiple appropriations within the series' various episodes.

As the *Star Trek* franchise has extended, so too has the range of material it quotes and reworks within its science-fiction setting. While Greek myth is revisited in *the Star Trek: Voyager* series in an episode I will turn to in depth, new sources of appropriation in the sequel series of *Star Trek* have included the legends of King Arthur and Robin Hood, the Medieval epic *Beowulf*, the Irish hero Brian Boru, the Bible, and *Moby Dick*. Ilsa Bick has argued that the *Star Trek* franchise continually alludes "to canonical texts such as Dickens, Twain, Doyle, and [...] Shakespeare [...] to legitimate and elevate its narrative to immutable *mythos*" (206). While critical of its textual strategies, Bick acknowledges that *Star Trek* holds a prime place within the history of popular culture, and is able to draw upon that sense of history in order, paradoxically, to suggest its own timelessness—creating a "cultural mythology" that aligns itself with the lasting quality of great works of literature and their esteemed *oeuvre* (Bick 206–7).

Given that the *Star Trek* franchise is over thirty years old and extends over many different media, it is particularly well placed to draw upon its own history and produce a (popular) "mythology" about itself. The *Star Trek* of the 1980s and beyond is aware of its textual past and place within popular culture, and occasionally displays this awareness in a heightened, deliberate manner. To coincide with the thirtieth anniversary of the series, for example, the *Star Trek: Deep Space Nine* (*DS9*) episode "Trials and Tribble-ations" (West 1996) has the crew of Deep Space Nine taken back in time to an incident depicted in the original series episode "The Trouble With Tribbles" (Pevney 1967).[6] With the benefit of digital technology, characters from the new series are able to rub shoulders with Captain Kirk and Mr. Spock of the original series. One of the *DS9* characters, an alien called Dax who has lived over the span of many human lifetimes, articulates the nostalgic aspect of this journey when she says "I remember this time. I lived in this time and it's—it's hard to not want to be a part of it again." Dax's sentiments echo those of many of the audience who, through rewatching the original episode and its reworking in "Trials and Tribble-ations" can "remember" the *Star Trek* of the 1960s, but only through the mediation of a 1990s perspective.[7] A retrospective understanding of the original series is filtered through the knowledge of its textual growth as a fictional realm and the emergence of its cult status in the history of popular culture.

While Dax yearns for the time of the original series, the episode also makes fun of this textual past. Attention is drawn to the fact that the alien Klingons look totally different in the new series to how they looked in the original series. Seated in a space station bar, the Klingon Worf looks uncomfortable as his *DS9* crewmates Odo, Miles O'Brien and Dr Julian Bashir survey the other Klingons in the bar. Worf, with his ridged forehead partially hidden by a scarf, uncomfortably avoids their gaze; the Klingons around him are distinguishable from humans only by a distinctive uniform and a predilection for goatee beards.

WORF: They *are* Klingons. And it is a long story.
O'BRIEN: What happened? Some kind of genetic engineering?
JULIAN: A viral mutation?
WORF: We do not discuss it with outsiders.

The seasoned *Star Trek* viewer, however, knows exactly what caused this racial transformation. Better make-up techniques and higher budgets led to a production decision that broke continuity between the original series of *Star Trek* and its subsequent film and television manifestations.

The changes between the original and sequel series of *Star Trek* are such that when viewed as a entire fictional world *Star Trek* does not merely revisit it's past, but rewrites it. The video sleeve of "Trials and Tribble-ations" includes a summary of the original "Trouble with Tribbles" episode. However the narrative of this "past" has been overwritten by the events depicted in the *DS9* episode. Tailing the description of the original episode, the video sleeve tells us that "Kirk was blissfully unaware [...] that a personal threat to him was being frantically averted by time-traveling Starfleet officers from a future century." The events of the *DS9* episode are thereby depicted as having had occurred all along, even though the episode itself makes clear that the presence of *DS9* characters in the past was not originally part of "history"—neither their twenty-third century history nor our 1960s television history. "Trials and Tribble-ations," more than merely a parody of the old *Star Trek* versus the new, combines self-reflexive highlighting of continuity changes with an attempt to weave *DS9* into the very fabric of this textual past. While Bick conceptualizes *Star Trek* as a type of master narrative that creates a "cultural mythology" through "the illusory, temporal seamlessness of sequels" (204, 207), the discontinuous elements between the various *Star Trek* texts combined with the quotation of outside texts produces a more complex, fractured textual array.

While "Trials and Tribble-ations" cites the original series in order to both parody and valorize it, "Way of the Warrior" (*DS9*, Conway 1995) in turn begins the process of turning *Star Trek: The Next Generation* (1987–1994) into a newly finished tradition which itself can be quoted in a mythic guise. Worf mourns the passing of his time on board the *Enterprise* both as an expression of nostalgia and as a means of articulating his new role. "We were like warriors from the ancient sagas," says Worf. "There was nothing we could not do [...]. The *Enterprise* I knew is gone. Those were good years. But now it is time for me to move on." In his nostalgia for that which has only just finished, Worf has already begun to idealize *The Next Generation* in terms of ancient legend and heroic deeds.[8] Reference to *Star Trek*'s own past here serves both nostalgia and product differentiation, as Worf eventually accepts his new role on the troubled space station (and actor Michael Dorn accepts his role on a different series).

Jim Collins argues that in the case of Batman, another franchise that has been retold over a number of decades, recent retellings have displayed an elevated level of self-awareness. The new Batman texts display a heightened acknowledgment of their own textual relations and past (Collins "Batman" 165, 167). In such a self-aware text, Collins argues, there can be no master narrative producing a myth, but rather only "myth" presented in quotation marks, forming a multitude of quotations of which audience members will have varying degrees of knowledge (Collins "Batman" 179–180).[9]

The *Star Trek* of the 1960s may quote non–*Star Trek* myths, but a popular culture mythology based around the series itself had not yet begun. By contrast, the *Star Trek* of the 1980s and beyond is aware of its own place within the history of popular culture, an awareness activated whenever it quotes itself. Within such a context, to retell a story appropriated from an outside source is to simultaneously and necessarily retell the *Star Trek* story in a new guise. When the *Star Trek* of the 1980s and beyond quotes an external myth, it is automatically at the very least a twofold endeavor, because it is aware not only of its source material, but also of its own status as (and deliberate construction of) a form of popular mythology. *Star Trek* not only contextualizes outside myths within *Star Trek*'s fictional realm, but also attempts to contextualize its own mythology through that quotation. The *Star Trek: Voyager* episode "Favorite Son" (Rush 1997), which retells the encounter of Odysseus with the Sirens, is an example of this form of mutual contextualizing.

Sci-Fi Sirens: "Favorite Son" and the Odyssey

Star Trek: Voyager is the most recent of the *Star Trek* sequel series. Set in the twenty-fourth century, it centers around the starship *Voyager*, which has been flung into distant space by a now-dead alien. The crew of *Voyager*, led by Captain Kathryn Janeway, embark on a seventy year journey home to Earth. The third season episode "Favorite Son" revises Odysseus' confrontation with the Sirens from Homer's *Odyssey* (c.750–700 BCE), a Greek epic that recounts individual heroic encounters occurring within the overall structure of the return home by Odysseus, his crew and his ship. In adapting the Sirens episode, "Favorite Son" situates *Voyager* in the context of Greek myth as well as situating Greek myth in the context of *Star Trek*.

In "Favorite Son," *Voyager* crew member Harry Kim begins to experience déjà vu, even though the ship is traveling through an area of space never before explored by *Voyager*. Undergoing a series of genetic transformations, Harry directs the ship to a planet on which he is warmly greeted. The inhabitants inform Harry that he is, in fact, not human, but rather an alien who has fulfilled his latent genetic urge to return home to take a mate. On a planet with a population of ninety per cent women, this revelation seems too good to be true. Unfortunately, the imbalances of the sexes on the planet Tauresia has led its people to infect male aliens such as Harry with a genetically altering virus, changing the victims to make them suitable for procreation. The combination of the virus and an abundance of women provides them with enough willing husbands. The men, however, are killed during the mating process—as Harry finds out just in time when he stumbles across the corpse of an unlucky husband.

In the tag of the episode, Harry sits in the Mess Hall telling fellow crew members about Odysseus and the Sirens. Harry tells them:

> But Odysseus had been warned that these women, the sirens, sang a song so beautiful that any man who heard it would be lured to his death. [...] He told his crew to cover their ears so they couldn't hear the sirens' song. But he also had them tie him to the mast of the ship so he could listen himself without being led astray as they sailed past.

Though remodeled to fit the concerns of a primarily science fiction program, ancient Greek myth forms the basic framework for this episode's narrative. Harry briefly retells the original source, providing not only a short lesson in the original myth but also another means of quotation.

The Sirens story is, therefore, told twice within the context of the episode, but it has a third resonance in relation to *Voyager*'s series structure of the return home. While Homer's *Odyssey* tells of Odysseus' encounter with the Sirens in flashback, the episodic nature of Odysseus' adventures within a quest to return home against great odds is a structure which *Voyager* follows as a series. Whether or not the viewer is aware of this alignment is another matter, given that "Favorite Son" gives no more information about the *Odyssey* than Harry's brief retelling of the Sirens at the end of the episode (quoted above). The use of the *Odyssey* nonetheless situates *Voyager* within its mythic framework, inviting the viewer to relate the two tales to one another and directing us specifically to Odysseus over a myriad of other Siren myths.

In the *Odyssey*, Odysseus is forewarned by Circe of the Sirens' deadly allure, and is, therefore, able to make preparations to protect himself and his men from the effects of their song. (12.39–54, 12.165–200). In "Favorite Son," Harry gradually gains knowledge of a different kind — a feeling of déjà vu and the gradual awareness of Tauresian knowledge. Yet this precognition is in fact part of the Tauresian's method of ensnarement.[10] Unlike Odysseus, whose characteristic use of intellect and craftiness allows him to pass by the Sirens unharmed (Neils 175), Harry is the youngster of the *Voyager* team, often depicted as talented but a little naïve due to lack of experience. He is not the captain of his ship, nor the leader of his crew as Odysseus is. Indeed, if for Odysseus the lure of the Sirens lies in their ability to sing for him an epic song in which his former heroic deeds will be praised (*Odyssey* 12.184–191; Pucci 196), Harry's temptation is to believe that he is more important than he has, as yet, become. As a young and upcoming officer, he longs to be special — an elevated status that the Tauresians can offer. Thus at the end of Harry's adventure he says that "[i]t wasn't just the women [...]. There was also something exciting about having a new identity. Being more than just young Ensign Kim." Although Harry becomes suspicious of the Tauresians, it is the combined efforts of the *Voyager* crew by which he is rescued, not his own cunning. Just as the *Odyssey* explicitly compares Odysseus' forthcoming adventures with those of Jason in the *Argonautika* (*Odyssey* 12.69–70), so too in "Favorite Son" Harry's encounter is modeled on and compared with that of Odysseus, but changed in order to accommodate a different heroic figure.

In their promise to tell Odysseus epic poetry, which will flatter his ego as a hero, the Sirens embody the "temptation of 'forgetting the return'" to his home and to the loved ones waiting there (Segal 215). Harry's false memories, which gradually emerge, operate in inverse to the possibility that he too may forget the return, and instead stay with the Tauresians. To "remember" the Tauresians is to forget *Voyager* and the desire to return to Earth. As Odysseus continually chooses the glory of *nostos* (return home) over the possible delights to be had elsewhere, so too the crew of *Voyager* consistently pass up opportunities to settle on hospitable alien planets. Although aliens often aid their journey, alien planets themselves always pose the potential of a replacement Earth that will divert the crew from their quest.

But the Sirens may pose a greater threat than merely their potential to halt the homeward journey. Odysseus is warned by Circe that those who listen to the Sirens do not depart again (*Odyssey* 12.40–46). Odysseus does not say whether there are indeed bones of the dead around the Sirens as Circe claims (*Odyssey* 12.45–6), and the Sirens themselves assert that one can listen and then freely depart (*Odyssey* 12.188). Unlike Odysseus, in "Favorite Son" Harry receives no warnings about the deadly intent of Tauresians,[11] and instead is lured by fake memories which make him believe he belongs with them. But while the presence of remains surrounding the Sirens is never corroborated in the *Odyssey*, the lethal nature of the Tauresians in "Favorite Son" is confirmed with the discovery of the corpse.

This threat is directly related to the Tauresians' sexuality. The viewer of *Star Trek* will be aware that love interests from outside the central spaceship usually last only for one episode (Blair 292), and are frequently treacherous or manipulative in nature. Despite the *Star Trek* edict of equality of races, this tendency seems little improved upon the *Odyssey*'s own distinction between Greek and non-Greek women.[12] Although the allure of Homer's Sirens lies in their promise of knowledge and epic poetry, the language they use is distinctly sexual, as is their location on a "flowery meadow" (*Odyssey* 12.159), a setting of sexual entanglements in early Greek poetry (Doherty 84, Schein 21). The Tauresians bypass such allusions, instead overtly offering the lure of no less than group sex. Their sexual drive is, however, channeled specifically for reproductive purposes.

Despite its twenty-fourth century setting, then, "Favorite Son" divests the Sirens of their role as holders of great knowledge, and instead depicts the Tauresians in terms of the dangerous nature of female reproductive power. While *Voyager* is much celebrated for having a female captain, it is a male ensign through which the Sirens story is told, not Captain Janeway. Although *Voyager*'s ensemble cast allows different characters to feature prominently in different episodes, Janeway is closer to Odysseus in rank and function as the leader of her crew. The choice of Harry as the hero, and the addition of procreation as the source of the Tauresian threat, suggests a return to the type of gender stereotyping often present in the original series.[13]

Indeed, the video sleeve for "Favorite Son" explicitly links the episode with earlier episodes from the original series and *The Next Generation*.[14] Under the heading of "Species Survival," the video sleeve notes that in the original series episode "Wink of an Eye" (Taylor 1968), the crew encounter a species whose men have been rendered sterile. The Queen of these aliens attempts to take all the men from the *Enterprise* in order to repopulate the planet. Just as the various alignments and discontinuities between Homer's description of Odysseus and the Sirens and *Voyager*'s version of the tale will be evident only if the viewer is in possession of specific knowledge, so too the episode's alignment with earlier *Star Trek* can only be appreciated if the viewer has seen the other episodes in question or has read the video sleeve.[15] Visually, however, the saturated reds and oranges of the Tauresian costumes with their black neck trim are reminiscent of the original series' Starfleet uniforms. While in "Who Mourns for Adonais?" Greek antiquity is suggested through the iconography of columns and (gold lamé) togas, in "Favorite Son" the iconography suggests not the *Odyssey* from which the plot is adapted but rather the original *Star Trek* series.

But if following explicit references can only take us so far, this by no means marks the boundaries of a possible intertextual array. In terms of Greek myth, the reproductive aspect of both "Wink of an Eye" and "Favorite Son" seems closer to the Lemnian women of the *Argonautika* (1.608–914) than the Sirens of the *Odyssey*. Similarly, a range of other *Star Trek* connections are possible, such as the animated series episode "The Lorelei Signal" (Sutherland 1973), which takes its name from the Germanic Siren. In this episode, a group of alien women whose own men have all died ensnare the men of other species through beautiful visions, and then drain them of their life force. The Taurean system in which these women live closely resembles the planet Tauresia from "Favorite Son" in name, and the plot and Siren theme are similar in both episodes. Yet the "Favorite Son" sleeve does not refer to this episode, thereby situating itself within a specific *Star Trek* array that privileges the live-action series over other media forms. But while the episode itself as well as the video sleeve suggest connections the viewer can make to other texts, this does not preclude other connections within or beyond the *Star Trek* array, as each viewer mobilizes their personal and shared popular culture memories.

As Irad Malkin notes in *The Returns of Odysseus*, "the *myth* of Odysseus" is made up not only of "the epic narrative of the *Odyssey*, but also alternative versions and 'sequels,' pictorial images [...] and forms of cult" (33). So although described in text, the myth of Odysseus is not contained in any single text, and by the early Classical period the Sirens in particular had been refashioned many times (Buitron-Oliver and Cohen 31–33). *Voyager*'s "Favorite Son" episode is but one in a long line of retellings which retains some aspects of the myth yet transforms others. But equally, the Sirens and the *Odyssey* are used in order to retell and construct *Star Trek*'s own form of a specifically twentieth century popular "mythology." Both *Star Trek* and the Sirens myth are retold in a continuous process of quotation, with each retelling situating itself in a much larger tradition that is made up of but ultimately not contained by its textual manifestations.

Voyager's quotation of, and alignment with myth as illustrated in the "Favorite Son" episode is but one of many quotation practices within *Star Trek*. These quotations simultaneously provide threads of other textual realms, yet rely upon varying audience awareness for their significance. *Voyager*'s second in command notes that out in the deep reaches of unknown space "every old trick is new again."¹⁶ More accurately, everything old is remade in a new form — both *Star Trek*, and the outside sources it quotes.

Notes

1. On the Paramount studio lot, the business of *Star Trek* as a whole is referred to collectively as "the franchise" (Poe 50).
2. "Classic *Trek*" is frequently used to indicate the original *Star Trek* series.
3. Part of this paper was presented at the inter-disciplinary symposium "The Use and Abuse of Antiquity: Interrogating the Classical Tradition," held at The University of Melbourne, Australia, October 7, 1999. I would like to express my thanks to the participants of the symposium for their comments. Responsibility for the interpretations contained herein lie with the author.
4. Dundes is a comprehensive anthology debating the definition (and function) of myth.
5. Collins uses the term "array" to give a geographically descriptive sense to numerous sets of texts and cultural knowledge interconnecting and existing simultaneously (*Architectures* 41; "Batman" 170–80).
6. The animated *Star Trek* revisited the Tribbles in "More Tribbles, More Troubles" (Sutherland 1973); it does not, however, revisit its past in the more literal sense embodied in "Trials and Tribble-ations."
7. Similarly, Peter Rose notes the way in which the first *Superman* feature film historicises its own myth by putting references to its 1930s original alongside its 1970s re-invention (33).
8. This characterisation is also drawn upon in *Star Trek* advertisements, one of which describes the passing of the tradition from the original series through to the sequels, so that *DS9* is "a place where legends are forged," and that "the legend continues with *Star Trek: Voyager*" (*Voyager* 4.12 containing "Living Witness" Russ 1998 and "Demon" Williams 1998).
9. As Rose notes in relation to *Superman*, for example, younger audience members may miss references to the *Superman* of the 1930s, changing the textual reading (33). Collins does not extensively develop his notion of "myth" and in *Architectures* develops a different construction of cultural mythology (47).
10. In another inversion, Odysseus is bound to protect himself against the Sirens (*Odyssey* 12.178–9), whereas the victims of the Tauresians are bound during the marriage ceremony.
11. *Voyager* later receives a warning about the Tauresians but is unable to contact Harry.
12. See for example Graham (13–4).
13. See for example Blair and Cranny-Francis.
14. *Star Trek: The Next Generation*, "When the Bough Breaks" (Manners 1988), in which a sterile alien race steal children from the *Enterprise*, and "Up the Long Ladder" (Kolbe 1989), in which a society which reproduces by cloning attempts to steal new DNA from *Enterprise* crew members.
15. Other episodes such as "Heroes and Demons" (*Voyager* Landau 1995) use the sleeve to provide information on the appropriated text, which in this case is the medieval epic *Beowulf*.
16. *Star Trek: Voyager*, "Ex Post Facto" (Burton 1995).

2009 Postscript

New Tricks

Since this article was written, the ongoing joke about the Klingons' changing appearance was finally laid to rest in the *Star Trek: Enterprise* episode "Divergence" (Allan Kroeker 2004). Taking its lead from the brief conversation in

Star Trek: Deep Space Nine, the non-ridged Klingons were retrospectively "revealed" to be the result of a viral genetic mutation. Because *Enterprise* is "before" the other television series in the *Star Trek* timeline, it could assert that this was the case all along!

Myth is a traditional story that must nonetheless—indeed necessarily—be updated for new generations. The most recent *Star Trek* film (directed by J. J. Abrams) is another case in point, noticeable particularly by the way it was marketed as "not your father's *Star Trek*." This represents a break from the type of marketing I identify in the article, which in the 1990s emphasized continuity from one *Star Trek* incarnation to the next in a type of mythic lineage. And yet of course the 2009 film is as much built on the pleasures of recognition as it is on rebooting the franchise. It is this continuing interplay between tradition and innovation that lies at the heart of mythic storytelling.

There is no single answer to why so many people find the world of *Star Trek* so appealing. To me, it resonates with questions long posed by our species—what's out there, and what is our place in this vast cosmos? By deliberately harking back to ancient tales of heroic quests, *Star Trek* suggests the timelessness of these questions, and yet myth in its various guises has always been indelibly tied to the moment in which it is retold.

This is true both of the stories and their audience. The original *Star Trek* had finished by the time I was born, but I grew up in the afterglow of the moon landing convinced that space travel would become commonplace. So the world of *Star Trek* for me perhaps embodies a type of nostalgia for a future imagined but never realized.

And for the next generation? My preschool daughter has a poster of the solar system in her bedroom, but there are two things about it that concern her. The first is the unsatisfactory name of the dwarf planet 2003 UB313. Second, is the equally unsatisfactory fact that humans have only traveled in person to the moon. We show her the opening title sequence to *Star Trek: Voyager* and she is appeased—this is much more like it. Impressive though real rocket launches may be, for now the dream of *Star Trek* trumps reality. A new generation waits in the wings, perhaps for the next installments in the *Star Trek* franchise, or perhaps for adventures of a different kind, yet to be imagined but undoubtedly tied in some way to all the quests that have come before it.

—Djoymi Baker, Melbourne, Australia, June 2009

Postscript Works Cited

"Divergence." *Star Trek: Enterprise*. Written by Judith and Garfield Reeves-Stevens. 25 February 2005.

Star Trek. Directed by J.J. Abrams. Screenplay by Roberto Orci and Alex Kurtzman. Paramount Pictures, 2009.

PART TWO

*Boldly Going Forward:
New Frontiers of Mythic
Star Trek Analysis*

7

Star Trek *as American Monomyth*

JOHN SHELTON LAWRENCE

I understand the American mythscape as a cultural space in which we can openly acknowledge the fictional narratives that excite senses of purpose and possibility. At times when enticing, affirmative beliefs resist scientific proof or philosophical demonstration, myth becomes a persuasive option.

For 1960s America, the United Space Ship *Enterprise* became a mythic transporter, taking its fans toward hope-saturated destinations. The improvements on the social and political realities of that era are apparent in several *Star Trek* features. The United Federation of Planets is the United Nations with a healthy budget and the power to modulate polar conflicts in less than sixty minutes—thus avoiding the cold and prolonged stalemates of Berlin, Korea, and Vietnam. In a time of race riots and military protection for black children, *Star Trek*'s crew calmly achieved ethnic harmonies. While U.S. astronauts of the Apollo program flew in the launch-by-rocket, land-by-parachute capsules, the luxurious *Enterprise* smoothly cruised the galaxy and always contained its crises. In telling its tales of space adventure, *Star Trek* reshaped our mythscape by blending some familiar American archetypes with futuristic visions. This essay sketches the mythic profile emerging from the narrative of *The Original Series* (*TOS*) and indicates its affinity to the paradigm of the American monomyth—especially its foreshortened vision of democracy. Although the resurrected franchises of *Star Trek* evolved into a more cosmopolitan outlook with *The Next Generation* (*TNG*), toward a feminist stance in *Voyager* (*VOY*), and a frequently respectful portrayal of alien religion in *Deep Space Nine* (*DS9*), the original American mythic imprint endured.

Despite the forward-looking fantasy so apparent in the early shows there was hesitation in the 1960s about calling *Star Trek* "mythic." The *New York Times*, for example, published two lengthy articles on the series that focused on directing, acting and Spock's ears (Prelutsky 1967; Diehl 1968). No *Times* author used the word "myth" until 1973 when Fay Beauchamp sarcastically remarked on the Kirk-Spock relationship: "America's Indians are organized enough to protest new Tontos, so the old Lone Ranger frontier myths are played out by exotic aliens" (71). The reticence in this period about recognizing myth was encouraged especially by the popular scholar Joseph Campbell, who maintained for five decades his conclusion from *The Hero with a Thousand Faces* (1949): "the invention of the power driven machine, and the development of the scientific method of research, have so transformed human life that the long-inherited, timeless universe of symbols has collapsed" (387). He repeated the view even more sharply in his late 1980s interviews with Bill Moyers for *The Power of Myth* television programs. "What we have today is a demythologized world" (Campbell and Moyers 9). Campbell, who paid little attention to popular culture, did not realize that *Star Trek* had constructed a mythic universe that freely employed scientific conceptualizations and technology. He would not acknowledge the presence of myth in American popular culture until George Lucas took him to Skywalker Ranch in the mid-1980s and forced him to watch the *Star Wars* trilogy (Lawrence 2006: 22; Larsen and Larsen, 541–43).

The ability to notice is often a function of what we look for. In his comparative studies for *Hero*, Campbell had concluded that there was but one myth-heroic story pattern, which he condensed into a now well-known formulation as the classical monomyth. "A hero ventures forth from the world of common day into a region of supernatural wonder: fabulous forces are there encountered and a decisive victory is won: the hero comes back from this mysterious adventure with the power to bestow boons on his fellow man" (30). One can find examples of this plot in the stories of Prometheus stealing fire from the gods to benefit mankind, of Ulysses undergoing his adventurous journey, of Aeneas visiting the underworld to discover the destiny of the nation he would found, of St. George and the dragon, and of Hansel and Gretel.

Joseph Campbell suggested that the archetype is molded according to rites of initiation, in which persons depart from their community, undergo trials, and later return to be integrated as mature adults who can serve in new ways. This training for permanent social responsibility, typically absent in American superhero tales, is important. The very idea of settling down, recently parodied in *The Incredibles* film (2004), is antithetical to the serial format, whose conventions dictate the hero's disappearance until the next crisis. In fact, that is the key to America's unique blend of heroic traits, formulated Campbell-style as the American monomyth Paradigm. Although there are significant variations, the following archetypal plot formula may be seen in thousands of popular-culture artifacts:

> A community in a harmonious paradise is threatened by evil; normal institutions fail to contend with this threat: a selfless superhero emerges to

renounce temptations and carry out the redemptive task: aided by fate, his decisive victory restores the community to its paradisiacal condition: the superhero then recedes into obscurity.

Whereas the classical monomyth seemed correlative to initiation rites, the American monomyth derives from tales of salvation. It secularizes the Judeo-Christian dramas of community redemption that have arisen on American soil, combining elements of the selfless servant who impassively gives his life for others and the zealous crusader who destroys evil. A major source of *Star Trek*'s appeal is rooted in its fidelity to this American monomythic archetype of plot, character, and communities in peril. *Star Trek* has given its selfless heroes an interstellar scope of responsibility, benignly joining science with redemptive tasks.

The duty to act as wise and virtuous saviors is the role that spans all the television series and the films. And although *Star Trek* has considerable popularity in our militantly anti-socialistic democracy, its political values amount to a form of "military socialism" that we see operating in the family-oriented teams who guide the voyages. The inner circle of leaders on a Starship and their living arrangements bear a clear resemblance to the philosophical "Guardian" class of Plato's *Republic*, a group deprived of private property and individual family relationships: thus freed from material temptations and the demanding distractions of an ordinary family life, the liberated Guardians were to rule society according to the principles of science (Plato 109–10).

From its very beginnings, *Star Trek* provocatively dramatized ideas about time, personal identity, emotion and reason, androids and their inner life, interspecies relationships, future technology, and alternative political forms. For those who lacked such philosophical or scientific interests, but were concerned about the intractable conflicts in American life and the Cold War, the program swept several centuries forward, leapfrogging beyond the fears of nuclear or racial Armageddons, and showed a multicultural spectrum of "survivors," confident and happy in their life work together. Fans of *TOS*, including its creator, Gene Roddenberry, believed that the program had abandoned a destructive mythic past in order to affirm a far healthier vision of the future.

Star Trek's *American Mission in* The Original Series

The United Star Ship *Enterprise* is on a five-year mission to explore the galaxy. Because of her speed in space — warp drive far exceeds that of light — the *Enterprise* explores and carries out its own assignments, making only infrequent contact with Federation authorities. Given this format, the episodes permit the *Enterprise* to intervene on her own initiative in the affairs of other planets. The leader of this semi-autonomous space probe is Captain James T. Kirk, a brilliant, irresistibly attractive, and hard-driving leader who pushes himself and his crew beyond human limits. He always leads the landing party on its perilous missions to unexplored planets but like a true superhero, regularly escapes after risking battle with monsters, seductresses, or enemy spaceships.

Kirk's main cohort, Mr. Spock, is cut even more clearly from superhero material. He is half-human and half-Vulcan, which gives him, in the well-chosen words of enthusiastic fans, "extra-keen senses, prodigious strength, an eidetic memory, the capacity to perform lightning calculations, telepathy, imperturbability, immunity to certain diseases and dangers, vast knowledge — especially of science" (Lichtenberg and Marshak 50). As played by Leonard Nimoy, Spock is a strong, ascetic character of pure rationality, his emotions kept strictly under control by his Vulcan temperament. The emotional tension is hinted at by his slightly Satanic appearance, including the famously pointed ears.

All the remarkable powers of Spock, Kirk, and their crew are required to deal with the adversaries of the *Enterprise*. The original *Star Trek* universe includes two vicious races of bad guys: the Romulans are similar to the Vulcans in ability and technological development but are "highly militaristic, aggressive by nature, ruthless in warfare, and do not take captives"; the Klingons are even worse, though seemingly less intelligent. Clearly such villains are "more symbolic than individual," threatening the peace of the galaxy in a way that requires constant vigilance by the *Enterprise*. In the evolution of *Star Trek*, the Klingons eventually became more tolerable, particularly in the heroic characters of Worf (*TNG*, *DS9*) and the half-Klingon B'Elanna Torres (*VOY*). Roddenberry had eventually concluded that the *TOS* Klingons were a convenient but crude mistake — favored by "writers who tended toward bad guys/good guys 'hack' scripting" (Alexander 516–17). But despite Roddenberry's professed aversion to bipolar moral thinking, Klingons retained their tendency to relapse into wicked hostility; they nearly destroy the medical ship *Pasteur* in *TNG*'s final episode, "All Good Things…" Their intractability in the expanding universe is matched by that of the Romulans, the Cardassians, and — most terrifying of all — the Borg, with their vicious Queen and pathetic hive mind.

To counter these threats and to cope with the weird and aggressive powers that seem to inhabit so many earth-like planets of the universe, the *Enterprise* of *TOS* acts as galactic redeemer in episode after episode. The format of *Star Trek* accentuates this role by keeping Kirk and his ship out of communication with Earth. The captain becomes "the sole arbiter of Federation law wherever he traveled … a law unto himself" (Gerrold 32). The stories of *TOS* thus fit the genre of the isolated zealous hero or nation, answerable only to a higher law and fighting for right whenever called to do so, a theme America has tried to act out repeatedly. And like a sophisticated American, Captain Kirk does not allow himself to become "paranoid" about the enemies who are out to get him or the planetary cultures he must alter in the fray.

The moral vision of *Star Trek* in its original incarnation thus partook of *Pax Americana*'s spirit and rhetoric. Its basic moral principle is zeal for the mission. This is in effect what the authors Lichtenberg, Marshak, and Winston celebrated in their early, comprehensive fan book *Star Trek Lives!* (1975) They affirm an admirable "equality of moral stature" on the parts of Spock and Kirk: "Each of them is that rarest of all things among men: a man of unbroken integrity ... each remains dedicated to the striving, extravagantly willing to pay the price" (99–100). But when this moral quality is measured against standards forbidding deceit, adultery, and violence, one notices a profound lack of restraint in the plots. What *Star Trek* presents is a moral zeal attached solely to the mission and to a particular vision of what amounts to "the American Way." It is a zeal transcending both due process and the moral code of the Federation's own "noninterference directive," which Kirk has sworn on pain of death to uphold. This directive is consistently broken in *TOS* episodes when it is "necessary" for the fulfillment of the mission. It was thus an effective format for reinstating in the realm of fantasy some of the American values that floundered in the 1960s against ugly obstacles in Vietnam.

The impact of this kind of uncompromising zeal on other cultures is worth noting. David Gerrold, writer for "The Trouble with Tribbles," notes that the cumulative message of the original *Star Trek* is that "if a local culture is tested and found wanting in the eyes of a starship captain, he may make such changes as he feels necessary" (256). This view was explicitly worked out as an apologetic for the Vietnam War in a backward time-travel episode entitled "The City on the Edge of Forever." McCoy has given himself an injection that results in his disoriented wandering around in the year 1930. Coming to his rescue, Kirk encounters and falls in love with a woman pacifist named Edith Keeler. When Spock looks into her background through newspaper research, he discovers that she will lead a peace movement that will delay U.S. entry into the Second World War. The logical conclusion comes when Spock says, "Jim, Edith Keeler must die." Kirk performs the deed that ultimately allows for the twenty-third century of *Star Trek*'s world.

H. Bruce Franklin, who studied the production history of that episode, questioned the producer, Robert Justman, about it. Was it "consciously intended to have the contemporaneous anti–Vietnam-war movement as subtext?" he asked. Justman replied: "Of course we did" (Franklin 38). And this episode was followed by "A Private Little War," where Kirk and McCoy have witnessed a war on the planet Neural between unequally armed participants and recall "twentieth-century brush wars on the Asian continent." Kirk asks McCoy whether he remembers the "Twentieth Century brush wars on the Asian content," explaining that there were "Two giant powers involved, much like the Klingons and ourselves. Neither side felt that they could pull out." McCoy replies: "I remember. It went on bloody year after bloody year." They eventually decide that they must intervene with armaments for the weaker side so that the resulting parity will result in the preservation of both. This episode appeared to be a symbolic affirmation of Cold War power politics (Franklin 40–42; also Worland 109–17).

In fairness to *TOS*, the stance of apologetics for the Vietnam War changed quickly after the Tet Offensive of 1968. With "Omega Glory" (March 1, 1968), written by Gene Roddenberry, the planet Omega IV rages a war without end between the dark-skinned "Kohms" and the lighter-skinned "Yangs"—Commies and Yankees, as Kirk and Spock deduce. This becomes even clearer when we see that the Yangs carry a tattered flag, their "Omega glory." But, as H. Bruce Franklin puts it, "Forgetting all the principles for which they were fighting in their endless war against the Communists, these Yankees have become savage barbarians teetering on the edge of bestiality. All they have left of the great American ideals are their worship words, garbled versions of the Pledge of Allegiance and the Preamble to the Constitution of the United States, which they recite as mere sacred gibberish" (43). The episode ends when Kirk takes the Preamble, reads it with emphasis on "We the people," chastising them for their inhuman zeal that results in the denial of rights. *Star Trek*'s creators had quickly devised a clever putdown of what they had so recently defended.

Given such an episode, it would be absurd to reduce a series like *TOS* to mere apologetics for U.S. military struggles. The dedication of fans is perhaps explained by Richard Slotkin's concept of "national mythology." He shows how the historical experience of a nation provides metaphors and stories that assume mythic proportions in literature and art, so that the resulting myth exercises a reciprocal pressure on succeeding generations. It shapes the sense of reality and is itself reshaped by subsequent experience (14–24). In this sense the original *Star Trek* appears to contain much reworking of traditional American myth. But as one might expect, there is a hitch to linking any notion of myth with the original *Star Trek*.

Star Trek's *Antimythic Bias and Its Own Mythic Ingredients*

On the surface level the *TOS* stories seem to defy interpretation as mythic. The series frequently takes a singularly dim view of myths, not to mention legends, fables, and their primitive religious accoutrements. *Star Trek* celebrates the freeing of the human spirit from both superstition and narrow-mindedness. It wears the cloak of empirical science. The antimythic bias in *TOS* is clearly visible in "Who Mourns for Adonais?" (Blish 1–27)

The U.S.S. *Enterprise* is approaching an unexplored M Class planet when an immense, masculine face appears on the scanner screen and stops the ship in place by a tremendous exertion of energy. Captain Kirk leads the exploration party of Spock, Chekov, McCoy, Scott, and the ravishingly beautiful archaeologist Carolyn Palamas. They find themselves in a Greek-like temple complex. A magnificent, muscular man, whose face they had seen on the scanner, rises to greet them with the words, "I am Apollo.... You are here to worship me as your fathers worshipped me before you." When Kirk asks what he requires, he insists he is Apollo and demands "loyalty," "tribute," and "worship" in return for a "human life as simple and pleasureful as it was those thousands of years ago on our beautiful Earth so far away." Kirk replies, "We're not in the habit of bending our knees to everyone we meet with a bag of tricks." When they refuse obeisance, Apollo's wrath melts their phaser guns and injures Scott, who has attempted to protect Carolyn from amorous advances. But Carolyn volunteers to go with Apollo, and she quickly falls in love with him. In the ensuing argument with her about her loyalty, Kirk insists: "He thrives on love, on worship.... We can't give him worship. None of us, especially you.... Reject him! You must!" Carolyn comes to her senses when she discovers that Apollo will not accept her liberated intellectual interests. This time the god lashes out in fury at her. But the incandescing phaser beams from the *Enterprise* strike his power source just in time, reducing him to a "man-size being."

"I would have loved you as a father his children," Apollo says, in anguish. "Did I ask so much of you?"

Kirk's reply is gentle: "We have outgrown you.... You asked for what we can no longer give."

Denied the worship so necessary for his being, Apollo's body begins to lose substance, and for the first time he admits that the time of the gods "is gone. Take me home to the stars on the wind."

This episode bears the clear message that the era of myths is over, that retreating into slavery to the gods of the past would be terrible. Moreover, the episode suggests that the ancient myths can be scientifically explained by assuming that space travelers played the role of gods. The episode implies that meaning is purely of this world; it denies any threshold to mysterious, transcendent reality. In contrast to the illusive message of myths and religions, the meaning of Carolyn Palamas' life is simply her "duty" to the only reality of which she can be sure, the "humanity" she shares. This conviction of Captain Kirk fits the spirit of the entire series. It is unthinkable that he or his crew, not to mention the strictly scientific Spock, would give credence to myths for a moment. As if to affirm a strongly anti-*mythos* for the series, a parallel plot of demythification was played out a quarter of a century later in the "Devil's Due" of *TNG*. There Picard's crew exposes the devilishly powered Ardra as a mere hoax.

Yet these story lines follow a mythic pattern. David Gerrold defined *Star Trek* as "a set of fables—morality plays, entertainments, and diversions about contemporary man, but set against a science-fiction background. *The back-*

ground is subordinate to the fable" (48; italics in original). This can be documented at those points in which dramatic coherence—that is, hewing to the mythic story line—caused scriptwriters to depart from the standards of scientific accuracy. For instance, the attractive young crew of the *Enterprise* never ages despite journeys through the light-year distances of outer space. Members of the bridge crew are regularly shaken off their seats by enemy torpedoes despite the fact that shock waves would not carry past a spaceship's artificial-gravity field. These scientific liberties are taken for dramatic effect, creating "action, adventure, fun, entertainment, and thought-provoking statements" (Whitfield 213). These are actually mythical elements that appeal to an audience schooled in a particular mythical tradition.

When one compares the themes of the series with the content of classical myths, we immediately three story telling patterns are apparent in "Who Mourns for Adonais?" The first is *saga*, which features a protagonist journeying to unknown and dangerous regions while undergoing trials to test his strength and wit. In the classical monomyth delineated by Joseph Campbell, a human undertakes a journey in response to the requirement to move from childhood to maturity through "the crooked lanes of his own spiritual labyrinth" (101). But in materials embodying the American monomyth, the saga of maturation tends to be replaced by the defense against malevolent attacks upon innocent communities. Gene Roddenberry's original prospectus for *Star Trek*, featuring the format of "Wagon Train to the Stars," aims at saga. He planned the series to be "built around characters who travel to other worlds and meet the jeopardy and adventure which become our stories" (Whitfield 23). This correlates with the announcement at the beginning of *TOS* programs that the mission of the *Enterprise* is "to explore strange new worlds, to seek out new civilizations, to boldly go where no man has gone before." Thus in the saga of Apollo's planet, the *Enterprise* had to be mortally endangered by the gigantic face on its scanner, and it was essential for protagonists Kirk and Spock to leave their command post and come face to face with the foe. It was obviously bad military and space-travel strategy, as many critics have pointed out. No sensible commander would send himself and the key technical officers on a landing party like this. But it is essential to the saga format and thus is characteristic of almost every episode.

The Mythic Call of Sexual Renunciation

The second mythic pattern visible in "Who Mourns for Adonais?"—and one very characteristic of the American monomyth—is sexual renunciation, a norm that reflects some distinctly religious aversions to intimacy. The protagonists in some mythical sagas must renounce previous sexual ties for the sake of their trials. They must avoid entanglements and temptations that inevitably arise from satyrs, sirens, or Loreleis in the course of their travels. Thus Lt. Palamas is tested in the episode with Apollo, her sexual liaison endangering the survival of the *Enterprise*. After she renounces her passion, the saga can get back on course. In the classical monomyth this theme plays a subsidiary role in the initiation or testing phase. The protagonist may encounter sexual temptation symbolizing "that pushing, self-protective, malodorous, carnivorous, lecherous fever which is the very nature of the organic cell," as Campbell points out (121). Yet the "ultimate adventure" is the "mystical marriage ... of the triumphant hero-soul with the Queen Goddess" of knowledge (109). In the current American embodiments of mythic renunciation there is a curious rejection of sexual union as a primary value.

In *Star Trek* each hero is locked into a renunciatory pattern closely related to the mission. On long expeditions in outer space there is, for example, no intrinsic reason why an intimate partner or family would not accompany the captain. This was customary for the masters of some large sailing vessels in the era of extended voyages. But that would violate the mythic paradigm. So Roddenberry describes the renunciation pattern: "Long ago Captain Kirk consciously ruled out any possibility of any romantic interest while aboard the ship. It is an involvement he feels he simply could never risk. In a very real sense he is 'married' to his ship and his responsibilities as captain of her" (Whitfield 217) In numerous episodes Kirk is in the situation Carolyn Palamas faced, forced to choose between an attractive sexual partner and his sense of duty to his mission. The authors of *Star Trek Lives!* report that female fans

> vicariously thrill to Kirk's sexual exploits with gorgeous females of every size, shape and type—from the stunning lady lawyers, biologists and doctors who have loved him, to the vicious and breath-taking Elaan of Troyius, who ruled a planet but was willing to risk destroying her entire solar system for him.... Many see Kirk's loves as having *a* tragic element. There is affection and warmth in his response, and evidently the capacity for deep love. But very often the situation is impossible. He loses not through his faults but through his virtues, because of the demanding life he has chosen [Lichtenberg and Marshak 41].

They go on to describe the renunciation of sexual bonds for the sake of loyalty to the *Enterprise* and its crew. "Time and again, he had to make a choice between a woman and his ship — and his ship always won" (151). An instructive exception to this pattern of isolation from family occurs in the move *Star Trek* (2009). There James T. Kirk's father chooses to remain aboard his ship while his wife in labor escapes to permit the birth of the future Captain Kirk. It is the renunciation of family intimacy for the sake of crew and the mission of thwarting the Romulans.

One episode of *TNG*, "The Inner Light," works out this connection between redemption and renunciation in opposition to familial commitment with great explicitness. The *Enterprise* is minding its own business when an apparently primitive "probe" begins to shadow it, eventually sending a shower of nucleons that causes Captain Picard to faint. As the crew examines him and tries to find a way to break the "beam" that has seized him, Picard begins to have experiences on another planet, Kataan, in a community called Ressic. Initially disoriented, he gradually realizes that he is having the experience of another man, Kamin, an "ironweaver" who has had a wife, Eline, for three years. After initial hesitations about going to bed with her, Picard fully accepts his role as her husband, responds to her desire to have children, fathering a son and daughter, and becomes an accepted member of his new community. Reflecting on his several years of experiencing these new human riches, Picard says to Eline: "I always believed that I didn't need children to complete my life.... Now, I couldn't imagine life without them."

At that moment, the crewmembers caring for Picard on the *Enterprise* break the beam, causing his counterpart on Kataan to experience a tremor and collapse. Crewmembers attending Picard's "original" body on the *Enterprise* decide that the beam must be re-established to stabilize him. Years more pass and Picard becomes a grandfather. As a citizen of Kataan, he gradually discovers that the planet is dying — a secret that the authorities have hidden. The episode is resolved in a peculiar twist of time. At a rocket-launching on the planet, a deceased friend, Batai, and Picard/Kamin's dead wife reappear in the flush of health. Responding to Picard's puzzlement, Batai tells him: "We hoped that our probe would find someone in the future, someone who could be a teacher, someone who would tell the others about us." Picard acknowledges: "I'm the someone it finds. That's what this launching is, a probe that finds me in the future." Having saved Kataan and safely retreated back to the *Enterprise*, Picard awakes after a mere 20 to 25 minutes of coma and is led to the medical facility by Dr. Crusher. The symbolic message here is: Picard may experience some of the pleasures of family, but they are subordinate to his planet-saving mission. His place is on the bridge of the *Enterprise*, not sitting at hearth with family responsibilities.

This renunciation of sexual love for the sake of loyalty to one's comrades goes far beyond the classical monomyth. It is seen perhaps most clearly in the person of Spock. He is loyal to Kirk and his comrades at the expense of risking his life for them again and again, but he persistently resists the temptation of entanglements with the opposite sex. Nurse Christine Chapel, a beautiful, talented crewmember who is hopelessly in love with Spock, gets the cold shoulder from him in episode after episode. Here is a man who is "capable of the prodigious outpouring of passion triggered by the irresistible *pon farr* and yet incapable of lasting emotional ties" with women (Lichtenberg and Marshak 80). Sex is an autonomous force here, distinct from Spock's personality and capable of destroying his ability to reason. Since he cannot integrate it with his personality, he must rigidly repress it until it overpowers him in the rutting season. Spock bears within his person the temptation that threatens every saga with disaster: he must fiercely renounce the temptation for the mission to succeed. Such a motif may not be true to life, and it is certainly improbable that there are sophisticated planets with *pon farr* rites derived from Puritan fantasies. But it is true to the mythic paradigm.

As the series matured in the more sexually liberated 1980s and '90s, *Star Trek*'s writers kept finding ways to keep their leaders hermetically sealed from intimacy. The film *Star Trek: Generations* (1994) contains several moments in which both Kirk and Picard meditate on their value system that excludes permanent partnerships with women and the families that might result. Picard reveals to the counselor Troi that his brother's children have died and that he is depressed because he had always thought they would carry on the family name. Now the name will die with him. Somewhat later, Picard's *Enterprise* is threatened by the Nexus, a "temporal disturbance" that can generate pleasant illusions for those who fall within its field. Picard drifts into the fantasy that he's having Christmas with his own large family; but he snaps out of it, realizing that his duty is real and this family is not.

Back at the bridge, the *Enterprise* battles against the Klingons near the planet Veridian III; in an abandon maneuver, Picard's saucer section crashes on its surface. Safely landed, the spirit of the guide figure Guinan leads Picard to find Captain Kirk, who is not dead as presumed in an accident seventy-eight years earlier, but living as a contented farmer in Iowa with "Antonia" and some rather satisfying horses. Picard, intent on recruiting heroic assistance, hectors him about duty, about the need for his participation in a rescue operation. Eventually, Kirk concedes that "Antonia isn't real." And he confesses his longing for the call of the old duties on the bridge: "Maybe it's about the empty chairs on the bridge of the *Enterprise*." He leaves Antonia and helps Picard defeat Zoran, who was only moments away from killing 240 million people. After helping defeat Zoran, the dying Kirk asks, "Did we make a difference?" Of course they did.

As did Captain Kathryn Janeway, also married in a lonely way to her ship in the *Voyager* series. In an interview with Jeff Greenwald, Kate Mulgrew, who plays the Janeway character, fiercely defended the need of her character to resist sexual intimacy: "Janeway wouldn't risk it. She loves the crew too much. I love the ship too much. I simply couldn't jeopardize it" (226). Only Captain Benjamin Sisko, who commands a static space station in *DS9*, is permitted to have a family; but, predictably, his wife has been dead for several years.

All of these triumphs of renunciatory duty over sexuality in *Star Trek* reflect Gene Roddenberry's philosophical views about the possibilities of intimacy. In an extended interview with Yvonne Fern, he explained:

> Romance is a product of not knowing each other. Friendship develops when you know each other.... Sex is not germane to intimacy.... Two men can be more intimate than a man and his wife. Or two women. Or a man and a woman who understand one another, perhaps share one another's dreams, but have no wish to live together or to share their bodies with one another [100].

Extending an essentially platonic notion of "true love" to the *Star Trek*–type settings, Roddenberry argues against marriage. Responding to Fern's question, "So when do two people marry?" he responded: "I think they don't, in a perfect world. I don't think there's that kind of mutual possession. Marriage in the form that it is now cannot possibly continue into the future. That's why we have so little of it in *Star Trek*" (100).

And then he added: "I think if we all lived in my *Star Trek* world, it would be pretty close to heaven." Thus the lonely marriage to the ship, in *Star Trek*'s ethos, is not a deprivation but a perfection. The duties of the bridge permit deeply satisfying friendships, unimpeded by the attractions and distractions of human desire and human bodies. A rare instance of sex among officers occurs in the film *Insurrection* (1998), when the "regenerative metaphasic particles" of the Ba'Ku people's planet stimulate good times between Commander Riker and Counselor Troi, who observes, "My boobs are beginning to feel firm again." Even Captain Picard feels randy with the beautiful Anij, a several-hundred-years-old woman, but chastely begs off because of pressing Starfleet business once he finally gets his chance to relax with her.

This skepticism about marriage as a possessiveness that works against military friendship is allied to the frequent sense that family authority must be rejected to permit Federation duty, that this duty is a higher calling than mere family can understand. When family members come into the vicinity of heroic crewmembers, they are disruptive and embarrassing. Deanna Troi's mother, Lwaxana, is domineering in the extreme. Deanna confronts her with these angry words in "Menage a Troi" (*TNG*): "Mother, look. Perhaps some day I will marry. But you have to let me make my own choices, live my own life, and not the life that you would choose for me." Data, the positronic, humanoid android officer of *TNG*, has an evil twin, "Lore." And in *Star Trek V: The Final Frontier* (1989), Spock has a wicked brother, Sybok, a religious charlatan who almost destroys them.

One sees enabling/crippling family dynamics worked out in some detail with the *VOY* episode "Tattoo," where Commander Chakotay explores his Native American roots as a descendant of Central American "Rubber Tree People." The background story shows him during a trip into the rain forest with his father. Chakotay expresses the idea that he is a "contrary" among his people since he believes that they "live in the past and myth." His father deeply disapproves of his decision to become a Starfleet cadet and predicts that he will be "caught between two worlds." This particular strand of the story emphasizes the idea that the Federation officer has the character to defy family authority to become a cadet. As the story works toward its resolution, Chakotay does use his native jungle lore to save his party from destruction when they encounter his ancestral people, initially hostile until they are reassured by his knowledge of them.

In this distancing from the threats that families pose for the spiritual perfection of the Federation military command, *Star Trek* stands with the Buddha, who abandoned his family in his search for enlightenment. It is also scriptural in echoing the spirit of Jesus' response to Peter, who tells him that "we have left everything and followed you." Jesus replies that the disciples will receive much greater rewards than the bonds of family: "Truly I tell you, there is no one who has left house or brothers or sisters or mother or father or children or fields, for my sake and for the sake of the good news, who will not receive a hundredfold now in this age ... and in the age to come, eternal life" (Mark 10:29–30, NRSV). Those who leave behind their earthly attachments for the heavenly life of *Star Trek* will harvest the heavenly friendships that transcend the ordinary intimacies of sexual commitment and family. In this regard, *Star Trek*'s myth system also reinstates the ethos of ancient religion while giving ancient narrative patterns a new lease.

Redemption

The third mythical pattern running through the episodes of *Star Trek* is redemption. In the classical monomyth, the beautiful maiden must be redeemed from the clutches of the sea monster, the endangered city spared from its peril, and the protagonist redeemed by fateful interventions in the nick of time. This pattern is much more diffuse in the classical monomyth than in modern materials that lie closer to the American pattern. A classical hero may experience supernatural aid as he crosses the threshold into the realm of initiatory adventure and then returns; and he may confront trials embodying the redemption of others. But his own redemption takes the form of gaining mature wisdom, achieving atonement with his father, enjoying union with the goddess, and returning home with benefits for his people. The redemption scheme in materials such as *Star Trek* has nothing to do with the maturation process; rather, it fits the pattern of crusading to redeem others. This form of selfless idealism has been elaborated most extensively by Ernest Tuveson in *Redeemer Nation*. As happens so frequently in American history, the *Enterprise*'s sense of high calling leads it to violate its own "noninterference directive" with great frequency. If Kirk and his crew encounter an endangered planet, their sense of duty impels them to intervene. It may not be legal, or right, or even sensible; but the zealous imperative to redeem is pervasive in *TOS*. While Gerrold overstated it in claiming that among the seventy-nine *TOS* episodes, "there never was a script in which the *Enterprise*'s mission or goals were questioned," he has accurately characterized the series (251).

This observation should be counterbalanced by the awareness that Star Trek's selfless crew never interfered with a culture in the spirit of conquest. They always intervened merely to set things right before they flew away in their spacecraft. In the successor series of the franchise, the writers became more self-conscious about violations of the Prime Directive and worked harder at maintaining the noninterventionist posture. But as Thomas Richards clearly explains, it is questionable whether non-intervention — apart from its dramatic undesirability — is even possible: "Behind the Prime Directive is the idea that it is possible to observe a society without affecting it" (Richards 15). *TNG* plays very self-consciously with this notion in its episode "Who Watches the Watchers?" Federation has established a "duck blind" that permits it to observe a primitive society. When their presence is accidentally revealed, a chain of events begins that compels them to realize that they have probably changed the society merely by making their presence known.

But the more usual role of the *Enterprise*, especially in *TOS*, is to intervene and to redeem some primitive society that has violated American norms of freedom and the challenge of self-development. Mr. Spock embodies the redemptive role in a particularly powerful way. His half–Vulcan origin makes him a godlike figure, peculiarly capable of effecting benevolent transformations. Spock consults his computer with superhuman speed to devise techniques for saving galaxies and men from prodigious threats, leading the audience to view him with a reverence that traditionally has been reserved for gods. Leonard Nimoy's interview, approvingly cited by the authors of *Star Trek Lives!*, points toward audience yearnings for an omniscient redeemer. In their perception, the viewer sees Spock as someone

> who knows something about me that nobody else knows. Here's a person that *understands* me in a way that nobody else understands me. Here's a person that I'd like to be able to spend time with and talk to because *he would know what I mean when I tell him how I feel*. He would have insight that nobody else seems to have [74].

In short, Spock is perceived as a god, which matches the requirements of the mythical pattern, namely that without a superhuman agency of some sort, there is no true redemption.

Captain Jean-Luc Picard carried the world-redemption theme to its fullest realization in the above-mentioned final episode of *TNG*, "All Good Things." But here it occurs with some irony, because the imminent destruction of the world was caused by an action of the *Enterprise* in bombarding an anomaly with "inverse tachyon beams" that set time rolling backward to destroy the primal soup that made all life possible. So, just as the future can be nullified by careless acts in the present, the past that made the present is pathetically susceptible to aggressively used tachyons. Q chastises Picard, who wants to hold *him* responsible: "I am not the one who causes the annihilation of mankind. You are!" Afflicted by his newly discovered anxiety that he alone is responsible for the whole world's past, present and future — and that he alone can save it — Picard struggles and juggles his roles at three moments in history. Just when everything seems to crash into nullity despite his efforts, Q presents himself again to tell him that it's over — but only for the moment. Picard has survived *this* existential challenge, which Q defines for him in this way:

> We wanted to see if you had the ability to expand your mind and your horizons, and for one brief moment you did.... For that one fraction of a second, you were open to options you'd never considered. That's the exploration that awaits you, not mapping stars and studying nebulae, but charting the unknown possibilities of existence.

In this moment of epiphany, when a god of chance reaffirms Picard's role as world redeemer, he seems to learn that he may have to save the world over and over again. A daunting task, but more prestigious than Sisyphus' job of endlessly pushing the boulder up a hill.

The Foreshortened Democracy of Star Trek

A final mythic feature to note in *Star Trek* is its utopianism, a topic given detailed consideration in detail in Bruce Isaacs' essay (Chapter 12). The escapist appeal for fans is the presumption that in the distant past Earth somehow abandoned poverty, racism, and war. In "Time's Arrow, Part II" of *TNG*, Deanna Troi explains to a skeptical Samuel Clemens/Mark Twain: "Poverty was eliminated on Earth a long time ago. And a lot of other things disappeared with it: hopelessness ... despair ... cruelty...." And in the film *First Contact*, Picard explains to the confused Lily, a person from the twenty-first century: "In my century we don't succumb to ... revenge. We have a more evolved sensibility." History's all-too-familiar conflicts regarding wealth, political power, and religious intolerance are all safely in the distant past. Life among humanoids affiliated with the United Federation of Planets has become abundant beyond our current imagination. The most evolved forms of the starships are outfitted like luxury hotels, with spacious personal quarters, magical food replicators, infinite entertainments on the fantastical Holodeck, and remarkable healing tools. The political and economic arrangements that make all this possible are vaguely democratic in the sense that occasionally there is a glimpse of elected Federation leaders as in *Star Trek IV: The Voyage Home* (1986) and *Star Trek VI: The Undiscovered Country* (1991).

But the focus of *Star Trek* is on the relationships among crewmembers and how they work as a redemptive team to save those communities that cannot save themselves. Does the *Enterprise*, in its organization and execution, exemplify the democratic ethos?

One could point to *Star Trek*'s well-known alignment with key values of recent democratic liberalism. Its pioneering efforts to include African-Americans in leading roles, albeit timidly at first, earned the praise of civil rights leaders such as Martin Luther King, Jr., Its expanding roles for women in commanding leadership positions have made *Star Trek* look far more egalitarian than the norm in American institutions. And the different series have all had moments when the crew eschewed violence, even if it required acquiescence. Kirk, the most belligerent and interfering of the *Trek* captains, puts it colorfully in "Elaan of Troyius," when he comments on his refusal to blast a Klingon ship: "If I can accomplish my mission by turning tail and running, I'll gladly do that." Among the later captains, Kathryn Janeway often takes perilous risks to preserve the sovereign autonomy of an alien adversary.

However, the political structures of all the starships are those of hierarchical military command. This is especially clear in the "All Good Things..." episode, which trumps every other superhero tale in redeeming existence itself. As the story works out, the family team that usually works together in consultation is subordinated to Picard's disoriented, obsessive sense of responsibility and the stress of saving the world while so little time remains. At several points, he angrily snaps at others who don't understand: "I don't have time to explain. Do it!" This aspect of the story emphasizes that the Federation *Starfleet* is a military organization with a top-down command hierarchy. *Star Trek*'s stories are not "militaristic" in the normal sense: the members of the crew are not conscripts; they do not fondle and gloat over the destructive power of their weapons; they do not scheme to usurp civilian authority. This is a different kind of military: soldiers don't spend a lot of time shining their shoes, clicking their heels, snapping stiff salutes against the brims of hats, shouting "Suh!" to their superiors.

But in the end, what is disappointing about *Star Trek*, as a supremely successful series of mythic tales for a democratic nation, is that its vision of perfection seems limited to men, women, and assorted aliens under a military command. They move rootlessly through the stars, as married to their starships as the Lone Ranger to the great horse Silver — and most of them as subordinate as Tonto. They show no signs of civic responsibility or leadership as that would be normally understood in a democracy with rooted citizens. *Star Trek*'s world is, of course, far closer to democracy in spirit than the stories of hereditary rule and restoration that we get in other workings of the myth such as the *Lion King* or *Star Wars*. Yet, despite the years of programming opportunities to create mythic texts that embody the fullest range of democratic aspirations, there is something important missing here.

The movie *Star Trek* (2009) is especially disappointing on this issue. It moves away from military meritocracy toward aristocracy. James T. Kirk is born to lead and rises to his captaincy by arrogant bullying and breaking rules whenever confronted with them. He cheats on the Kobayashi Maru test, connives to get back on the *Enterprise* after being banned, and takes on Spock, his commanding officer, in a brawling fist fight. Egotism and brash risk taking are the foundation of his leadership, not demonstrated competence and judgment. Spock conveniently defers because the time-traveling older Spock counsels him to accept a subordinate role.

Despite these limitations of democratic ethos limited by distinctive American mythic convictions, the early *Star Trek* became an internationally recognized and loved program. Jeff Greenwald, who traveled around the world in the mid–1990s searching for *Star Trek*'s most serious fans, discovered people lauding it for its heroic view of science, the richness of its philosophical exploration of technological issues, and its vision of interplanetary cooperation — where "kindness, tolerance, and patience have superseded brutality and greed" (99). In Hungary he met Szolt Sàrközy ("Federation alias Lieutenant Commander Q"), who reflected on how his life would be different without *Star Trek*: "I think something would fail, would miss, in my life. I would be empty.... I'm happy that I'm a Trekker. It gives meaning to my life" (95). Consistent with this sort of tribute, Yvonne Fern, who lived with Gene Roddenberry's family during the last months of his life in 1991, reported constant references to altered visions and lives in the letters of condolences that flooded in when Roddenberry died. She reported: "Every letter said the same thing: 'Star Trek changed my life.'" (215). Such testimonies suggest that the *Star Trek* series, however stamped as American by the concerns of their respective eras, achieved a compelling myth that could be globally shared. Fans who responded to *Star Trek*'s excitement at exploring for the sake of knowledge, its provocative philosophical meditations, its expanding visions of equality and tolerance — they grasped the positive elements that will always guarantee a hopeful audience for the programs.

Works Cited

Alexander, David. Star Trek *Creator: The Authorized Biography of Gene Roddenberry*. New York: ROC/Dutton Signet, 1994.
Beauchamp, Fay. "Is This Why We Go on Raising Cain?" *New York Times* 23 December 1973: 71.
Blish, James *Star Trek 7*. New York: Bantam, 1972.
Campbell, Joseph. *The Hero with a Thousand Faces*. New York: Meridian, 1956.
Diehl, Digby. "Girls All Want to Touch the Ears." *New York Times* 25 August 1968: D17.
Fern, Yvonne. *Gene Roddenberry: The Last Conversation*. Berkeley: University of California Press, 1994.
Franklin, H. Bruce. "*Star Trek* in the Vietnam Era." *Film and History: An Interdisciplinary Journal of Film and Television Studies* 24 (1–2) 1994: 36–46.

Gerrold, David. *The World of Star Trek*. New York: Ballantine, 1973.
Greenwald, Jeff. *Future Perfect: How* Star Trek *Conquered Planet Earth*. New York: Viking, 1998.
Jewett, Robert, and John Shelton Lawrence. *Captain America and the Crusade against Evil: The Dilemmas of Zealous Nationalism*. Grand Rapids, MI: Eerdmans, 2003.
Larsen, Stephen, and Robin Larsen. *A Fire in the Mind: The Life of Joseph Campbell*. New York: Doubleday, 1991.
Lawrence, John Shelton. "Joseph Campbell, George Lucas, and the Monomyth." *Finding the Force of the* Star Wars *Franchise: Fans, Merchandise, & Critics*. Ed. Matthew Wilhelm Kapell and John Shelton Lawrence. New York: Peter Lang, 2006. 21–34.
Lichtenberg, Jacqueline, Sondra Marshak and Joan Winston. *Star Trek Lives!* New York: Bantam, 1975.
Plato. *The Republic*. Ed. G.R.F. Ferrari. Cambridge: Cambridge University Press, 2000.
Prelutsky, Burt. Untitled. *New York Times* 15 Oct 1967: 141.
Slotkin, Richard. *Regeneration Through Violence: The Mythology of the American Frontier, 1600-1860*. Middletown, NH: Wesleyan University Press, 1973.
Tuveson, Ernest Lee. *Redeemer Nation: The Idea of America's Millennial Role*. Chicago: University of Chicago Press.
Worland, Rick. "Captain Kirk: Cold Warrior," *Journal of Popular Film and Television*, 16.3 (Fall 1988): 109–117.

Star Trek *Media Cited*

Star Trek *Films*

Star Trek IV: The Voyage Home. Directed by Leonard Nimoy. Screenplay by Steve Meerson, Peter Krikes, Harve Bennet and Nicholas Meyer. Paramount Pictures, 1986.
Star Trek V: The Final Frontier. Directed by William Shatner. Screenplay by David Loughry. Paramount Pictures, 1989.
Star Trek VI: The Undiscovered Country. Directed by Nicholas Meyer. Screenplay by Nicholas Meyer and Denny Martin Flynn. Paramount Pictures, 1991.
Star Trek: First Contact. Directed by Jonathan Frakes. Screenplay by Brannon Braga and Ronald D. Moore. Paramount Pictures, 1996.
Star Trek: Generations. Directed by David Carson. Screenplay by Ronald D. Moore and Brannon Braga. Paramount Pictures, 1994.
Star Trek: Insurrection. Directed by J.J. Abrams. Screenplay by Roberto Orci and Alex Kurtzman. Paramount Pictures, 2009.

Star Trek: The Original Series

"The City on the Edge of Forever." Written by Harlan Ellison. 6 May 1967.
"Elaan of Troyius." Written by John Meredyth Lucas. 20 December 1968.
"Omega Glory." Written by Gene Roddenberry. 1 March 1968.
"A Private Little War." Story by Jud Crucis. Teleplay by Gene Roddenberry. 2 February 1968.
"Who Mourns for Adonais." Written by Gilbert Ralston. 22 September 1967.

Star Trek: The Next Generation

"All Good Things..." Written by Brannon Braga and Ronald D. Moore. 23 May 1994.
"Devil's Due." Story by Philip LaZebnick and William Douglas Lansford. Teleplay by Philip LaZebnick. 4 February 1991.
"Inner Light, The." Story by Morgan Gendel. Teleplay by Morgan Gendel and Peter Alan Fields. 1 June 1992.

"Ménage á Troi." Written by Fred Bronson and Susan Sackett. 26 May 1990.
"Time's Arrow, Part II." Story by Joe Monosky. Teleplay by Jeri Taylor. 21 September 1992.
"Who Watches the Watchers." Written by Richard Manning and Hans Beimler. 16 October 1989.

Star Trek: Voyager

"Tattoo." Story by Larry Brody. Teleplay by Michael Piller. 6 October 1995.

8

The Sisko, the Christ

A Comparison of Messiah Figures in the *Star Trek* Universe and the New Testament

JEFFREY S. LAMP

The topic of religion plays an important role in the development of the *Star Trek* vision of the universe (Lamp 193–214). This is especially true in *Star Trek: the Next Generation* and even more so in *Star Trek: Deep Space Nine* and *Star Trek: Voyager*. What makes *Star Trek: Deep Space Nine* especially intriguing is the more permanent proximity of the presence of the United Federation of Planets to a planetary culture rich in religious faith and expression, that of Bajor. The interaction of the "secular" Federation and the "spiritual" Bajorans makes for telling insights into the role of religion envisioned in the *Star Trek* universe. And there is no more focal figure to this aspect of the *Star Trek* universe than Benjamin Sisko, who is both a commissioned Starfleet officer in command of the space station Deep Space Nine and who has also been labeled by the Bajoran spiritual establishment as the messianic "Emissary of the Prophets."

This discussion explores the handling of this rather unique pairing of roles in the person of Sisko to two ends. First, it draws comparisons and contrasts between this picture and the presentation of Jesus as a messiah figure in the New Testament.

Second, it focuses on how a messiah figure is defined and perceived within the framework of a secular, materialistic view of the universe as represented by the Federation.

The discussion consists of three major sections. The first deals with methodological considerations that provide the contours for the discussion. The second compares and contrasts the messianic caricatures of Sisko and Jesus within their respective narrative worlds. The final section draws conclusions from these comparisons and summarizes how the messianic depictions of Sisko and Jesus are appropriate within their respective narrative frameworks and world views.

Preliminary Matters

Methodological Considerations for This Study

A couple of important controls must be addressed before this discussion proceeds. First, a working definition of "messiah" is necessary. The term "messiah" is the English transliteration of the Hebrew word *mašiaḥ*, which means "anointed (with oil)," owing to the practice of anointing with oil a person consecrated to a special position, such as priest or king (Aaron as priest, Exod 28:41; David as king, 1 Sam 16:3, 12–13). The sign of anointing with oil designated a person as one set aside by God for a task.

In the Intertestamental Period *mašiaḥ* came to be associated with the hope that God would send an agent to free Israel from the yoke of foreign oppression and to restore righteousness. In the New Testament, the term *Christos*, from which derives the English word "Christ," similarly means "anointed (with oil)." In some texts the connection of *Christos* with the person of Jesus casts him in the role of the promised messianic deliverer, though in a sense not commensurate with contemporary Jewish messianic expectations (Hurtado 106–17; Wise).

Of special note in helping define the term for our purposes is the reference to king Cyrus of Persia in Isaiah 45:1 as "[the Lord's] anointed." Cyrus is the one through whom God will rebuild Jerusalem following the Exile, and as one set apart for a purpose in the divine will, Cyrus can be defined as a *mašiaḥ* in the true sense of the word. What is noteworthy here is that a person can be designated as "anointed" by God even though the person is not an adherent to the religion of that deity. This is pertinent in our study of Sisko, who by Bajoran reckoning is the "anointed one," but who is not a follower of Bajoran religion.

The data in this study suggests that a useful working definition for "messiah" in the present discussion would be *a figure of religious significance within a religious tradition who is deemed designated by the deity of that tradition to perform a redemptive mission for a particular group of people*. Granted, the definition is loose.

Yet it retains enough of its biblical significance to make possible the comparison of a modern fictional character (Sisko) with Jesus. It allows for the figure to be human/non-divine or ascribed with the characteristics of deity; it allows for the figure to be a faithful worshiper of the deity or a non-believer;

it allows for the holders of the religious tradition to identify the figure to be messianic whether the figure accepts that role or not.

The second methodological control is the delineation of those sources that provide the substance for our study. In the case of Sisko, the choice is rather self-evident: several episodes of *Deep Space Nine* in which the religious significance of Sisko is addressed. In the case of Jesus, however, the choice of source material must be justified to some extent. However, my justification of the use of biblical sources will be highly unsatisfying to many of my colleagues. I will use the writings of the New Testament *in their canonical form* as the source data in discussing Jesus' messiahship. I do not deny the usefulness or insights of critical biblical scholarship. Rather, I choose this source data in order to maintain a level of consistency with that chosen for information about Sisko.

In the case of the television series, we are interested in the portrayal of the character in the final produced form of the episodes. There may be many interesting background features behind these episodes, many scenes that started as one thing and ended up as another, but the material with which we must work is the product that aired. To be consistent, it seems reasonable to deal with the sources about Jesus that "aired" in their final forms. While this may be viewed by some as naive and uncritical, it is arguably the most manageable tack given the scope of the present discussion.

Religious World View of the *Star Trek* Universe

I have outlined six points that describe the religious world view of the *Star Trek* universe (Lamp 196–200):

- It is secular and materialistic;
- It is optimistic;
- It understands deity to be a matter of relative superiority;
- It views the "supernatural" as "natural";
- It views religion as fulfilling a functional social role; and
- It is religiously pluralistic.

It has been widely noted that the *Star Trek* universe is not only a description of a fictional universe, but is also a prescription of how contemporary and future human society should evolve. The overarching framework for such a society is epitomized in the United Federation of Planets, of which Starfleet is the narrative representative. This is the quintessential secular society, governed by a nearly religious commitment to science and technology as the "savior" and solution for all situations.

Within this secular utopia all phenomena are explainable in scientific terms, and from the viewpoint of the dominant secular world view, there is no true divinity or supernatural. This does not preclude, however, particular cultural expressions of religious faith and practice within the framework of the dominant secular paradigm. Rather, the celebration of diversity within an overarching unity is celebrated, so long as the social order is not compromised and absolutist claims are not made across cultural and religious boundaries. The faith of one cultural group may be meaningful and appropriate for that group, but it may not be so for another group, and the personal preferential nature of religion must be respected.

In light of this sketch of the religious world view of the *Star Trek* universe, it is apparent that Benjamin Sisko represents a somewhat enigmatic figure. He is committed to the secular position and agenda of the Federation. Yet he finds himself, against his will, thrust into the role of religious deliverer in a religion that is not his own. He does not believe in the gods of the Bajorans, the Prophets, nor does he consider them gods. Nevertheless, he is the Bajoran Emissary. We now turn our attention to the religious and messianic aspirations of the Bajoran people for whom Sisko is a venerated personality.

Linford has earlier described Bajoran religion in greater detail than is possible here (77–100). Here we note a few characteristics of Bajoran religion, especially in terms of its "messianic expectations" of its Emissary of the Prophets.

The religion of the Bajorans is based on worship of the "Prophets," beings to whom divinity is ascribed and who dwell in the "Celestial Temple." The Prophets are mysteriously said to be "of Bajor," and they take an active, benevolent interest in the Bajoran people. The Prophets have communicated with the Bajorans via two means: through a series of "Orbs" that mediate "spiritual" encounters specific to the purpose of the Orb, and through a collection of "scriptures" called "Prophecies." A group of religious leaders known as "Vedeks" governs access to the Orbs and interprets the Prophecies. The supreme religious leader, the "Kai," is elected by the Vedeks and functions as the religious spokesperson for the Bajoran people. The spirituality of individual Bajorans appears to be based upon seeking and following the "will of the Prophets" in their experience. The practice of spirituality includes private ritual ("The Homecoming"), regular attendance in corporate worship ("Accession"), and prayer ("Ties of Blood and Water"), the aim of which is the sustenance and enrichment of an individual's "pagh," roughly the Bajoran equivalent of a soul.

In terms of "messianic expectation," the Bajoran prophecies foretell of the coming of the Emissary of the Prophets, one who will save and unite the Bajoran people by discovering the Celestial Temple (Okuda et al. 88). When Sisko is assigned to command Deep Space Nine, he discovers a stable wormhole and encounters the mysterious race of aliens that the Bajorans worship as the Prophets ("Emissary"). To Sisko, however, they are simply an advanced race of beings for whom the concept of "linear time" has no meaning. Upon securing regular passage for ships through the wormhole and upon returning to the station following his encounter with the wormhole aliens, Sisko is tabbed by the Bajoran religious establishment as the prophesied Emissary of the Prophets. This ascription is based upon Sisko's contact with the Prophets, the first known direct encounter as far as anyone in the religious establishment can determine.

Two things are noteworthy about Sisko's designation as Emissary. First, at the time of this designation, it is unclear why a non–Bajoran would be chosen as the Emissary. Sisko's relationship with the Bajorans and the Prophets will eventually become explicit by the final season of the series, but at the outset, it remains enigmatic. Second, Sisko, the consummate Starfleet officer, is uneasy with the status of "religious icon," but plays the role of Emissary, not for reasons sympathetic with Bajoran spirituality, but for the pragmatic benefits it has for gaining the Federation's chief goal — admission of Bajor into the United Federation of Planets. The tension between Sisko's dual roles as Starfleet officer and Bajoran religious persona figures prominently in the story line of the series and helps define the *Star Trek* universe's vision of proper religious faith and practice.

Messianic Depictions of Sisko and Jesus Christ

This discussion consists of comparisons and contrasts of messianic depictions in three areas: messianic consciousness, messianic disposition, and messianic program.

Messianic Consciousness

In discussing the concept of messianic consciousness, we describe two related issues. First, the person so designated must be aware that in some sense the notion of messiahship is ascribed to him. It is clear that following the event of his encounter with the wormhole aliens Sisko is aware that the Bajorans view him as the Emissary.

This leads to the second issue, that of personal acceptance of the mantle ascribed to him. Sisko is a reluctant messiah, evidenced by his vacillating acceptance of the role confirmed upon him by virtue of his encounter with the inhabitants of the wormhole ("Emissary"). It is to Sisko's ambivalence in accepting the role of Emissary that this discussion now turns.

For the first few years of the series, Sisko is depicted as balking repeatedly at his designation as a religious figure. His only reason for accepting the role is pragmatic — for the purpose of gaining Bajor's admission into the Federation.

It is with the episode "Destiny" that Sisko begins to develop some level of genuine respect for Bajoran religion, for the first time entertaining the idea that the prophecies allegedly referring to him may actually do so. As a result he accepts his role as Emissary in a bit more meaningful way. In "Accession" Sisko's acceptance of the role of Emissary takes a couple of significant turns. At the appearance of an ancient Bajoran poet claiming to be the Emissary, Sisko expends great energy, even searching the prophecies themselves, to transfer the mantle to the newcomer. However, once the new Emissary begins re-establishing the old caste system of family-determined occupations, Sisko seeks to regain the title for himself. What is noteworthy is the motivation for this effort. It is not out of some theological conviction that he is truly the Emissary, but because the reformed social order would keep Bajor from gaining admission into the Federation. The contest over who is truly Emissary is eventually settled by the Prophets themselves, who affirm Sisko's claim to the position. Here, too, Sisko takes another step toward embracing the role of Emissary.

With the episode "Rapture" Sisko shows a growing acceptance of his role. At first this is exercised rather cynically as he uses his position to allow him to survey an ancient Bajoran artifact. Through an accident, Sisko discovers the lost city of B'hala. This discovery is a sign to the Bajorans, proof that he is indeed the Emissary. He receives a series of visions, ostensibly from the Prophets, visions that "make sense" of "everything." When the visions threaten his life, he initially resists treatment in order to receive further insights. The visionary experiences even cause Sisko to embrace his role as Emissary over that of Starfleet officer, keeping Bajor from joining the Federation at the time. He begins to speak in religious terms, offering his own prophecies and blessings to the people. Nevertheless, Sisko is not truly converted to the Bajoran faith. When his visionary episodes cease as a result of a medical procedure, Sisko remains a Starfleet officer with its concomitant commitments. Sisko is willing to be used by the Prophets in the course of events, but he does so as a religious outsider.

Another step toward acceptance is taken in "The Reckoning." Sisko is told in a vision that a "reckoning" is at hand. A tablet is discovered, and Sisko again uses his status to take possession of the tablet, stating that "the Prophets want him to take it." The tablet is partially translated, indicating that a disaster will destroy the station and Bajor. Sisko angrily breaks the tablet before it is to be returned. In the meantime, Kira, Sisko's first officer, is possessed by a Prophet, while an evil Pagh Wraith possesses Jake, Sisko's son. A battle is to ensue, the result of which, if Kira wins, is to be a Golden Age for Bajor. Sisko is told in a vision that "he will not waiver." In response he orders the Promenade cleared for the battle.

As the battle between Kira and Jake occurs, Sisko watches, knowing that for the will of the Prophets to be done, Jake must die. Winn prevents the battle from concluding, saving the station but releasing both entities. Two features of this episode indicate a growing acceptance by Sisko of his role as

Emissary. The first is a comment by Jake voicing concern that his father is willing to die for his role as Emissary. The second is that Sisko is willing to let Jake die to fulfill the will of the Prophets.

The beginning of the seventh season finds two episodes that relate significantly to Sisko's role as Emissary. In "Image in the Sand," Sisko learns that the woman who raised him was not in fact his birth mother. "Shadows and Symbols" reveals that Sisko was born to a Prophet, called "Sarah," who inhabited a human body to give him birth. At this revelation, Sarah calls Sisko "Emissary," a moment that marks a turning point in Sisko's perception and acceptance of his destiny. This revelation further clarifies earlier enigmatic statements by the Prophets that "the Sisko is of Bajor" ("Favor the Bold"; "Sacrifice of Angels").

By the end of the series, Sisko is portrayed as alternately cooperative and uncooperative with the Prophets. But in the series finale, "What You Leave Behind," following the Federation's victory over the Dominion, Sisko is dancing with Kasidy when he is struck with the realization that he knows what the Emissary must do, at which point he goes to the Fire Caves to face Dukat and the Pagh Wraiths in a climactic showdown. Upon his triumph over Dukat, Sisko finds himself in the Celestial Temple with Sarah, who tells him, "The Emissary has completed his task." Sisko further learns that he must remain in the Celestial Temple. He explains to Kasidy that the Prophets have saved him and that he has much to learn and do because the Prophets still have work for their Emissary to perform. In the end, Sisko has fully embraced his status as Emissary of the Prophets.

In comparing the messianic consciousness of Sisko to that of Jesus, a few points are noteworthy. One is the relative timing of messianic awareness. Sisko is not aware that he has any such status until he is so named following his encounter with the wormhole aliens. While his *preparation* for this role is eventually revealed to him to have begun with his birth, his awareness of this fact is rather late in the series narrative. Jesus, on the other hand, is identified as the pre-existent divine lord and agent of creation (John 1:3; 1 Cor 8:6; Col 1:16), even as God (John 1:1, 18; 20:28; Rom 9:5; Titus 2:13; Heb 1:8; 2 Pet 1:1; cf. Harris). Moreover, Jesus is depicted as being aware of his pre-existence, having chosen to come into the world to fulfill the redemptive plan of God (John 17:5; Phil 2:6–8).

The only canonical account of the childhood of Jesus shows awareness of his unique status (Luke 2:41–52). Jesus is seen sitting in the temple courts in Jerusalem speaking with the teachers, later informing his searching parents that "he had to be in his Father's house" (v. 49). In contrast to Sisko, when others acknowledge Jesus' unique religious status to him (John the Baptist, Matt 3:14; God, Matt 3:16; demons, Mark 1:24 and 5:7; Peter, Mark 8:29), Jesus affirms this, whether explicitly or implicitly. At his appearance before Pilate, Jesus responds to Pilate's question as to whether Jesus is the king of the Jews (Matt 27:11) with the words, "Yes, it is as you say" (v. 11).

In summary, Sisko is depicted as one who wrestles with the religious status ascribed to him, gradually coming to terms with its meaning for his life until he fully embraces it. Jesus, on the other hand, is pictured as one who is eternally aware of his nature and mission and who embraces it fully. We now turn to discuss the "spiritual" dispositions of these messianic figures.

Messianic Disposition

We now discuss two qualities pertinent to the messianic pictures of Sisko and Jesus: obedience to the divine will and personal communion with the deity.

Obedience to the Divine Will: The depictions of obedience to the divine will of Sisko and Jesus are in large measure direct opposites. In Sisko is the constant tension between his roles as a Starfleet officer and as a religious figure within Bajoran religion. So in an important sense, Sisko by definition is disobedient to the "divine will" of the Prophets because he does not consider them to be deities. When Sisko does cooperate with the desires of the Prophets he does so not out of a sense of obedience or submission to the will of a god, but for reasons that are deemed commensurate with his role as a Starfleet officer.

From the perspective of the wormhole aliens, Sisko can be labeled, on the one hand, as one who "will not waiver" ("The Reckoning"), and on the other hand, as "belligerent, aggressive, adversarial" ("Sacrifice of Angels"). He demonstrates obedience to the desires of the Prophets to the point of great personal loss and sacrifice, risking his own life ("Rapture") and the life of his son ("The Reckoning") to pursue a course given him by the Prophets, and embarking on a sort of religious quest in his pursuit of the lost Orb of the Emissary ("Image in the Sand," "Shadows and Symbols"). He appears to reach a point of unequivocal obedience when he states in "What You Leave Behind" that he knows what the Emissary "must do."

Yet Sisko often resists the desires of the Prophets, sometimes resulting in personal loss. He often appears to the Bajoran religious establishment as disobedient to the will of the Prophets when he chooses his role as Starfleet officer over what the religious leaders perceive to be proper for the Emissary ("In the Hands of the Prophets"; "Destiny"). In "Tears of the Prophets," Sisko rejects the warning of the Prophets and follows Starfleet orders to launch an attack on Dominion forces, resulting in the death of one of his officers, Jadzia Dax. Even with this event in recent memory, Sisko again rejects the warning of the Prophets regarding his marriage to Kasidy, opting to proceed with the marriage and uttering in defiance, "to hell with the Prophets" ("Penumbra"), also allaying Kasidy's fears that the Prophets' warning has to do with the child she is carrying ("The Dogs of War").

Comparing Sisko's obedience to the divine will with that of Jesus shows a fundamental difference in disposition. Jesus is depicted as obedient from eternity, choosing to submit to God's will to enter human history (Phil 2:6–8). Jesus is said to have "learned obedience" through his suffering and submission to God's will (Heb 5:7–9). This is perhaps an apt way of regarding Sisko's pilgrimage of response to the leading of the Prophets, but the fundamental paradigm of Jesus' response to God's desires is his prayer in Gethsemane, "not what I will, but what you will" (Mark 14:36).

In summary, Sisko's obedience to the divine will is better characterized from his perspective as selective cooperation with an alien race. Even in the series finale, when Sisko is "saved" by the Prophets and remains in the Celestial Temple because he has work yet to do, it is not stated that he has embraced the religion of the Bajorans. In light of this silence, it is probably best to see here another instance in which he is cooperating with the desires of the wormhole aliens rather than submitting to the will of the Bajoran deities. Jesus, on the other hand, believes in the deity of his narrative world and is pictured as the exemplar of obedience to the divine will, an integral component to his messianic depiction. This state of affairs is largely based upon the relationships of Sisko and Jesus with the deities they are seen as serving.

Personal Communion with the Deity: Since Sisko does not regard the wormhole aliens as deities, his state of personal "spiritual" communion with them must be interpreted in this light. Though he is known as the Emissary of the Prophets, Sisko is not regularly depicted as a participant in the ritual practice of the faithful. His primary mode of communication with the Prophets is through numerous visionary experiences, and these occur primarily at the impetus of the Prophets. Sisko does not pray in the conventional sense — a noteworthy exception being his nearly mocking tone in beseeching the Prophets to intervene on his behalf in "Sacrifice of Angels." Rather, he communicates directly in his visionary experiences, though the substance of the communications frequently leaves Sisko baffled. While this mode of communication was initially the fact that led to his identification as Emissary, Sisko gives the impression that the visions are sometimes unwelcome.

In terms of other religious practices, Sisko's attitude toward the Prophecies of the Bajorans is pragmatic rather than devotional. In "Destiny" he refuses to allow the prophecies to influence his joint mission with the Cardassians concerning the wormhole, though he comes to see that they may indeed be referring to him in some way. In "Accession" he somewhat cynically uses the prophecies to try to relieve himself of the role of Emissary. In short, his view toward reading Bajoran scripture is encapsulated in his stated goal while reading in "Favor the Bold": "guidance, insight, loopholes." As for Sisko's use of ritual and symbol, he again largely abstains from such Bajoran religious practices, with a few exceptions. Following the Prophets' abandonment of Sisko and Bajor in "Tears of the Prophets," Sisko becomes obsessive in his quest to locate the lost Orb of the Emissary ("Shadows and Symbols"). Moreover, the artifact that leads to his discovery of B'hala functions sacramentally in allowing him further visionary experiences and insights ("Rapture"). To be sure, these are indeed exceptional rather than typical uses of religious symbols, symbols peculiar to his role alone and not those of the religious experience of the typical Bajoran.

Jesus, in contrast, believes in the deity for whom he functions messianically. As such, he desires and experiences personal intimacy with his God, a relationship described in terms of the father-son relationship. This intimacy is grounded in Jesus' assertion that he and the Father are one and that the Father is "in" him (John 17:22–23). Moreover, Jesus is pictured as a man of prayer who seeks solitude in which to pray (Mark 1:35). Some of his prayers are preserved (Mark 14:36; John 17:1–26) and he gives instruction to his disciples as to how to pray (Luke 11:2–4). Jesus is not depicted as a man of frequent visionary experiences, a notable exception being the Transfiguration (Mark 9:2–10), though this experience was more for the benefit of Peter, James, and John than for himself. Jesus' approach to Scripture is one of reverence. He sees it as speaking of his own ministry (Luke 4:14–21) and he sees himself as its authoritative interpreter (Matt 5:17–48). As for ritual and symbol, Jesus is pictured as a participant in several Jewish feasts (Tabernacles, John 7:1–52; Passover, Mark 14:12–26), accepts symbolic anointing as prefiguring his death (Mark 14:1–11), rides into Jerusalem in a way that incites messianic fervor (Mark 11:1–11), symbolically purifies the temple (Mark 11:12–18), and pays the temple tax (Matt 17:24–27). Jesus can be critical of ritual practice in the religious establishment, but the focus of his criticism is not the practice itself but rather the hypocrisy with which it is practiced (Mark 7:1–23).

In summary, the matter of personal communion with the deity is governed by the belief, or lack of it, on the part of the figure in question. Sisko does not personally believe in the religion of the Bajorans. Therefore, his relationship is one more of occasional interaction rather than communion. It is not until the series finale that Sisko experiences anything like joyful communion with the Prophets. Jesus, on the other hand, believes in his God and gladly participates in the means of grace present in his religious tradition.

Messianic Program

By messianic program we mean the mission of redemption undertaken by each of the messianic figures. Messianic expectations of the faith communities play prominently in this portrayal, as does, in the case of Sisko, the political agenda of the Federation.

Sisko's messianic mission begins with his encounter with the wormhole aliens and subsequent identification by the Bajoran religious establishment as

Emissary of the Prophets. This moment fulfilled prophecy and tabbed Sisko as the one who would save and unite the Bajorans. Though Sisko rejects the religious significance of this position, it proves useful to the Federation in securing their objectives: initially, the admission of Bajor into the Federation, and subsequently, winning the war against the Dominion. The resulting tension creates conflict between Sisko and the Bajoran religious leaders over fulfilling the messianic expectations of the Prophecies. Sisko does not fit the mold of what the religious leaders expect of him, leading to conflicts with certain Vedeks ("In the Hands of the Prophets," "Destiny"). The narrative history of the series is filled with instances where these competing agendas regarding Sisko's role on the station converge and diverge, where the desired end results of both agendas find varying degrees of completion, though at times not in the manner foreseen by the Federation or the Bajorans.

Jesus' messianic program proper begins with his baptism, endowment of the Spirit, and divine sanction (Mark 1:9–11). He is then led by the Spirit into the desert where he fasts for forty days and nights, after which he is tempted by the devil (Mark 1:12–13). After these days of commissioning and preparation, he embarks on his mission of proclaiming the kingdom of God (Mark 1:14–15). As was the case with Sisko, differing messianic expectations led to episodes of conflict between Jesus and the Jewish religious authorities (Mark 2:23–28). The difference between Sisko's and Jesus' conflicts with religious leaders is that Sisko, by virtue of his unbelief in the religion of the Prophets, balks at and frequently openly rejects the mantle of Emissary, while Jesus embraces his messianic role, albeit in a fashion unfamiliar to the Jewish religious authorities.

Sisko and Jesus both face what might be termed "spiritual" conflicts when viewed from the perspective of the Bajoran and New Testament world views. Sisko sets the stage for the battle between the Prophets and Pagh Wraiths ("The Reckoning"), Dax is killed by Dukat and the Pagh Wraiths due to Sisko's rejection of the Prophets' warnings ("Tears of the Prophets"), Sisko is attacked by a member of the Pagh Wraith cult while on Earth ("Image in the Sand"), and Sisko battles Dukat and the Pagh Wraiths directly ("What You Leave Behind"). Jesus, in his desert experience, resists the temptations of the devil. He performs exorcisms of demons (Mark 1:21–28), heals the sick (Mark 1:29–34), and triumphs over spiritual powers through his death on the cross (Col 2:15). Moreover, both Sisko and Jesus suffer betrayal at the hands of those who have professed allegiance at some point. Sisko's longtime antagonist Winn openly rejects Sisko's status as Emissary ("Till Death Do Us Part," "Strange Bedfellows"), setting the stage for Sisko's climactic battle in the series finale, while Jesus is betrayed into the hands of his enemies by Judas (Mark 14:42–50). One final form of "spiritual" conflict that is noteworthy in both figures might be labeled "internal conflict," or more religiously, "divine abandonment." After disobeying the warnings of the Prophets in "Tears of the Prophets," Sisko senses that the Prophets have left him and forsaken Bajor, a suspicion confirmed by the darkening of the Orbs. Just prior to his death on the cross, Jesus cries out, "My God, My God, why have you forsaken me?" (Mark 15:34) It is interesting that the motif of darkness is present at this moment, having covered the face of the earth during the daytime (v. 33). A significant difference between these experiences of abandonment is that in Sisko's case, he experiences abandonment due to disobedience, while Jesus experiences it because he obediently bears the sins of humanity on the cross, becoming a curse on humanity's behalf (Gal 3:13).

Again, these observations are made from the perspective of the religious world views of the Bajorans and the New Testament. From these perspectives, these conflicts are spiritual oppositions to the messianic missions of Sisko and Jesus. From the perspective of Sisko the Starfleet officer, they are conflicts with alien races that arise within the scope of his official duties as space station commander.

A further area of comparison is that of the nature of the salvation provided by the messianic figures. Again, Sisko's provision of salvation for the Bajorans is motivated by his commitment to Federation objectives, the protection of Bajor for its eventual admission into the Federation. This agenda is interpreted from the Bajoran perspective to be, at least in part, the proper function of the Emissary. The Prophets have the well being of Bajor at the heart of their actions, and their interaction with Sisko is done in benevolence toward the Bajorans. Yet the series depicts the Prophets' concern for Bajor primarily in terms of protection from her enemies, whether the Dominion/Cardassian alliance or the Pagh Wraiths. Though Bajoran religion has rituals, symbols, and a theology derived from the Prophecies and the Orbs, there is lacking any real sense of a personal soteriology in the Prophets' dealings with the Bajorans. While it is true that the triumph over the Pagh Wraiths would, from the Bajoran religious perspective, constitute a deliverance from evil in spiritual terms, even from that perspective it is not cast in terms of personal spiritual salvation. The focus is on the temporal and spatial experience of redemption, not eternal and spiritual.

On the other hand, Jesus' redemptive mission is portrayed as a victory over sin that provides the redeemed with personal, spiritual, eternal salvation. To achieve this, Jesus must die as a ransom for the ungodly and be raised from the dead as vindication of his messianic mission (Mark 10:32–34, 45; Acts 2:31–36). To be sure, there is a spatial component to the salvation of Christ described in eschatological terms of establishing the effective reign and realm of the kingdom of God (1 Cor 15:24). Nor does the personal, spiritual, eternal focus of this salvation deny temporal implications for the redeemed, who are to emulate their savior in works of compassion for others (Matt 25:31–46; Gal 6:10).

Nevertheless, the portrayal of Jesus' redemptive work is given in terms that are in contrast with Sisko's work.

Other comparisons and contrasts between Sisko's and Jesus' messianic program are possible. Jesus is frequently depicted as a teacher. Preserved teachings such as the Sermon on the Mount (Matt 5–7), several discourses in John, and his numerous parables all point to the importance of teaching in Jesus' program. Sisko, on the other hand, is rarely pictured speaking as the religious Emissary, primarily because he does not view his role in religious terms. His advice to Winn in "In the Cards" to sign a non-aggression pact with the Dominion to insure Bajor's survival may be an exception to this tendency. In the series finale, several motifs similar to the redemptive mission of Jesus are found in the portrayal of Sisko's mission: the apparent victory of evil over the messianic figure (Mark 14:37); an "ascension" to "heavenly" realms (Luke 24:51); and a promise to return from the heavenly realms (John 14:3). In Sisko's portrayal, however, there is no necessity for a sacrificial death to provide the desired redemptive results, nor is there any concomitant need for a resurrection from the dead, though the imagery of Sisko falling with Dukat into the fire pits and finding himself in the Celestial Temple may evoke comparison with the death and resurrection of Jesus. And the extensive accounts of Jesus' arrest, trial, and crucifixion (Mark 14:43–15:41), which serve to show Jesus as one unjustly condemned dying for the unrighteous (1 Pet 3:18), find no parallel in Sisko's depiction.

In summary, the redemption wrought by Sisko for the Bajorans eventuated, from his perspective, as an incidental byproduct of the performance of his Starfleet duties. This does not preclude the Bajorans, however, from interpreting the results of these duties as fulfilling certain prophesied religious ends. Jesus, on the other hand, is intentional in following the program that will bring about the desired redemptive will of God. The portrayals of these messianic figures unfold in such a way as to allow the various world views in play to assess their messianic programs in such a way as to maintain consistency and integrity within their respective narrative worlds.

The Nature and Significance of Messianic Depictions

We now reach the point where we must synthesize the results of the foregoing discussion in order to arrive at a picture of the nature and significance of the messianic depictions of Sisko and Jesus within their respective narrative contexts. We begin this discussion by summarizing the messianic depiction of Jesus in the New Testament.

Given the religious world view of the New Testament, it is perhaps not surprising that the messianic depiction of Jesus would include as foundational his characterization in highly exalted language that attributes to him qualities of deity. In fact, a handful of passages go so far as to call Jesus "God." This messiah Jesus was the Son of God before the world began and was himself the agency of creation. He enjoys an intimate relationship with God akin to that of son and father. Jesus is the one sent by God to be the savior of the world (John 3:16) and is the perfect, unblemished sacrifice for the purchase of redemption (Heb 9:14) as well as the perfect High Priest who mediatorially offers himself as this sacrifice (Heb 7:23–28). Having been crucified for the sins of humanity, raised from the dead, and ascended to heavenly glory, the exalted Christ continues to intercede on behalf of faithful believers before God (Rom 8:34). He is the Lord over all things (Eph 1:20–23) and will return to exercise judgment and consummate the kingdom of God (1 Cor 15:25–26).

While Jesus is depicted as a divine messiah, he is also clearly depicted as a human being, albeit a perfect one. He assumed human nature and "became flesh and made his dwelling among us" (John 1:14). He was tempted by Satan with those things that entice fallen human beings (Matt 4:1–11) and resisted every temptation common to human beings (Heb 4:15). Though divine in nature, Jesus learned obedience through suffering and submission, thus establishing his perfection. His birth to a human woman allows his lineage to be established by human reckoning (Matt 1:1–17; Luke 3:23–38). He is depicted as showing the very human emotions of sorrow (John 11:33, 28) and indignation (Mark 11:15–17).

This picture of Jesus as both divine and human, both cosmic and terrestrial, is fit for the world view of the New Testament. If the plight of humanity is cast in terms of spiritual inability to attain communion with God because of sin and rebellion against God, the solution must occur through divine initiative and provision. Yet shedding blood is required for the forgiveness of sin, and if God is to judge sin justly, then an appropriate sacrifice must be offered. A major strand of argumentation in the letter to the Hebrews is that the sacrifice must be perfect and spotless, not an animal, but a perfect human being, one that reflects the original intention of God for humanity. So Jesus the messiah could not come strictly as an exalted heavenly figure; he had also to come as a human being to model ideal humanity as the "Second Adam" and to triumph over temptation, sin, and their effects. And the victory over sin is won in both the personal and systemic spheres. Personal redemption is attained by faith in the sacrificial work of messiah Jesus; systemic sin is eradicated in the eschaton. This messianic depiction of Jesus makes sense in light of the narrative world of the New Testament.

If the messianic depiction of Jesus in the New Testament is portrayed in exalted and idealized terms, it is clear that the messianic depiction of Sisko in *Star Trek: Deep Space Nine* pales significantly in comparison. Sisko is all too human. There is no claim to perfection or absolute missional devotion made for him; there is no need to purify Sisko for his task. Even up to the very end of the series, Sisko is found in defiance of the desires of the Prophets. The fact that Sisko was "born of a Prophet" does not endow him with extraordinary moral, religious, or spiritual senses. Though the Bajoran religious tradition ascribes to him the venerable status of the Emissary of the Prophets, in the eyes of Sisko and the world view of the *Star Trek* universe, he is simply an imperfect human being who has had rather unusual experiences with an alien life form.

Sisko embodies the collision of diametrically opposed world views in his personal tension of functioning in the dual roles of Starfleet officer and Bajoran Emissary of the Prophets. From the perspective of the Federation and its secular/materialistic vision of the universe, whatever religious status is ascribed to Sisko by the Bajorans has no basis in objective reality. Sisko can function in this role without lending Bajoran religious claims any credence because there is something to be gained from it. Even in those moments where Sisko embraced his role as Emissary, often to the detriment of his role as Starfleet officer ("Rapture"), he could do so without any intimation that he personally ascribed to the Bajoran religious world view. From the perspective of the Federation, and Sisko, the role of Emissary was simply that — a role. Sisko's unbelief in the religion of the Prophets was immaterial in fulfilling his role as Emissary as he pursued the agenda of the Federation.

From the perspective of the Bajorans, however, Sisko is the prophesied Emissary who has come to unite the Bajoran people through discovering the Celestial Temple of the Prophets. He has delivered the people from the threat of the Cardassians and the Dominion and he has saved them from the wrath of the Pagh Wraiths. Sisko's unbelief in the religion of the Bajorans, the appearance of an apparent rival for his role as Emissary ("Accession"), and Winn's open rejection of Sisko as Emissary in the series' final story arc aside, there is no indication that either the religious establishment or the general populace of Bajor ever doubted that Sisko was their prophesied Emissary. In the end, Sisko fulfilled the messianic expectations of the Bajorans, though often in ways that they may not have fully understood.

The tension created in the figure of Sisko within these two fictional narrative worlds contributes significantly to the prescriptive vision of the *Star Trek* universe. The *Star Trek* universe's utopian vision of the future is one in which the dominant paradigm of reality is secular though tolerant of cultural and religious diversity to a point. The vision allows the Bajorans, a religious subculture within the *Star Trek* universe, to ascribe to Sisko religious significance, while allowing the Federation to interpret his role apart from the viewpoint of that religious subculture. The subculture can interpret persons and events in a manner appropriate and meaningful to its world view, while the dominant cultural paradigm is permitted to interpret the same persons and events in a manner appropriate to its own world view. The net effect of this portrayal of

Sisko achieves for the framers of the *Star Trek* vision of the universe a profound result: *it removes from the religious subculture the right to make absolute claims about truth and reality for anyone beyond its own subculture.* In this respect, the messianic portrayal of Sisko more closely resembles the messianic portrayal of Cyrus, the Persian king who was chosen by God to fulfill a redemptive role for the exiled Israelites, than he does the messianic depiction of Jesus, the cosmic ruler of all creation whose claims are absolute. Sisko is a mere human being who, because of his position, is able to function redemptively for a faith community to which he does not himself belong. All parties may evaluate the figure and interpret him in a way meaningful to the interpreter.

I have argued elsewhere that the vision of the *Star Trek* universe has within it a hermeneutical agenda for handling sacred texts in such a way as to remain meaningful for the faith community while eliminating claims to absolute truth on those outside the community (Lamp 193–214). It seems apparent that in the person of Benjamin Sisko, Starfleet captain and Bajoran Emissary of the Prophets, the vision has done the same thing with respect to messianic figures.

Works Cited

Harris, Murray J. *Jesus as God*. Grand Rapids, MI: Baker, 1992.
Hurtado, Larry W. "Christ." In *Dictionary of Jesus and the Gospels*. Ed. Joel B. Green, Scot McKnight and I. Howard Marshall. Downers Grove, IL: IVP, 1993. 106–17.
Lamp, Jeffrey S. "Biblical Interpretation in the *Star Trek* Universe: Going Where Some Have Gone Before." In Star Trek *and Sacred Ground: Explorations of* Star Trek, *Religion, and American Culture*. Ed. Jennifer E. Porter and Darcee L. McLaren. Albany: State University of New York Press, 1999. 193–214.
Linford, Peter. "Deeds of Power: Respect for Religion in *Star Trek: Deep Space Nine*." In Star Trek *and Sacred Ground: Explorations of* Star Trek, *Religion, and American Culture*. Ed. Jennifer E. Porter and Darcee L. McLaren. Albany: State University of New York, 1999. 77–100.
Okuda, Michael, Denise Okuda and Debbie Mirek. *The Star Trek Encyclopedia: A Reference Guide to the Future*. New York: Pocket, 1994.

Star Trek *Media Cited*

Star Trek: Deep Space Nine

"Emissary." Written by Michael Pillar. 3 Jan. 1993.
"In the Hands of the Prophets." Written by Robert Hewitt Wolfe. 20 Jun. 1993.
"The Homecoming." Written by Ira Steven Behr. 26 Sept. 1993.
"Destiny." Written by David S. Cohen and Martin A. Winer. 13 Feb. 1995.
"Accession." Written by Jane Espenson. 26 Feb. 1996.
"Rapture." Written by Hans Beimler. 30 Dec. 1996.
"Ties of Blood and Water." Written by Robert Hewitt Wolfe. 14 Apr. 1997.
"In the Cards." Written by Ronald D. Moore. 9 Jun. 1997.
"Favor the Bold." Written by Ira Steven Behr and Hans Beimler. 27 Oct. 1997.
"Sacrifice of Angels." Written by Ira Steven Behr and Hans Beimler. 3 Nov. 1997.

"The Reckoning." Written by David Weddle and Bradley Thompson. 29 Apr. 1998.
"Tears of the Prophets." Written by Ira Steven Behr and Hans Beimler. 17 Jun. 1998.
"Image in the Sand." Written by Ira Steven Behr and Hans Beimler. 30 Sept. 1998.
"Shadows and Symbols." Written by Ira Steven Behr and Hans Beimler. 7 Oct. 1998.
"Penumbra." Written by Rene Echevarria. 7 Apr. 1999.
"Till Death Do Us Part." Written by David Weddle and Bradley Thompson. 14 Apr. 1999.
"Strange Bedfellows." Written by Ronald D. Moore. 21 Apr. 1999.
"The Dogs of War." Written by Rene Echevarria and Ronald D. Moore. 26 May 1999.
"What You Leave Behind." Written by Ira Steven Behr and Hans Beimler. 2 Jun. 1999.

9

Course in Federation Linguistics

Richard R. Jones

> *qayajbe', joHwI'.*
> *("I understand you not, my Lord.")*
> — Rosencrantz, Hamlet, Act IV,
> Scene II (Nicholas and Strader 122)

Two native Klingon speakers who also happen to be fluent speakers of Spanish and English are conversing in a bar and one says to the other, "Did you hear about the woman who cheated on her fiancé eight months before they were married and her husband found out on her wedding day?" Dramatic pause. "ShHHe was very *embarazada*."

All criticisms regarding the lameness and sexism of the joke aside — they are Klingons after all — this bilingual pun illustrates some of the significant challenges that would face us should we ever encounter an intelligent alien species. Playing on the different meanings of "embarrassed," in English, and "*embarazada*," (pregnant) in Spanish, the joke depends on both the speaker and the hearer knowing the two languages. If the joke were told in German, to bilingual German and Spanish speakers, it would make no sense, because *schwanger* (pregnant) does not have a phonetic structure similar to "*embarazada*." Consequently, there can be no pun.

The ability to structure meaning across two languages depends on knowing both languages and exploiting the correspondences between the two. Such correspondences go far beyond just playing on sound similarities between languages. Translation from one language to another, at least initially, depends on some sort of conscious evaluation of the translation process that involves our capacity to create hypotheses about the structure of a language one is trying to learn. All human languages are structured within a narrow range of possibilities that make forming hypotheses about other unknown human languages productive. For example, we can hypothesize, *a priori*, that any human language we may encounter will have nouns and verbs. On the other hand, those assumptions may be wholly inapplicable to the acquisition of an extraterrestrial (ET) language, which may be structured in ways that human languages are not. Also, there is significant evidence that some aspects of human language are innate, which means that some elements of language do not have to be *learned* because they are imprinted on the structure of our brains at birth.

In addition to being able to infer the structure of languages, and in addition to the fact that much of human language seems to be innate in us, there are also all the connoted meanings attached to the structures of language, such as metaphor, cultural symbolism, and unspoken rules of conversation. All of these things pose formidable barriers to learning other human languages, in spite of the fact that human languages and cultures share great similarities. How much more formidable would be the challenge to learning a language that shares few, if any, of these similarities?

English and Spanish share many culturally connected meanings that are similar. Ideas about engagement, marriage, out-of-wedlock pregnancies, and sexual fidelity are pretty much the same between English and Spanish speaking cultures. Those culturally connected meanings make the Klingons' pun understandable — just as much as the homophony of the words "embarrassed," and "*embarazada.*" It is possible to imagine two languages with structures and homophonies that allow for punning, but if there are no similar meanings associated with those structures, there is no way to construct a meaningful pun.

Considering the things just discussed communication between us and ETs may prove to be very difficult — or even impossible. The writers of *Star Trek* were, however, aware of some of these difficulties, and have proposed some solutions, as we shall see.

Briefly, we will survey linguistic interaction in the *Star Trek* universe, then take a look at what we know about human languages, and, finally, evaluate real world possibilities for communications with ETs, should the *Star Trek* vision for space travel ever be achieved.

Federation Linguistics: Myth and Modes of Linguistic Interaction

Language in the *Star Trek* universe is performed within the framework of a grand utopian myth about a future that symbolically speaks to our world in many different ways. This myth illuminates the struggle between good and evil, defines humanity's place in the universe, and it prophetically reveals what humanity is destined to become, once it overcomes many of its current moral and ethical shortcomings. And, of course, the myth celebrates the idea of "infinite diversity in infinite combinations" (IDIC), which has become a mantra of sorts celebrating the entire *Star Trek* mythic vision. Unfortunately, a story — or stories — based only on the idea of things being different and existing in different combinations is not very interesting for very long; sort of like watching several different kaleidoscopes at the same time. IDIC, ironically, demands a resolution to, and an equalization across, all that diversity for the sake of story telling. From IDIC must be forged a coherent and shared whole.

Linguistic interaction is the most fundamental part of the *Star Trek* myth where diversity must be bridged across and equalized. A *Trek* episode that consisted only of a number of different languages being spoken, with no translation occurring, no matter how exotic or beautifully staged, would not be very popular or meaningful. People must communicate in order for there to be a story.

The *Star Trek* myth offers at least one historical claim and a technological solution to overcome the problem posed by too much diversity. Part of the background story for the *Star Trek* universe, which is hinted at in a number of episodes, is that all humanoid life-forms are somehow related by descent or seeding from some ancient race that once populated the galaxy. This means that all humanoid life-forms are similar enough that we would expect language to work similarly across species. Thus, learning Klingon or Romulan should be no more difficult than learning Swahili or Arabic. Equally important for dealing with interspecies linguistic interaction is the development of powerful computing and sensor technologies. These magical technologies of the *Star Trek* universe allow the universal translator to sense brainwaves and, in conjunction with powerful computing ability, to be able to parse translations from the most meager linguistic data.

That being said, within the *Star Trek* universe, by virtue of a shared biological history, humanoids have linguistic structures and mythical structures that are similar enough to allow communication to be possible. No further analysis of mythical structures is offered here. It goes beyond the scope of this article to analyze the structure of myth itself. For a detailed and erudite discussion of the structure of myth, see Peter J. Claus' classic essay (Chapter 2).

Here, briefly, we will survey linguistic interaction in the *Star Trek* universe. After that, we will evaluate the linguistic aspect of the *Star Trek* myth against what is known in modern linguistics.

Beginning with the pilot of *Star Trek* the original series (*TOS*) and continuing and expanding through *Star Trek: The Next Generation* (*TNG*), *Deep Space Nine* (*DS9*), *Star Trek Voyager* (*VOY*), *Enterprise* (*ENT*), and 11 feature films (so far), fans are introduced to a large number of intelligent beings on other planets or living in space itself. The entire *Star Trek* franchise depicts extraterrestrials that are frequently good, but which are occasionally bent on the destruction of humans or other species. Of course those beings speak different languages.

During the filming of the pilot — and even before — Gene Roddenberry knew he had to have a way to speed up communication between earthlings and ETs. In the *TOS* pilot story outline of *The Cage*, Captain April is allowed to retain "a simple language translator device" by his captors (Whitfield and Roddenberry 51). This technological device is never completely explained. In the original outline for the series, Roddenberry describes a device that is "carried in a pocket, little more complicated than a small transistor radio, it is a 'two-way scrambler' that appears to be converting all alien language into English and vice versa" (Whitfield and Roddenberry 27).

Star Trek, in all of its media manifestations, is drama — a kind of space opera. In space opera, everything is on a grand scale; technology is incredibly powerful, speeds and distances are vast. Likewise, characters are larger than life and good and evil are clearly depicted. Consequently, all the limitations of that genre determine to a great degree what can be done in front of the camera. This is not a slight to the franchise. I think *Star Trek* is not only frequently good, solid drama, but occasionally, even rises to the level of great drama. But *Star Trek* is also a little more. It has a visionary utopian component that asserts an optimistic view of humanity in general and technology in particular. So, in order to maintain the pacing of good drama and in order to depict technological aspects of this futuristic utopia, it is not surprising that there are various practical production shortcuts that enable us to get straight to the dialogue with other life forms. Consequently, the idea of language translating technology is a pragmatic invention that facilitates communication in both the myth and reality.

Star Trek introduces us to a rich variety of different beings who speak as many different languages.

The first non-human introduced in the *Star Trek* universe is the Vulcan, Spock, who appears at the very beginning of the *TOS* pilot, and who is at that time a fully integrated member of the *Enterprise* team. The Vulcan language and its various dialects have been described and elaborated on by fans (and linguists!) since the 1970s.[1]

Klingons, who are definitely in competition with Vulcans for "most popular alien," are first encountered in the *TOS* episode "Errand of Mercy."[2] The grammar of Klingon has been worked out and a respectable vocabulary documented.[3] Nicholas and Strader have even translated *Hamlet* into Klingon. Our understanding of Klingon even includes the description of many sociolinguistic patterns, such as the practice of eschewing any form of social pleasantry like greetings and partings.

Then there are the Romulans, distant cousins to the Vulcans, whose martial culture keeps them isolated and removed from most Federation activities. Their language is related to that of Vulcan. Fans have also invested a great deal of effort in describing the Romulan language, *Rihannsu*.[4]

In addition to Vulcan, Klingon, and Romulan, there are a large number of other humanoid languages depicted or implied in the franchise: Tellurian, Ferengi, Edo, Terellian, Binarian, Aldean, Onarian, and a host others. There are also a number of non-humanoid sentient life forms with languages, such as the Horta in *TOS* "Devil in the Dark," the Harada in *TNG* "The Big Goodbye," Armus in *TNG* "Skin of Evil," the Crystalline Entity in *TNG* "Datalore," the Nanites in *TNG* "Evolution," and many other named and unnamed intelligences encountered in open space or on planet surfaces.

We know that the Harada, insectoid creatures, demand perfect pronunciation of their tongue, which puts tremendous pressure on Captain Picard to memorize a greeting correctly in *TNG* "The Big Goodbye." The Darmok have a language that is entirely metaphorical in *TNG* "Darmok." The Binars, in *TNG* "11001001," apparently have a binary, digitally based language they use among themselves. Other examples could be given. Indeed, the list of examples, alone, would be quite long.

Among this diversity of alien species, however, there are really only four modes of linguistic interaction in the *Star Trek* universe: 1) By the modulation of radiation of various energies, such as radio, light, and so on, 2) By the modulation of space or "subspace," 3) By the modulation of sound waves in an atmosphere, just as we do — incredibly most within our narrow range of sound perception and, finally, 4) By telepathy that presumably modulates thought waves. Regardless of the medium — radiation, space, atmosphere, or mental ether — or the mode — frequency modulation, amplitude modulation, intensity modulation, space modulation, or etheric/thought modulation — all these languages operate within parameters understandable to humans. That is, *most importantly*, the grammatical rules that govern the modulation and organization of the signals through the medium work in such a way those rules can be applied in reverse to translate the communication by humans. For the linguist, just constructing and sending modulated signals is not language. Language senders must also be language receivers. Coding and decoding must be able to be done by the same organism. Language is dependant on this dual ability.

The question naturally arises, how can humans come to know these rules? Human languages operate according to rules that are structured and constrained by the biology of our brains, which makes human languages a species-specific ability. Why would we expect extraterrestrials with quite different biological processes to have languages with structures that are similar to own, such that our brains can learn them? Learning the rules of an extraterrestrial language would be a lot like trying to determine the rules of a complex game that you can only observe, and where no one can talk to you. In some cases, through long association and dedicated linguistic inquiry with different species humans might eventually be able to describe many linguistic rules from observation, linguistic experimentation, and trial-and-error efforts at communication. On the other hand, unless the rules of the non-human language are fairly similar to those of human languages, it may be extraordinarily difficult, if not impossible, for humans to really understand the new language. Mediation by a machine, such as a computer, could certainly help, but, at the present time, computers demonstrate a remarkable inability to capture much of the subtle, but essential, characteristics of even human languages. Part of the difficulty is due to the fact that human minds do not work like computers and computer software is not totally able to compensate for that, at least not yet.

It is fitting at this point to present an overview of what constitutes a human language, in order to evaluate the problems that would face us should we ever encounter a non-human species with a language of their own.

Human Language

What is language?

Ferdinand de Saussure (1857–1913), considered by many to be the founder of modern linguistics, suggests a possible answer to this question that has profound implications for how beings communicate in *Star Trek*, or anywhere else. In a collection of his work, compiled by his students shortly after his death, known as the *Course in General Linguistics* — hence the title of this essay — Saussure carefully distinguishes between the structure of languages and how individuals use those structures to communicate. So, in answering what language is, Saussure makes an important distinction between what we say, which he refers to as *speech*, and the underlying structure of language, which he refers to as *language:*

> By distinguishing between the language itself and speech, we distinguish at the same time: (1) what is the social from what is the individual, and (2) what is essential from what is ancillary and more or less accidental. (13–14)
>
> The language itself is not a function of the speaker. It is the product passively registered by the individual...
>
> Speech, on the contrary, is an individual act of the will and intelligence.

By this Saussure means that all the rules and knowledge of a *language*, and the ability to produce an infinite set of understandable utterances, is acquired and internalized unconsciously by us as we develop. Children do not choose to learn a language, they just *do* language. The famous linguist, Noam Chomksy, after careful consideration of various theories of language acquisition in children, asserted that children must possess an innate ability to acquire language, an assertion that he successfully defended in debates with Jean Piaget in 1975 at Abbaye de Royaumont in France. The idea that humans possess an innate language acquisition device (LAD) is now generally accepted by linguists.[5]

On the other hand, Saussure points out that *speech*, which is what we say, is done willfully. It follows logically then that what we say is always a miniscule subset and representation of what it is possible for us to say. At any given moment in time one can potentially say anything, but what we say is always something finite and constrained by the social situation. For Saussure, the inquiry into what language *is* must first focus on understanding *language* (what is possible in language), as opposed to *speech* (what is performed in language), because the former precedes the latter. Not that *speech* is unimportant. *Language* and *speech* are two aspects of the same thing, but *speech* can only be properly understood as a product of *language*. Chomsky calls the same distinction competence (*language*) and performance (*speech*).

The work of Saussure and Chomsky provide the basis for the modern structural view of language that will be briefly reviewed here.

At the level of sounds, human *language* works on the contrast between sounds, not on absolute differences. For example, in Klingon, the sound [p] contrasts with the Klingon sound [q]. The sounds contrast because they are produced in different parts of the vocal tract. The [p] is produced at the front of the mouth by blocking air with the lips, while the [q] is produced at the back of the mouth by blocking air with the back of ones tongue raised to the velum — or whatever is the Klingon equivalent. The pitch of the two sounds does not matter; neither does the quality of the voice of the speaker, nor the volume.[6] This contrast is important because it signals a change in meaning when one or the other is used to form words. The Klingon words, *poH*, and *qoH*, mean "period of time" and "fool," respectively. Klingon resembles human languages in this way. Sounds that contrast and which distinguish meaning are called phonemes. Because the sounds, [p] and [q], change the meaning of the word when they are exchanged for each other, they are phonemes in Klingon. Phonemes are written like this: /p/, /q/. The sound system or phonology of a language consists of a small set of such phonemes. English has about 37 phonemes; Arabic about 31; and Klingon about 30.[7]

Looking more closely, things get a bit more complicated in both human languages and in Klingon. Not only do human languages have phonemes, but each phoneme has a set of allophones, which are variations of the phoneme in different linguistic environments. For example, "tip" and "hat" both have the phoneme /t/, but the actual sounds we produce in the two words in speech is different. The [t] in "tip" is aspirated, that is, we produce it with a puff of air. Consequently, we transcribe it [t^h], where the superscript indicates the aspiration. The [t] in "hat" does not, in normal speech, get any aspiration. It is, instead unreleased. It is transcribed [t^-]. You can test this yourself by placing your hand in front of your mouth as you say each word — be careful not to artificially emphasize, and thus aspirate, the [t] in "hat."

Thus, in English, the phoneme, /t/, is said to have two allophones: [t^h] and [t^-]. Fortunately, the distribution of the two different allophones is entirely predictable in English; [t^h] always occurs at the beginning of words, and [t^-] always occurs at the end of words. This distribution of allophones can be written as a rule. Such a rule is called a phonological rule. Phonological rules describe the distribution of allophones in words and in phrases. Because the rules are consistently followed by language speakers, deducing the phoneme is easy for a native speaker who has internalized those rules. Depending on the dialect, there are about 22 consonant phonemes and 15 vowel phonemes in English. Each of these 37 phonemes has at least one allophone. Some have three, or four, or five allophones! Each human language has a finite set of phonemes, which are subset of all possible human phonemes. Most languages have 30 to 40 of the about 200 possible phonemes that exist collectively in all human languages.

The phonological system, or sound system, of a human language is governed by phonological rules which relate phonemes and allophones and thereby encode and decode speech, that is, what we actually say. The process of language that goes on in our minds works, however, on the contrast of phonemes. Phonemes must be converted, via phonological rules, to the appropriate allophones when we speak, and they must be converted from allophones to phonemes when we hear someone talk.

Even if non-human languages have a similar underlying structure with phonemes and allophones, it would still be a difficult task to determine which allophones are associated with which phonemes. What would the first Vulcan to visit Earth make of the somewhat phonetically rendered, "Jeetyet?," which every speaker of American English knows means, "Did you eat yet?" A series of phonological rules compresses the 10 phonemes in "Did you eat yet?" [dId yu it yɛt] to only 6 in "Jeet yet?" [jityɛt]. Without knowing the phonological rules involved, which also entails knowing the phonemes from their allophones, the Vulcan cannot even begin to decipher the sound system of the English language.

Understanding all this is a tedious exercise, but essential to understanding the problem. Humans speak primarily in allophones, but think in phonemes. From this, it can be seen that *speech* (what we say) is distinct from, but related in a rule governed way, to *language* (the knowledge of language in our minds).

Individual sounds organize into units called morphemes, which are words, or suffixes, or prefixes that have meaning associated with them. The ways is which sounds can combine is always limited, however, in a particular language. There are constraints in every human language as to what is allowed in the sequence of sound units that can be used to form a morpheme. For example, Arabic never allows 3 consonants in a row, even across word boundaries; English never allows words to begin with [sr]; and Spanish does not allow 3 consonant clusters like [str] or [skl] to begin words. The study of the rules that order the sounds in a language is called phonotactics. The study of the meaning bearing units of the language — the morphemes — is called morphology.

Morphological units are organized into another level of relationships called syntax. Syntax consists of the rules that govern the placement of morphemes in relation to each other to construct utterances. Language typologists have also observed that, just like the sound system, the syntactical structure of human languages is highly constrained. For example, the number of word categories (Noun, verb, etc.) is finite; the organization of main constituents in a sentence is limited to Subject-Verb-Object (SVO), VSO, VOS, OVS, OSV, and SOV; each level of syntactical organization is limited to about 5 bits of information, probably due to the limitations of human short term memory; and that there are a finite number of rules that order syntactic relations. Structural linguistics identifies two general types of rules in syntax: 1) transformational rules, such as relative clause formation, yes/no question formation, fronting, etc., and 2) phrase structure rules that order the word elements in noun phrases, prepositional phrases, etc. Such rules are small in total number — perhaps only 40 or so rules, depending on how they are written — but such rules are able to generate most of the grammatical utterances of the language they describe.

Finally, complete syntactical units, sentences, are spoken as part of a larger discourse, which provides the context for attributing the correct meaning to what a speaker is saying. Identically uttered statements can mean completely different things depending on the context. "We are going to kill you!" means different things depending on whether it is spoken by one football team captain to another before the game, or by a criminal gang leader to a lone pedestrian at night. Therefore, meaning in language, the semantic content, is contingent on many factors that go beyond the string of speech produced by the speaker. Essentially, speakers construct meaning by orchestrating a masterful symphony of linguistic and social knowledge. Consequently, utterances must not only be grammatically correct — that is, they must follow the rules of phonology, phonotactics, morphology, and syntax — but must also articulate coherently into larger systems and patterns of connotation and denotation, metaphor, myth, social ritual, interpersonal relations, genre, immediate context, and individual will in a way that makes them significant.

Every human language operates within the domain just described. Every human *language* can be analyzed in terms of its phonology, morphology, and syntax, but that only provides the framework upon which *speech* constructs meaning by actively and creatively manipulating a huge body of social knowledge to a desired end. Understanding the formal rules of the *language* itself will not guarantee mutually intelligible translation, because *speech* refers to, and plays on, a huge body of social knowledge, and associations between elements of that knowledge, that must be known to in order to make what is said understood.

This is, briefly, how human languages work. Now let us put into practice how this issue of language will affect the ways in which humanoids in *Star Trek* will communicate.

ET Languages and Communication

When Captains Archer, Janeway, Kirk, Picard, or Sisko encounter unknown life forms communication with those life forms usually seems to be the least of their problems. But what would the problems really be in trying to communicate with a new life form? If we were fortunate enough to be equipped with the latest Federation technology, how could we use that technology to help us effectively communicate? Surely, both theoretical and pragmatic aspects of communication between species must be an important part of every cadet's education at Starfleet Academy.

All languages used by a species that has some type of collective lifestyle and communication (i.e. a culture) must be based on the ability to send and receive signals of some sort. It follows that senders of signals must also be receivers of signals and that there must be some biological apparatus dedicated to the production and processing of those signals. Additionally, those signals must be propagated by one organism across space to some other organism.[8] The most common carriers for signals would probably be some form of radiation (light or radio, for example) or sound waves.[9]

Signals must be modulated in some way in order to provide contrast between them. This modulation can be in the form of stopping and starting the signal — sort of like Morse Code — or by varying the signal's frequency, amplitude, strength, or by bundling together a group of signals of varying frequency, amplitude or strength to form a complex signal. This is what happens in human languages where any given phoneme is actually the product of a constellation of features that produces a unique sound. A set of such contrasting symbols provides the basis for constructing linguistic communication. For humans, the set of phonemes are produced as sounds.[10] Phonemes could just as easily be constructed from complex bundles of modulated light or radio signals as long as the organisms that use them are biologically equipped to be able to produce such signals and to receive such signals and to linguistically process them.

Once there are a contrasting set of signals, they can be used in different combinations to associate with various meanings. In turn, those meaning bearing units can be organized in relation to each other to form sentences, and those sentences can be ordered in relation to each other to form complex discourse.

There are, however, some potential problems.

The basic foundation of any linguistic system must be somewhat like what has just been described. Such a system plays on the relative (not absolute) differences between signals; on the arbitrary association of meaning to collections of signals; and on the hierarchical ordering of meaning bearing units in relation to each other. An ET language may work in much the same way as earth based languages, but what if it differs in scale at any or all of the linguistic levels. In other words, what if the ET language has 800 phonemes, instead of the approximately 30 or so that are found in human languages? What if their collection of meaning bearing units—their vocabulary—is hundreds of times greater than most human languages? What if their sentence structure allows for multiple subjects and objects with differing attribution of agency for each of them via complex verbs? What if their discourse requires the perfect and exact repetition of earlier phrases, or portions of phrases, and does not allow referential phrases such as "*They* said," or "*It* was exciting."? So, it is possible for immensely complex languages to emerge from within the general kinds of patterns established in human languages. Humans could possibly encounter languages that, even though they work much like ours, are far beyond the processing capability of our minds.

The technical evolution of the Universal Language Translator (UTL) in *Star Trek* shows that the device was refined over a considerable period of time and suggests that it developed in response to the Federation encountering more and more different species. In *ENT*, Hoshi frequently struggled with limitations of the, then, new UTL technology. She often had to resort to her personal skills as a linguist. By the time of *TOS*, the UTL is seen once as a portable device, in the episode, "Metamorphosis," but the device has developed and is reliable enough by this time so that it is rarely mentioned or seen.

Unfortunately, it is not all clear exactly how the ULT works. From *ENT* we know that the ULT gets more accurate with increasing language input. Indeed, large samples of language signals would help in sorting out phonotactic patters, and in identifying the allophones and phones, and in identifying some words. However, knowing what all those signals *mean* is an entirely different matter. Of course, none of this is a problem in *Star Trek* as myth, but in the real world it matters very much.

Meaning, at least in human languages, is arbitrarily associated with strings of sound signals. How does the ULT get at the meaning of what is being said? Meaning is only associated with the signals—the signals in and of themselves do not contain the meaning.

For example, in the *TNG* episode "Datalore," how could Lore understand the transmissions of the Crystalline Entity? Whatever signals were produced by the entity could be analyzed for patterns, but how would Lore ever know what the signals meant? There are no bilinguals to help translate. Of course, linguists might be able to work out the meaning of some of the signals, but only through a long process of interaction with the entity that would require its cooperative participation.

Going back to the beginning of this essay, there is one other important aspect of language that must be taken into account. All languages are embedded in culture. Culture imposes a huge number of explicit and implied associations of meaning on what is said. Every culture has its own myths, too. The bilingual Klingons punning on the words "embarrassed" and "*embarazada*" had to also know that a bride found to be pregnant, by someone other than the groom, on her wedding was in an awkward social situation. If they did not understand that, the joke would not have been funny in spite of the similarity in the sounds of the words. It is not enough to know just the rules of a language in order to communicate effectively; one must also know the culture of the language and all the social knowledge that is drawn upon during the performance of the language.

Consequently, first contact situations should always be confusing, even with the aid of the ULT, because the ULT has no way of knowing the cultural or mythical information of the native speakers. That is indeed the case in one particular *TNG* episode. In "Darmok," Captain Picard and a Tamarian, named Dathon, face a situation in which they must learn to communicate with each other in order to confront a common threat. Dathon utters the phrase, "Darmok and Jalad at Tanagra," many times in an effort to get Picard to understand. The ULT is able to render the Tamarian language into recognizable English sounds and syntax, but the phrase has no apparent meaning to Picard. The problem is that Dathon's myths and metaphors are not the same as Picard's myths and metaphors. Picard is eventually able to unravel the meaning of the myth connected to the metaphor and to effectively communicate with the Tamarians. The point is that this level of linguistic confusion should occur in nearly every first contact situation and there would undoubtedly be ongoing problems with the cultural and mythical allusions in language.

While it is possible to imagine a language with no cultural metaphor in which there is a one-to-one correspondence between signal (word) and meaning, such a language would have a huge vocabulary (i.e. one word for every object; 100 pencils would have to have 100 different names), and it would probably take a long time to say anything, since you could not use words categorically. For example, you could not use the word, "words." Instead, you would have to list all the words in the language if that is what you are talking about.

Human languages, Vulcan, Romulan, Klingon, and Tamarian are all languages rich in metaphor. In all of those languages, words are categorical and cultural metaphors abound. The *TOS* episode, "The Trouble with Tribbles," shows that Klingons have clearly grasped some metaphors of Federation English when one calls Captain Kirk a "swaggering, overbearing, tin-plated dictator with delusions of godhood," and refers to the U.S.S. *Enterprise* as a "sagging old rust bucket ... designed like a garbage scow."

A UTL—some kind of computer based device that enhances our ability to manipulate the sounds, words, and rules of a language we do not know—might just be possible at some time in the future. However, we may always have problems with more subtle matters of communication found in *speech* that are connected to our culture.

While it seems that the fundamental structure of languages may be similar in some ways across the universe, communication with aliens—should we ever encounter them —will probably always be difficult, even with computers to help mediate that communication. It is at least possible that we will develop the technology to help us parse alien languages grammatically, but what will always get us in trouble is the performance of the language within a cultural context.

Conclusion

Within the mythical universe inhabited by the U.S.S. *Enterprise* and its crew, efficient and effective communication between various life-forms is routine and facilitated by a sophisticated mythical technology. In the real world, the problems posed by communication between two different species are not so easily overcome. The very nature of human language, as we understand it, suggests that if ETs have some form of language, it may be so different than our language that effective communication would be either difficult or impossible.

There is an oft told joke at Starfleet Academy that illustrates the distinction between *language* and *speech* and the difficulty of generating effective communication between two different species, a difficulty not often considered by the writers of *Star Trek*.

A Vulcan walks into a bar and sees a Klingon tactical officer drinking Romulan ale. The Vulcan raises his hand and says, "Na'shaya!" So, the Klingon kills him.[11]

Notes

1. The Vulcan Language Institute can be found at www.vulcanlanguage.org.
2. First aired March 23, 1967. The "mind sifter" device used by Klingons to read the mind of Spock in this episode is the first major example in *Star Trek* that the underlying grammar of alien language is the same as that of humans.
3. The Klingon Language Institute can be found at http://www.kli.org/. Also, see Marc Okrand, *The Klingon Dictionary*. New York: Simon & Schuster, 1992.
4. The Rihannsu Encyclopedia, which contains a dictionary and grammar, can be found at *http://pfrpg.org/RH/*.
5. Jean Piaget and Noam Chomsky debated whether or not language learning began with a brain that was essentially a blank slate (Piaget), or whether or not the human brain has some innate structuring (knowledge) that acts to organize language acquisition (Chomsky). Chomsky won the debate. For more see, Piattelli-Palmarini.
6. Features such as pitch are used in human languages, like Chinese, to contrast, but that is ignored here to keep the discussion moving.
7. The reason for saying "about" is due, in the majority of cases, to dialectical variation

and, in a few cases, to linguistic debates about specific sounds. Information about Klingon words and sounds is taken from Okrand, *The Klingon Dictionary*.

8. Of course we can imagine a social organism consisting of a large number of individual brains joined by a biological framework, like some huge slime-mold, but signals would still have to move around inside it in order for it to establish the basis for a language.

9. Touch, odors, sub-space modulation (whatever that is), and mental waves—if they exist—might also be used, each having its own unique limitations, but the most widespread carriers of linguistic signals in the universe will probably turn out to be radiation and sound, since both are found on planets with oceans and/or atmospheres that are orbiting stars, which conditions I assume are prerequisites for life to develop.

10. For the sake of brevity, I am ignoring human gestural languages, such as American Sign Language, here. Such languages work just like spoken languages, but they are not just gestural representations of spoken languages. Visual units are used phonemically and morphemically, in gestural languages, instead of sound units.

11. "na'shaya" is a greeting in Vulcan (http://www.starbase-10.de/vld/) while the phonetically similar "naS'a' ya" means, "A tactical officer is vicious?" Such a question is a clear insult to the Klingon at the bar. (The Klingon phrase is constructed from information in *The Klingon Dictionary*. Any errors in interpretation are my own.)

Works Cited

Nicholas, Nick, and A. Strader. *The Klingon Hamlet: The Restored Klingon Version*. Ed. M. Shoulson, W. Martin and d'Armond Speers. New York: Pocket, 2000.
Okrand, Marc. *The Klingon Dictionary*. New York: Pocket, 1985.
Piattelli-Palmarini, Massimo, ed. *Language and Learning: The Debate between Jean Piaget and Noam Chomsky*. Cambridge, MA: Harvard University Press, 1980.
Saussure, Ferdinand de. *Course in General Linguistics*. Ed. C. Bally and A. Sechehaye. Trans. R. Harris. Chicago, IL: Open Court, 1997.
Whitfield, Stephen E., and Gene Roddenberry. *The Making of Star Trek*. New York: Ballantine, 1968.

Star Trek *Media Cited*

Star Trek: The Original Series

"The Cage." Written by Gene Roddenberry. October 4, 1988.
"Devil in the Dark." Written by Gene L. Coon. 9 March 1967.
"Errand of Mercy." Written by Gene L. Coon. 23 March 1967.
"Metamorphosis." Written by Gene L. Coon. 10 November 1967.
"The Trouble with Tribbles." Written by David Gerrold. 29 December 1967.

Star Trek: The Next Generation

"The Big Goodbye." Written by Tracy Tormé. 11 January 1988.
"Darmok." Story by Philip LaZebnik and Joe Menosky. Teleplay by Joe Menosky. 30 September 1991.
"Datalore." Story by Robert Lewin and Maurice Hurley. Teleplay by Robert Lewin and Gene Roddenberry. 18 January 1988.
"Evolution." Story by Michael Piller and Michael Wagner. Teleplay by Michael Piller. 25 September 1991.
"11001001." Written by Maurice Hurley and Robert Lewin. 1 February 1988.

"Skin of Evil." Story by Joseph Stephano. Teleplay by Joseph Stephano and Hannah Louise Shearer. 25 April 1988.

Star Trek *Linguistics Web Sources*

The Klingon Language Institute. *http://www.kli.org/.*
The Rihannsu Encyclopedia. *http://pfrpg.org/RH/.*
Vulcan Language Dictionary. *http://www.starbase-10.de/vld/.*
The Vulcan Language Institute. *www.vulcanlanguage.org.*

10

Evocations and Evasions of Archetypal Lesbian Love in Star Trek: Voyager

ROGER KAUFMAN

A valiant female starship captain of the twenty-fourth century, Kathryn Janeway (Kate Mulgrew), encounters a flesh-and-blood duplicate of herself, and together the two women must negotiate their unwavering compassion for one another when they realize that only one of them can survive the deadly aftereffects of a spatial anomaly. Soon thereafter, the surviving Janeway resolutely carries another grown woman in her arms through a lethal energy field, gravely risking her own life in order to save her friend. A few months later, more daring than ever, this same starship captain separates a cybernetic organism from a vast hive of high-tech drones, and devotes herself tirelessly to liberate the young human woman found underneath multiple layers of grafted technology and almost two decades of group-mind indoctrination. These are just a few of the many vivid scenes throughout *Star Trek: Voyager (VOY)* that portrays indomitable women heroically defending and fostering the well-being of other vigorous women.

In *VOY,* women not only save each other's lives—as well as those of their male comrades—but they develop caring and affectionate bonds with one another and actively encourage each other's psychological development. Although none of these relationships are shown to be overtly sexual or romantic, the *lesbian-centered* psychological perspective to be employed in this essay has the potential to "read between the lines" to possibly reveal erotic undercurrents as well as prominent symbolic imagery that may evoke archetypal aspects of same-sex romantic love.

As a gay man, my ability to effectively consider lesbian themes in *VOY* will inevitably be limited, but the effort seems worthy in order to foster a much-needed dialogue that is mutually supportive of developing profound gay-centered and lesbian-centered psychologies, along the same lines of a lively exchange I enjoyed for many years with my lesbian colleague, psychotherapist Sandra Lee Golvin, who was just beginning her pioneering efforts to articulate a depthful lesbian-centered psychology when she was prematurely felled by terminal cancer in 2006. Her germinal ideas were based on the work of psychologist and scholar Mitch Walker, founder of the Institute for Contemporary Uranian Psychoanalysis, whose comprehensive elucidation of a gay-centered psychology is both ground and container for the analysis of this paper.

Theoretical Foundation: An Archetypal View of Lesbian Love

It's easy enough to recognize chaotic aspects of existence, but what seems much more noteworthy to me is how highly ordered our universe appears to be (Hogenson 271). Although it has always been controversial (Samuels 23), C.G. Jung's concept of *archetypes* as pre-existing meaningful patterns that are universal in structuring the human mind ("Psyche" 213) aligns well with a basic observation of the structured form that pervades our bodies and also makes possible a coherent experience of personal subjectivity. Recent efforts to integrate dynamic systems theory with Jungian psychology demonstrate that the "self-organizing" process that allows highly complex organisms to develop from much simpler ones features highly stable "principles of organization" that do not "exist" anywhere and yet are highly predictable and reliable, in a remarkable parallel with Jung's idea about archetypes (McDowell 651).

Jung proposed that archetypal patterns guide the transmutation of instinctual *libido* into advanced forms of personality and consciousness. As he describes in *Symbols of Transformation*, this occurs because libido has an inherent "intentionality" (137) and intelligence, exemplified metaphorically by the Greek god Eros, predisposing it to draw into the mind particular images of persons from the outer world, which then function as living *symbols* for underlying archetypes that spur the development of the mind forward. "The symbols act as *transformers*," writes Jung, "their function being to convert libido from a 'lower' into a 'higher' form" (232). This dynamic is exemplified by the experience of romantic love, where an attractive woman functions for a heterosexual man as the symbol of his own central feminine *soul*, resulting in the coalescence of an inner *soul-figure complex* or sub-personality based on the archetype of the *anima* ("Aion" 13). Likewise, (heterosexual) women are understood to project their inner masculine ideal or *animus* onto men they find attractive. If this symbol-making experience can be made conscious, then the person can better integrate the contrasexual into his or her own personality, spurring the metamorphic process of *individuation*, leading toward the experience of wholeness through the reconciliation of psychic opposites and realization of the archetype of the *Self*, the unconscious center of the personality, also understood as the "god-image" in the mind ("Aion" 26–27).

Jung's vision of the psyche as "the world's pivot" ("Psyche" 217) honors human subjectivity with a dignity and depth not found, to my knowledge, in other modern or postmodern conceptualizations of being a person, but his emphasis on the contrasexual archetype does not recognize a viable path of individuation for people who are primarily attracted to members of the same sex.

To address this problem, Mitch Walker has articulated in his 1991 paper, "Jung and Homophobia," a far-reaching gay soul psychology which recognizes an intelligent *homosexual Eros* who inspires men to be sexually attracted to other men. Walker further articulates, drawing from his own earlier 1976 paper, "The Double: An Archetypal Configuration," how homosexual Eros attracts to "himself" a genital twin image as a soul-figure for the ego-personality, a living presence within who is given form by the archetype of the *double*. This double soul-figure, who can be understood as an individual's personal muse, functions even when still unconscious as the erotic inspiration for the development of a healthful gay identity, also leading further toward initiation into the mysteries of the inner world, and when apprehended consciously is "experienced as profound, godly, joyous" ("Double" 167). Walker has stated his belief "that a corresponding women's perspective also exists," including a female double as soul-figure and a "lesbian homosexual libidinal Intelligence" ("Revolutionary" 26), which I will tentatively refer to in this paper as *lesbian eros*, a phrasing that Sandra Golvin used and which has been occasionally employed in other contexts (for example, see Ginzberg). I am keeping the *e* in *eros* lowercase to acknowledge some awkwardness in designating a phenomenon in and between women with a word derived from the name of a male god.

In contrast with the ubiquitous power differentials of male-female dynamics, same-sex love relationships inspired by homosexual forms of *eros* can be seen to feature a distinctive quality of *libidinal twinship mutuality*, which can also activate within an individual's mind a symbolic "romance" between the ego and the double soul as representative of the archetypal Self, revealing homosexual love's significant role as primary catalyst for shamanic endeavors moving toward enlightenment ("Double" 170; "Jung" 64). In *Myth and Mysteries of Same-Sex Love*, Christine Downing captures some of these aspirational feelings for women when she writes about Aphrodite as "a goddess who models women's affirmation of their own sexuality—as powerful, beautiful, and sacred" (213). She further explains:

> The myths about women loving women help us see what deep human longings are expressed in such love ... the longing for relationships free of that struggle for dominance so often characteristic of heterosexual bonds, the longing for permanent connections that are genuinely mutual and egali-

tarian, the longing to fully validate one's own female being and to celebrate that with others ... the longing to encourage another's creativity and find one's own inspired by it, the longing to deal with and overcome one's own misogyny and homophobia, the longing to become all one might be [214].

In alignment with these sentiments, the overarching purpose of both gay-centered and lesbian-centered theory is what Walker calls the "facilitation" of homosexual Self-realization ("Uranian Soul" 38), especially using the Jungian technique of *active imagination* in order to dialogue with different internal figures, in particular for gay people the same-sex double soul-figure, who, once engaged, can inspire the cultivation of meaningful interiority, personhood, creativity, love, and the ecstasy of spiritual awakening.

Such a contemporary "essentialist" perspective argues for the immensely positive meaning of words like *lesbian* and *gay*, featuring a heartfelt appreciation for the salutary nature of achieving a personal identity supported by these words, in opposition to postmodern "social constructionist" perspectives which argue that such "labels" and related identities are restrictive categories imposed by the pervasive power dynamics effected by the "deployment of sexuality" through the "discourses" of language (Foucault 106). Sandra Lee Golvin's thoughts are helpful here: "When we use the word Lesbian, we can begin to understand it not as an exclusionary category, but rather as a 'person' of the psyche, a metaphor for an archetypal force with its own elaborate and fantastic mythology with whom we are being invited into imaginative engagement and relationship" (11).

Grassroots Activism: How Lesbian and Gay Fans Have Engaged with the Series

In the following discussion, I will be pinpointing analogical aspects of relationships in *VOY* that suggest parallels with what I see as the archetypal underpinnings of lesbian love. However, I will not attempt to somehow *prove* that certain characters secretly engage in homosexual sex or are *really* lesbians. It has been long publicly known that Paramount Pictures, which has produced the various *Star Trek* series since the franchise's inception in 1966, has explicitly avoided portraying homosexuality or a character who overtly identifies as gay, lesbian, or bisexual. And this stance has persisted despite a long tradition of enthusiastic public efforts by fans to request that such characters be included (Sinclair). For example, in 1995, the Voyager Visibility Project was formed to persuade Paramount to include a lesbian or gay character on the new show, an effort which was intensified in 1997 when it became public that a new primary player would be introduced. This effort was supported by the Gay and Lesbian Association Against Defamation as well as by *VOY* executive producer Jeri Taylor, who explained in *TV Guide* (March 10, 1998) that the show's new character, Seven of Nine (Jeri Ryan), was definitely not a lesbian, but that the idea "is something I am absolutely sympathetic with, and I have tried several times to do it. But for various reasons there has been opposition, and it gradually became clear that this is a fight I could not win" (qtd. in Sinclair).

Despite these failures, *VOY* is ripe with scenarios that, as Debra Bonita Shaw has written, make it easily available for "resistant readings" (71), meaning those perspectives that challenge the "compulsory heterosexuality" (81) that's officially portrayed in the series. Indeed, *VOY*'s numerous scenes that portray fondness and bonding between women have sparked a vast burgeoning of "slash" fan fiction, or "femslash," showing *VOY* characters in romantic lesbian relationships. Perhaps the largest category is "J/7," filling in all the luscious details of sex, love, and marriage between Captain Janeway and Seven of Nine, as illustrated, for example, in the *Just Between* series by G.L. Dartt, as Michèle Bowring has previously discussed. While the *VOY* producers made repeated efforts to show that their characters were heterosexual, it is clear that many aspects of the show have made it easy for fans to interpret it in a strikingly different, overtly lesbian way.

In the same spirit but moving in an alternative direction, the inquiry in this paper seeks to support lesbian love and self-actualization by directing attention to what same-sex romantic themes might be found lurking in the interpersonal dynamics actually shown in the series itself.

The Archetypal Double as Primary Symbol of Lesbian Eros

Mitch Walker's conceptualization of how a homosexual organization of the libido constellates the archetypal double in an overtly romantic way to birth a primary soul-figure complex is supported by myriad mythological and literary references. These range from Plato's invocation of the inherent creativity of "heavenly" same-sex love to the twin *ka* soul of ancient Egypt ("Jung" 62–66). In my own previous essays, I have spotlighted homosexual manifestations of the double in many of the most prominent science fiction and fantasy films of the past three decades, including the *Star Wars* space opera (Kaufman, "Star Wars"), *The Lord of the Rings* trilogy (Kaufman, "Lord"), and the *Alien* saga (Kaufman, "Heroes"), which with its intrepid female hero, Lieutenant Ellen Ripley (Sigourney Weaver), offers many parallel themes with *VOY*.

However, the double has been understood quite differently in much of Western literature, film, and psychological analysis, where it is often seen as a malicious, usurping adversary at war with the individual, sometimes referred to as a *doppleganger*. Perhaps the most well-known examples in literature are Fyodor Dostoevsky's *The Double* and Robert Louis Stevenson's *Strange Case of*

Dr. Jekyll and Mr. Hyde. A 1913 German film, *The Student of Prague*, in which a young man dies when he kills his vehemently hated double, brought fresh awareness of the motif as newly invented film effects allowed the creation of an "identical twin" of an actor. This captured the attention of early psychologists such as Otto Rank and Jung, who in 1929 called it "the best movie I ever saw," and which he described as showing "the separation of the conscious man and his shadow, so that the shadow moves by itself" ("Dream" 259). Here Jung is referencing the most morally inferior "dark aspects of the personality" ("Aion" 8), which contrast specifically with the positive inspirational qualities of an erotic soul-figure.

In *Deep Space and Sacred Time: Star Trek in the American Mythos*, Jon Wagner and Jan Lundeen emphasize how Jung used the term *double* as synonym for *shadow* (70), and they have identified multiple instances where doubles in the *Star Trek* franchise do develop this quality. Walker incorporates this understanding of the double in his own theory by articulating what he calls the "competitor" motif ("Double" 173), but Wagner and Lundeen miss the more positive aspects of the double that Walker emphasizes and that do also appear in numerous *Star Trek* episodes. Furthermore, they fail to make any connection between double imagery and same-sex romantic love, even though they discuss inferred aspects of homosexuality in the franchise (106). Although it is beyond the scope of this paper, a hypothesis to be considered for future research is that the currents of cultural homophobia in recent centuries have influenced these conflations of the double with the shadow. For now, what's possible to state is that *VOY* is abundantly rich with a predominantly positive portrayal of double figures, providing support for Mitch Walker's appreciation of the archetype as fundamentally beneficial, especially when it functions as the crucial underlying structure for a soul-figure complex.

Key Themes Anticipated in This Analysis

On the pages that follow, I will describe numerous different manifestations of the double in *VOY*, especially in the form of what I am calling the "identical twin" motif, as well as in significant intimate partnerships between Captain Kathryn Janeway and two attractive, young, brilliant female members of her crew, Kes (Jennifer Lien) and Seven of Nine.

My goal is to hopefully show that almost all of these relationships demonstrate prominent features consistent with the constellation of the double as erotically alluring lesbian soul-figure, providing lesbian viewers in particular with helpful imagery for development of an "inner romance" with their own double soul. To support this aim, I will highlight several notable qualities that are consistently shown in these relationships, drawing in part from an earlier analysis I conducted in my essay, "How the *Star Wars* Saga Evokes the Creative

Promise of Homosexual Love." In *VOY*, twinship partnerships are consistently *passionate, affectionate, mutual, lifesaving, transformative,* and *transcendent*. In contrast with these positive qualities and the patterns found in *Star Wars*, my secondary hypothesis is that double relationships in *VOY* are usually *not* particularly *enduring*, often ending with the death or departure of the twin figure, and rarely lead to a true *coniunctio* or union with the character representing the ego-personality, suggesting the possibility that the psychological limitations of the creative team prevented them from "going all the way" with the powerful libidinal themes that they were invoking. It's true that throughout mythology and literature, inspiring double figures *do* often die, as Mitch Walker has explained, in order to provide "a fateful momentum to the ego" ("Double" 172), and this dynamic is sometimes demonstrated in *VOY*, but more often the resolution of these scenarios ends on a negative note in the series, which tends to dilute but not completely destroy the more positive imagery that does repeatedly appear.

Captain Janeway's Unshakable Empathy for Her Own Double

In Mitch Walker's theory, whenever two people in a relationship have the same genital sexual characteristics, the double is present in some manner, even if they don't look so much like each other. That said, the image of "identical twins," especially when they are seen caring for one another instead of acting as enemies, has its own uncanny valence that epitomizes important qualities of the double, especially when it manifests homosexually as soul-figure. All of the *Star Trek* television series have used the motif of the twins repeatedly, and *VOY* is no exception.

For a brief orientation, in the first episode of the seven-year series, the starship U.S.S. *Voyager* is thrown 70,000 light-years away from Earth by a vastly powerful extraterrestrial entity, and Captain Janeway makes a fateful decision to ensure the safety of another, more vulnerable alien species they have encountered, which has the dismal side-effect of ruining her ability to get her crew back to Earth in a reasonable time frame. The series follows the adventures of the Captain and her crew as they embark on what could possibly be a 70-year journey home through the galaxy's "Delta Quadrant" territory almost never before visited by human beings. During their adventure, the entire crew gets duplicated on two separate occasions, and particular characters experience various forms of doubling many more times.

One of the most pronounced examples of the twinning theme is in "Deadlock," a Season Two episode in which *Voyager* hides from the organ-harvesting aliens called Vidiians in a plasma cloud, but when it appears safe to move on, the primary warp engines fail, and mysterious, repeating proton bursts threaten to tear the ship apart. Amidst the chaos, Ensign Samantha Wildman (Nancy Hower) gives birth to a girl who dies soon after delivery when the ship's medical support systems fail. Ensign Harry Kim (Garrett Wang) gets sucked out of a hull breach into outer space, and Lieutenant B'Elanna Torres (Roxann Dawson) watches Kes vanish into a spatial rift. As the senior crew is evacuating the disintegrating bridge, Captain Janeway sees a ghost image of herself, but in a much calmer state, seated in her chair. Now the perspective shifts to the other Janeway on an undamaged *Voyager* who witnesses a disheveled version of herself leaving the bridge, "almost like a ghost image." Walker has described the double soul-figure as a "ghost-twin" of the ego ("Uranian Soul" 205), and sure enough, as demonstrated by Janeway's spooked reaction, there is something haunting but fascinating about seeing another iteration of herself. Meanwhile, a real live duplicate of Kes has been found and brought to the sickbay. After the visiting Kes describes what's happened on *her* version of the ship, the Captain and her crew realize that due to a subspace divergence field, all the matter in the ship has been duplicated, but the anti-matter which drives the two ships' propulsion systems did not get copied, so *Voyager* has become, as Janeway puts it, "like Siamese twins linked at the chest, with only one heart." Working with B'Elanna, the Captain manages to create a visual link with the other *Voyager*. Back on that other, wounded *Voyager*, Captain Janeway is surprised to see another version of herself on the video screen, saying, "Captain, this isn't an illusion. What you're seeing is real, but it's going to take some explaining." Janeway #1 is not immediately convinced, but within a few minutes she is actively engaged with her counterpart to find a solution to their shared predicament.

After a failed attempt to merge the two ships, the Captain from the undamaged *Voyager* decides to cross the spatial rift, and thanks to the cleverness of special effects, the two Janeways encounter one another in person and debate what the next steps should be. This scene is shot intimately, in profile, the two Janeways close together, looking directly into each other's eyes. The Janeway from the badly wounded *Voyager* announces that she is going to sacrifice herself and her ship, because logically it is the only viable option. There is heightened tension between the two Janeways, but it is only because they have such consummate empathy for one another. As Mitch Walker describes it, there is a "rapport" in this kind of double relationship that generates "an atmosphere between the friends of profound equality and deep familiarity" ("Double" 169). As it turns out, the nefarious Vidiians discover and attack the undamaged *Voyager*, but do not detect the wounded *Voyager*, so the tables turn, and it is the Janeway on the less damaged ship who now volunteers to sacrifice herself and her crew, using the ship's explosive self-destruct mechanism. However, she sends her iterations of Harry Kim and Samantha Wildman's baby over to the other ship, effecting a kind of resurrection for them both along with the odd result that Samantha will mother a child she did not actually give birth to, providing a symbol of the creativity of twinship mutuality, in line with Otto Rank's statement: "As the twins appear to have created themselves independently of natural procreation, so they were believed to be able to create things which formerly did not exist" (qtd. in Walker, "Jung" 66). As the two Janeways poignantly say farewell via their video connection, the one who is preparing to die says to the other, "Make me a promise, Kathryn. Just get your crew home." The remaining Janeway is distraught when it is confirmed that the other *Voyager* has been destroyed along with her double, though naturally relieved to hear that the hostile alien ship was also obliterated, meaning that the other Janeway's sacrifice was not in vain, and at least one *Voyager* has survived. During an informal debriefing with Lieutenant Tuvok (Tim Russ), after he says that he did not envy the decision-making predicament the Captain was in with her counterpart, Janeway demonstrates her intuitive connection with her twin when she replies wistfully, "Neither did I, and neither did she."

Already in this first example, there is ample evidence for the primary themes of my discussion. The relationship between the two Janeways is visibly *passionate* and gradually *affectionate*, as they demonstrate heroic concerns for one another's welfare. They are exquisitely balanced in equal power, persuasive capacities, and self-awareness, showing that their bond is supremely *mutual*. Clearly, this is also a *lifesaving* twinship, where each is willing to sacrifice herself for the survival of the other, which can also be described as a *transcendent* quality, further symbolized by the "magical" resurrection of Harry Kim and Ensign Wildman's baby. One category that does not appear to be fully met in this situation is *transformative*, as the surviving Janeway seems touched and sobered by her encounter, but after it is all over, she displays a matter-of-fact attitude about the experience. This provides support for my secondary hypothesis, that the demise of the double in *VOY* often has a nihilistic, cynical edge, almost as if to say, "It was all for naught."

However, Captain Janeway meets her double many more times through the course of *Voyager*'s journey, often with more impactful results, especially in the series finale to be discussed toward the end of this essay.

Spiritual Transformations: Captain Janeway and Kes

In the first *VOY* episode, one of the refugees that joins the *Voyager* crew is an eager young woman from the planet Ocampa named Kes. During her three years on *Voyager*, she develops a warmhearted bond with Captain Janeway in a pattern that Mitch Walker calls the "youth-adult" variation of the double ("Double" 171).

The depth of Captain Janeway's growing fondness for Kes is perhaps best demonstrated by events that transpire in the episode "Sacred Ground" from

Season Three, which also relevantly shows a particularly significant interaction between Janeway and a female spiritual guide. While touring a religious shrine on the Nechani homeworld, Kes naively wanders up some steps toward a bright light where she is rendered comatose by a sudden surge in a biogenic energy field. Janeway decides that the only way she can save Kes is by subjecting herself to an arduous initiatory ritual that supposedly prepares monks to pass unaffected through the deadly energy. Perhaps in the process of her journey she can collect scientific readings about how the ritual creates resilience in the body through a subdermal bioprobe that will provide the information needed to treat Kes. Janeway is led through a grueling process for three days and nights by a friendly if mysterious female guide (Becky Ann Baker), who is clearly bemused by her initiate's uptight sense of urgency. At the beginning, three women attendants come toward Janeway, gently gesturing that they will remove her clothes. Perhaps for the first time, the starship captain who has so frequently and fearlessly battled vicious aliens looks really nervous, initially jumping back in fear. To be disrobed, stark naked, surrounded and touched gracefully by handsome women! Now the stakes really are high! Her guide gently but firmly encourages her to allow the experience to unfold, and she is taken on a descent that, as Wagner and Lundeen point out, is reminiscent of the myth of the Greek goddess Demeter as well as the Sumerian goddess Inanna (37).

In *Myth and Mysteries of Same-Sex Love,* Christine Downing explores the lesbianic aspects of the Demeter myth, focusing in particular on the goddess Baubo, who succeeds in breaking Demeter's deep depression by making her smile and laugh. Sometimes described as having a vulva for a mouth, Baubo takes off her clothes, spreads her legs, does a lewd dance, and, as Downing explains it, "communicates her joy in her own body, her pride in her female organs, her conviction that her sexuality is hers.... Conventional beauty, youth, reproductive capacity are all beside the point — she celebrates the pleasure her body can receive and give" (201–2). Downing further explains that Baubo was often portrayed by the Greeks as "seated on a pig with legs outspread, holding a ladder by which one might mount to the gods" (202). Janeway's guide is admittedly more self-contained than Baubo, and yet she has many Baubo-like qualities. As a hefty woman with short hair, she lacks conventional beauty yet seems supremely comfortable in her own skin, and takes genuine delight in helping the starship captain to become more embodied and humble in relation to the divine. In lesbian colloquial terms, she could be described as a "soft butch," who is most definitely "topping" Kathryn in a strenuous ordeal, breaking Starfleet protocol by intentionally calling her by her first name. Ultimately, all of Kathryn's scientific research efforts have to be abandoned so she can discover a basic inner trust that she will be able to withstand the neuroleptic shock, and she realizes that she herself must bring Kes into the energy field one more time in order to cure her. It's a moving, all-too-rare image to see a woman carrying another woman in her arms through a potentially deadly situation, but sure enough, they both survive and Kes smiles beatifically looking into Janeway's eyes as she awakens in the Captain's arms.

The warm intimacy between Janeway and Kes is most clearly shown in their tearful good-bye when Kes decides that it is time for her to leave *Voyager* in the climactic Season Four episode, "The Gift." She is rapidly developing psychokinetic abilities to the point where she can now see below the subatomic level of material reality, empowering her to demolecularize objects, and it seems that she herself is coming apart in some sort of metamorphosis to a higher level of consciousness, with the growing risk that her mere presence might tear *Voyager* apart.

Kes sounds quite a bit like a lesbian who is coming out to her parents when she tells Janeway, "Something important is happening to me and I want to explore it, but I can't stay here any longer. I'm a danger to all of you." This sense of feeling like a "danger" echoes strongly Sandra Golvin's discussion of the experience many lesbians have of being seen as "trouble" in their family-of-origin: "Attempting to be seen for who she is, which is Lesbian, inevitably lands her in trouble, for she does not conform in the profoundest of ways, a disturbing presence to those around her" (3–4). For a moment, Janeway sounds like a homophobic mother who sees her daughter's homosexuality as something to be fixed when she says, "We're going to get to the bottom of this. The Doctor's already working on a new approach." But then Kes responds with new self-confidence: "Everybody thinks that what's happening is a medical condition; that's not it at all. I'm going through a transformation. I don't know how or why, but every cell in my body is telling me I'm changing into something more." These words have been spoken almost verbatim by many lesbians and gay men as they come out of the closet and begin to assert their hard-won identity. Janeway realizes she can't convince Kes to stay, and places her hand gently on Kes's face as her eyes well up with tears and her voice shakes as she plaintively cries, "Oh, I'm going to miss you!" They give one another a long, deep hug, and then Kes starts to dematerialize. Hallway walls shredding in their wake, Janeway rushes her to a shuttle, which quickly launches and Kes soon dematerializes into a blinding burst of light. As a final gift, she uses her newfound god-like powers to hurl *Voyager* 9,500 light-years, or ten years, closer to home.

However, the story is not over, as Kes returns for one more episode, "Fury," in Season Six, when she comes back two years later as an enraged, paranoid old woman who crashes her shuttlecraft into *Voyager* and then comes aboard, still ripping apart walls just by walking down the hallway, but this time unconcerned for the welfare of *Voyager*. She uses the ship's power source in order to travel back in time to the earlier *Voyager* where she sedates her younger self, hides her in a drawer, takes on the visage of that familiar version of Kes, and then proceeds to terrorize the ship. Evidently, her transmutation into a greater form of consciousness did not end up going very well. Now she acts out the more clichéd portrayal of the "evil twin" form of the double, and Janeway is forced to kill her in order to save the younger, sweeter version of Kes. On a more positive note, the nature of time travel provides an opportunity to achieve a better outcome for the future. The more youthful Kes records a holographic full-body-image message to her older, more scornful self, which Janeway plays for the elderly Kes when she arrives in her vengeful mode in the new version of the future. This message allows the angry old Kes, who had forgotten having made the recording, to reconnect with her younger self, in a youth-adult pattern where, as Walker writes, "the younger person inspires new strength in the principles or the particular quest of the older" ("Double" 171).

The overall message of this episode is a mixed bag. On the one hand, the *VOY* creators seem to be saying, "Don't play with higher levels of awareness. You'll just turn old, bitter, and destructive." On the other hand, the double is shown to yet again save the day.

Notwithstanding the painful coda of their relationship, Captain Janeway and Kes do definitely achieve a warmhearted intimacy. The *passionate* and *life-saving* aspects of their relationship can be found in Janeway's willingness to risk her own life to preserve Kes's, and Kes's huge gesture of tossing *Voyager* out of hostile territory and ten years closer to home. They are frequently *affectionate* toward one another, and the *mutual* nature of their dynamic can be seen in the fact that, although Janeway wields all the power on *Voyager*, Kes as an alien refugee has no "rank" in the ship's hierarchy and is free to go whenever she wants, as she makes clear when the Captain tries to convince her to stay. The *transformative* aspect of their bond is well illustrated by how Janeway provides a safe home aboard *Voyager* for Kes to develop the psychokinetic abilities that were previously dormant in her species, as well as by the incident in which, as one of her last acts on *Voyager*, Kes saves the life of Seven of Nine, who has just arrived on *Voyager*, by psychokinetically removing an implant deep in Seven's brain, making possible an even more impactful soul-figure relationship for Janeway. Finally, the *transcendent* aspect of their relationship is demonstrated in Kes's breathtaking transfiguration beyond physical reality, but also in Janeway working with the younger version of Kes to get older Kes back on course when she loses her way.

Becoming Human: Janeway and Seven of Nine

Perhaps the most symbolically and emotionally resonant relationship between two women in *VOY*, or for that matter in any *Star Trek* production, is the fateful alliance between Captain Janeway and the cybernetic organism whose humanity she restores, Seven of Nine. In the same episode discussed above in which Kes departs *Voyager*, "The Gift," viewers witness the early stages of the metamorphosis of Seven of Nine from bald androgynous cyborg to human female. When we first lay eyes on her, she appears as a grotesque assemblage of futuristic technology, including a massive ocular implant where an eye should be, a large metallic box on the side of her head, and plated armor clamped permanently on much of her skull and body. Until a few days ago, she was a part of a vast hive mind of trillions of drones who have been "assimilated" from thousands of other species, but now she has become separated from the Borg collective, and Janeway is determined to help Seven regain her individuality, despite the drone's vehement protests. The Captain shows Seven a photo of herself found in the ship's database as a pretty six-year-old girl named Annika Hansen, taken just before her parents and she were abducted by the Borg, but Seven forcefully pushes the image away, and is clearly in agony having lost the security of being an integrated member of a harmonious, unified neural network.

"One voice can be stronger than a thousand voices," Janeway exclaims. "Your mind is independent, with its own unique identity."

"You are forcing that identity on me. It's not mine," Seven replies.

"I'm just giving back what was stolen from you," Janeway counters. "The existence you were denied. The child who never had a chance. That life is yours to live now!"

"I don't want that life," Seven cries out in anguish.

"It's what you are, don't resist it," Janeway replies.

Seven attempts to hit Janeway away, but she falters, overwhelmed with unfamiliar emotions, and collapses on a bench. Janeway drops down behind her, and places her hands affectionately on Seven's back, who is now too weak to reject the Captain's kindness.

In this scene, viewers are given a relatively rare vivid image of two women physically and emotionally wrestling passionately with each other over the crucial issue of becoming an authentic autonomous person. Janeway is initiating Seven into an accelerated version of the journey of *individuation*, which William G. Doty describes as "the process by which selfhood is attained by an individual" (209). Moreover, I would suggest that the dialogue spoken between Janeway and Seven is particularly resonant for many lesbians and gay men, succinctly hitting some notable aspects of *homosexual identity formation* (Ritter & Terndrup 90). In this instance, Janeway is speaking in a non-parental role as what Alice Miller calls an "enlightened witness" (167), especially when she says, "I'm just giving back what was stolen from you, the existence you were denied." And Seven sounds like a still-closeted lesbian in the stage of *identity confusion* (Ritter & Terndrup 91) when she says, "I don't want that life!" But Janeway pushes the issue of Seven's particular identity when she insists that, "It's what you are, don't resist it." Many a lesbian and gay man have spoken these words to themselves as they struggle to accept their homosexuality.

During this episode, Seven's body continues to reject her Borg implants and the Doctor must remove the majority of them. The ugly duckling becomes a beautiful swan, as Seven is revealed to be a tall, blond woman in a sheer, form-fitting uniform. She is an arresting combination of "feminine" beauty with a "butch" interior, tough as nails and ruthlessly logical. She has a brilliant mind and a pursuit of "perfection" that has survived from her Borg days. Janeway and Seven very quickly develop a robust relationship that grows beyond the roles of mentor, mother, daughter, or sister.

A prime example of the steadfast caring between Janeway and Seven occurs in the two-part episode "Dark Frontier," where they take turns risking their own lives to save the other. It all begins when Janeway hatches a plot to invade a Borg cube spaceship in order to steal a trans-warp drive which when fitted into *Voyager* will allow them to get home much faster. What Janeway doesn't know is that Seven has been secretly contacted by the Borg Queen (Susanna Thompson) via the Borg regeneration alcove Seven still uses for sleep, and has been told that the Borg know all about Janeway's scheme, but that if Seven surrenders herself to the collective during the mission, the vastly more powerful Borg will let the *Voyager* crew live. Janeway, Seven, and other crew members beam over to the Borg cube, and successfully steal the trans-warp drive, but then at the last minute, Seven announces her intention to return to the collective, and demands that Janeway leave without her or the *Voyager* crew will be assimilated. Janeway is deeply troubled, but soon figures out that Seven had been covertly contacted by the Borg and coerced to rejoin the collective.

Meanwhile, Seven is brought into the Borg Queen's chamber, who appears as a humanoid head, neck, shoulders, and spinal column that descends from on high through a central column into a cybernetic female-shaped body. Multiple cables coming out of her hairless skull connect her to the hive mind. This Borg Queen is actively seductive toward Seven, gently stroking Seven's face with overt sensuality and is "all-eyes" as she stares into Seven's pretty orbs. She hopes to exploit Seven's recent experience of individuality in order to learn how to assimilate the rest of humanity.

As documented in *The Celluloid Closet* (1995), Hollywood has frequently portrayed female and male villains as "lecherous homosexuals," which can be seen, for example, in *Dracula's Daughter* (1936), *Rebecca* (1940), and *Supergirl* (1984). This stereotypical pattern is all-too-predictably replicated here. Furthermore, I have discussed in earlier papers how homosexual eros between two main characters often gets more blatantly expressed through the villain between them, as can be seen in *Star Wars: Episode III— Revenge of the Sith* (2005) with the queeny Emperor inserting himself between Anakin and Obi-Wan (Kaufman, "Star Wars" 146) or in *The Lord of the Rings: The Two Towers* (2002), where Gollum manifests much of the erotic tension inherent in the relationship between Frodo and Sam (Kaufman, "Lord" 32). A similar dynamic is occurring here between the threesome of Seven, Janeway, and the Borg Queen.

The Captain dauntlessly breaks her way into the Borg Queen's chamber and there is a fierce battle of minds as the Borg Queen and Janeway fight over Seven's fate. Janeway exclaims, "Don't listen to her, Seven. She's irrelevant." And Seven replies to Janeway, "Our thoughts are one," echoing Mitch Walker's observation that, "Double fuses the fate of two into one" ("Double" 169). Working together, they are able to blast away the Borg Queen's connection to the neural network, rendering her temporarily harmless, and they escape to safety.

The episode ends intimately back on *Voyager* as Janeway affectionately orders Seven to regenerate, and gently walks her to her sleeping alcove, where the Captain "tucks her in" by turning on the regeneration cycle and saying, "Sweet dreams." The final tableau is not, however, of a mother looking down on her daughter in bed but rather of Janeway looking up with deep affection and perhaps even admiration at the statuesque Seven, who sleeps standing up.

Janeway and Seven experience many intense adventures together, especially during the final episode of *VOY*, which also features a new encounter Janeway has with an older iteration of herself. "Endgame" begins in a future in which *Voyager* made it back to Earth 23 years after arriving in the Delta Quadrant, and Janeway has become an admiral, but Seven has long since died in one of their many battles with alien species. Admiral Janeway now realizes she could have gotten her crew home 16 years earlier, avoiding Seven's death along with many other consequences if she had used one of the Borg-controlled wormholes they had discovered, so she brazenly procures a time-travel device, and suddenly appears in the Delta Quadrant, announcing to her younger self, "I've come to take *Voyager* home!" Much of the passion in this episode actually occurs between the older and younger Janeways, but there is still considerable emotional intensity between Janeway and Seven, or in this case, between the *two* Janeways and Seven. When Admiral Janeway first sees Seven after 13 years, there is visible emotion in her eyes as she says, simply, "Hello, Seven," the tone of her voice a mixture of grief and joy and hope, as if seeing the ghost of a fondly remembered friend (ex-lover?) after many long years. When Admiral Janeway and Captain Janeway are debating about whether to go straight home quickly or make a devastating but risky blow to the villainous Borg collective along the way, Admiral Janeway begins her argument in favor of the faster, safer path by announcing to Captain Janeway that "Seven of Nine is going to die three years from now," and the Captain is visibly shaken by this news. Soon thereafter, Admiral Janeway is speaking alone with Seven, trying to persuade Seven to go along with her plan in opposition to Captain Janeway. She tells the former Borg that she will die in three years, and urges her to think of the effect that will have "on people who love you." The "official" subtext here is Chakotay (Robert Beltran), who has recently fallen in love with Seven, but the Admiral does *not* name him in this scene. Instead, we see only the two women looking at each other, and it seems clear by the *gravitas* with which Admiral Janeway speaks that she is experiencing her own continuing sorrow at the loss of Seven. After climactic action mostly involving the two Janeways and the Borg Queen, the seven-year series concludes with a close-up of Captain Janeway in her chair on the bridge, with Seven standing at her station directly above her, just out of the camera frame, and then, at last, an image of the big blue Earth on the viewscreen.

Now looking back, it is evident that the partnership between Janeway and Seven is extraordinarily *passionate*, and in many ways also *affectionate*. Although Captain Janeway initially makes decisions for Seven, their relationship swiftly becomes *mutual* and equal as Seven demonstrates her formidable intellect, valor, and strength, in more than one case in order to save the Captain's life, acts of courage which Janeway frequently returns, revealing the *lifesaving* nature of their bond. The *transformative* nature of their relationship is evident not only in Seven's remarkable evolution from Borg drone to human, but also in Captain Janeway's total dedication to that project, in effect making it her life's work, second only to getting *Voyager* back to Earth. And clearly, the *transcendent* dynamic is involved in Seven's ability, with Janeway's help, to integrate her gruesome but highly educational experience as a Borg into her humanity. And yet, as prominent as they are, these themes of female intimacy are dampened by efforts in Seasons Six and Seven to show Janeway and Seven having heterosexual romances, further evidence of *VOY*'s pattern of ultimately stifling lesbian eros.

Finally, the *Voyager* storyline comes full circle to Captain Janeway's relationship with another "identical twin" version of herself, in this case offering another illustration of the youth-adult motif, where Admiral Janeway is 16 years older than the Captain. This situation is somewhat different from the Janeway twin experience discussed above in "Deadlock," because Admiral Janeway has many years more experience, knowledge, and even technology than Captain Janeway, but Captain Janeway has her own inspiring attributes, as she is far less cynical than Admiral Janeway. After much debate and getting "re-acquainted," it is secretly agreed between them that Admiral Janeway will function as an elaborate decoy and Trojan horse by allowing herself to get caught and assimilated by the Borg Queen (Alice Krige), which will disperse a nanovirus she has been injected with, seriously crippling the Borg empire and enabling *Voyager* to escape through a Borg wormhole to make it back safely to Earth. As the two Janeways say good-bye, just before they hatch their plot, the Admiral says, "Captain, I'm glad I got to know you again," and the camera moves up close to capture the younger Janeway's indelible, ebullient expression, beaming with a big smile and a joyful glint in her eyes.

Once again, here is a relationship between two exceptional women that is definitely *passionate*, and ultimately, *affectionate*. The *mutual* quality of their interaction can be seen in the fact that, although Admiral Janeway may outrank Captain Janeway, the younger one still has the loyalty of her crew, and persuades her older self to follow her plan of attack, which they then refine together, leading the Admiral to sacrifice herself for the younger Janeway, demonstrating the *lifesaving* nature of their alliance. Meeting one another is definitely *transformative* for both, as Captain Janeway manages to get her crew back to Earth 16 years earlier than history dictates, and Admiral Janeway reconnects with the idealism of her own youth, healing her cynicism and grief, and empowering her to commit one last selfless, *transcendent* act.

Conclusion: Tantalizing Intimations of Lesbian Love and Individuation

Now it can be seen that almost all of the encounters described between women in *Star Trek: Voyager* portray relationships that are *passionate, affectionate, mutual, lifesaving, transformative,* and *transcendent.* These qualities richly demonstrate Mitch Walker's conceptualization of the archetypal double, especially in its role as erotically alluring soul-figure leading the personality toward Self-realization, and suggest that these double relationships are rooted in the feminine intelligence of lesbian eros. In many cases, these salutary aspects of the twinships shown meet an abrupt end, preventing the development of blatant romantic involvement or further self-development, and yet the potent imagery depicted is remarkable, especially in the context of a large-scale Hollywood television production that assiduously avoided having overt homosexual love or identity depicted. By placing center-stage throughout its 171 episodes many striking scenarios of extremely courageous, exceedingly intelligent, physically attractive, highly cultured women who demonstrate visible devotion to one another, *Star Trek: Voyager* evokes what can reasonably be deemed the inspiring power of lesbian love, as well as its many laudable attributes, especially its vast *transformative* potential for sparking *transcendent* spiritual awakening. We can hope that some day the love that still dares not speak its name out loud in the *Star Trek* universe will be more fully celebrated, offering hope for lesbians, gay men, and ultimately, all human beings who seek non-violent, humane ways of living in *mutual* harmony with one another and with Planet Earth, which, as the journey of *Voyager* through the frightening expanses of outer space so clearly shows, is our only viable home, at least for the foreseeable future.

Works Cited

Bowring, Michèle. "Resistance Is *Not* Futile: Liberating Captain Janeway from the Masculine-Feminine Dualism of Leadership. *Gender, Work and Organization* 11.4 (July 2004): 381–405.

Dart, G.L. *Just Between...* 24 August 2008 <http://www.northco.net/~janeway/fanfic.htm#JBStories>.
Downing, Christine. *Myth and Mysteries of Same-Sex Love*. New York: Continuum, 1989.
Foucault, Michel. *The History of Sexuality — Volume I: An Introduction*. New York: Vintage, 1978.
Ginzberg, Ruth. "Audre Lorde's (Nonessentialist) Lesbian Eros." *Hypatia* 7.4 (1992): 73–90.
Golvin, Sandra Lee. "Gender Trouble: Lesbian Psyche as Revealed in the Writing of Judith Butler." Unpublished manuscript, 1999.
Hogenson, George. "The Self, the Symbolic and Synchronicity: Virtual Realities and the Emergence of the Psyche." *Journal of Analytical Psychology* 50 (2005): 271–284.
Jung, C.G. *Aion: Researches into the Phenomenology of the Self, Second Edition*. Princeton, NJ: Princeton University Press, 1969.
_____. *Dream Analysis: Notes of the Seminar Given in 1928–1930*. Ed. William McGuire. Princeton, NJ: Princeton University Press, 1984.
_____. "On the Nature of the Psyche." *The Structure and Dynamics of the Psyche, Second Edition*. Princeton, NJ: Princeton University Press, 1969.
_____. *Symbols of Transformation*. Princeton, NJ: Princeton University Press, 1956.
Kaufman, Roger. "Heroes Who Learn to Love Their Monsters: How Fantasy Film Characters Can Inspire the Journey of Individuation for Gay and Lesbian Clients in Psychotherapy." In *Using Superheroes in Counseling and Play Therapy*. Ed. Lawrence Rubin. New York: Springer, 2007.
_____. "How the *Star Wars* Saga Evokes the Creative Promise of Homosexual Love: A Gay-Centered Psychological Perspective." In *Finding the Force of the Star Wars Franchise: Fans, Merchandise, & Critics*. Ed. Matthew Wilhelm Kapell and John Shelton Lawrence. New York: Peter Lang, 2006.
_____. "*Lord of the Ring* Taps a Gay Archetype." *Gay & Lesbian Review Worldwide* 10.4 (2003): 31–33.
McDowell, Maxson. "Principle of Organization: A Dynamic-Systems View of the Archetype-asS." *Journal of Analytical Psychology* 46 (2001): 637–654.
Miller, Alice. *Banished Knowledge: Facing Childhood Injuries*. New York: Anchor, 1990.
Plato. *Symposium*. Trans. Robin Waterfield. New York: Oxford University Press, 1994.
Ritter, Kathleen, and Anthony Terndrup. *Handbook of Affirmative Psychotherapy with Lesbians and Gay Men*. New York: Guilford, 2002.
Samuels, Andrew. *Jung and the Post-Jungians*. New York: Brunner-Routledge, 1985.
Shaw, Debra Bonita. "Sex and the Single Starship Captain: Compulsory Heterosexuality and *Star Trek: Voyager*." *Femspec* 7.1 (2006): 66–85.
Sinclair, David. *Gay, Lesbian & Bisexual Characters in Star Trek*. 26 May 2008. <http://www.webpan.com/dsinclair/trek.html>.
Wagner, John, and Jan Lundeen. *Deep Space and Sacred Time:* Star Trek *in the American Mythos*. Westport, CT: Praeger, 1998.
Walker, Mitchell. "The Double: An Archetypal Configuration." *Spring: A Journal of Archetypal Psychology* (1976): 165–175.
_____. "Jung and Homophobia." *Spring: A Journal of Archetypal Psychology* (1991): 55–70.
_____. *The Revolutionary Psychology of Gay-Centeredness in Men*. Self-published pamphlet, 1999.
_____. *The Uranian Soul: A Gay-Centered Jungian Psychology of Male Homosexual Personhood for a New Era of Gay Liberation Politics With Universal Implicational Import*, Unpublished manuscript, 2008.

Films Cited

Alien. Dir. Ridley Scott. Twentieth Century–Fox, 1979.
Alien: Resurrection (1997). Dir. Jean-Pierre Jeunet. Twentieth Century–Fox, 1997.

Aliens. Dir. James Cameron. Twentieth Century-Fox, 1986.
Alien³. Dir. David Fincher. Twentieth Century-Fox, 1992.
The Celluloid Closet. Dir. Rob Epstein and Jeffrey Friedman. Brillstein-Grey, Channel 4 Films, HBO, 1995.
Dracula's Daughter. Dir. Lambert Hillyer. Universal Pictures, 1936.
The Lord of the Rings: The Fellowship of the Ring. Dir. Peter Jackson. New Line Cinema, 2001.
The Lord of the Rings: The Return of the King. Dir. Peter Jackson. New Line Cinema, 2003.
The Lord of the Rings: The Two Towers. Dir. Peter Jackson. New Line Cinema, 2002.
Rebecca. Dir. Alfred Hitchcock. Selznick International Pictures, 1940.
Star Wars: Episode I — The Phantom Menace. Dir. George Lucas. Twentieth Century-Fox, 1999.
Star Wars: Episode II — Attack of the Clones. Dir. George Lucas. Twentieth Century-Fox, 2002.
Star Wars: Episode III — Revenge of the Sith. Dir. George Lucas. Twentieth Century-Fox, 2005.
Star Wars: Episode IV — A New Hope. Dir. George Lucas. Twentieth Century-Fox, 1977.
Star Wars: Episode V — The Empire Strikes Back. Dir. Irvin Kershner. Twentieth Century-Fox, 1980.
Star Wars: Episode VI — Return of the Jedi. Dir. Richard Marquand. Twentieth Century-Fox, 1983.
The Student of Prague. Dir. Stella Rye and Paul Wegener. Deutsche Bioscop GmbH, 1913.
Supergirl. Dir. Jeannot Sward. Artistry Limited, 1984.

Star Trek: Voyager *Episodes Cited*

"Caretaker." Story by Rick Berman, Michael Piller and Jeri Taylor. Teleplay by Michael Piller and Jeri Taylor. 16 January 1995.
"Dark Frontier, Parts I & II." Written by Brannon Braga and Joe Menosky. 17 February 1999.
"Deadlock." Written by Brannon Braga. 18 March 1996.
"Endgame, Parts I & II." Story by Rick Berman, Kenneth Biller and Brannon Braga. Teleplay by Kenneth Biller and Robert Doherty. 23 May 2001.
"Fury." Story by Rick Berman and Brannon Braga. Teleplay by Bryan Fuller and Michael Taylor. 3 May 2000.
"The Gift." Written by Joe Menosky. 10 September 1997.
"Sacred Ground." Story by Geo Cameron. Teleplay by Lisa Klink. 30 October 1996.

11

The Protestant Ethic and the Spirit of Surak

Star Trek: Enterprise, Anti-Catholicism and the Vulcan Reformation

JENNIFER E. PORTER

> *What does it mean to have a god? Or, what is God? Answer: A god means that from which we are to expect all good and to which we are to take refuge in all distress, so that to have a God is nothing else than to trust and believe Him from the heart; as I have often said that the confidence and faith of the heart alone make both God and an idol. If your faith and trust be right, then is your god also true; and, on the other hand, if your trust be false and wrong, then you have not the true God; for these two belong together faith and God. That now, I say, upon which you set your heart and put your trust is properly your god.*
> — Martin Luther, Large Catechism, 565
>
> *After the devil himself, there is no worse folk than the pope and his followers.*
> — Martin Luther, "Against the Roman Papacy," 279

Star Trek: Enterprise is the problem child of the *Star Trek* franchise. Originally titled simply "*Enterprise*," the fifth and (to date) final television series lasted for only four television seasons before being cancelled, the first series in the franchise to have been cancelled since the original *Star Trek* series. *Enterprise* encountered ambivalent responses from fans beginning with the original announcement of its prequel concept. Ratings dropped noticeably over the four years of its run, with average viewership falling from 5.9 million viewers per episode in Season One, to 2.81 million viewers per episode in Season Four ("Star Trek: Enterprise" para 51). When cancelled, the series left unresolved plot issues and a general feeling of dissatisfaction among the fan base it had managed to build. According to producers, the failure of the series was the result of "franchise fatigue" (Hark 41.) *Star Trek*, it was suggested, had simply worn out its appeal. According to general fan consensus, however, the series was just "too different" to appeal to hard-core *Star Trek* fans, and "simply didn't feel like a [*Star*] *Trek* [series]" (True Edge 2).

Was *Star Trek: Enterprise* really so different from other *Star Trek* series, however? Conceptually, the series is a prequel, and according to producers Brannon Braga and Rick Berman, was intended to be "dramatically different" from other *Star Trek* series, while simultaneously utilizing "a lot of the things that people have come to appreciate about *Star Trek*" ("Enterprise Cast" para. 20, 22). The prequel concept allowed the series to explore the early developmental stages of beloved *Star Trek* technologies, such as the transporter and the warp drive; show the influential events leading to the development of *Star Trek*'s ideological principles, most notably the non-interference or "prime" directive; and introduce "first contact" and early relationship narratives with alien races familiar from other *Star Trek* series. Of significant prominence in the series is the Vulcan species, familiar to fans since Mr. Spock graced television screens in the 1960s. Vulcans figure prominently in the pilot episode of *Enterprise*, but in a more antagonistic, arrogant portrayal than fans expected. In trying to account for the demise of the series, one fan writes: "...even the Vulcans weren't quite like the ones we were used to seeing. It was quite an adjustment to make for many of us solid *Trek* fans" (True Edge 1).

Vulcans are central to the entire *Star Trek: Enterprise* series and it is through the Vulcans that one can see that, ideologically, the series is very much in keeping with other series in the franchise. Story arcs involving Vulcans, however, reveal the dark side of *Star Trek*'s utopian message of hope and promise of a better future. Recast in *Enterprise* as the force of obstruction against which human ingenuity, autonomy and destiny must struggle, the Vulcans—or, more accurately, the Vulcan High Command—resonate with themes drawn from the history of American anti–Catholicism. In depicting the struggle for human independence, scientific and moral advancement, and intellectual and moral freedom, *Enterprise* situates itself in a long-standing American protestant rhetoric that elevates individual moral choice, the primacy of text over tradition, the moral supremacy of dissent, and the need for individual experience of the divine, while condemning the "evils" of ritualistic, hierarchical, authoritarian, and foreign-controlled systems of belief. Although the Vulcans in *Enterprise* are clearly not Catholics, their portrayal and treatment is imbued with the stereotypes of anti–Catholic rhetoric.

Star Trek's *City on a Hill*

According to media scholar Lincoln Geraghty, *Star Trek* draws upon a Puritan heritage in casting its utopian message of hope for the future within the frame of the American Jeremiad, where past sins are overcome and pave the way to a brighter, destined future. He writes:

> the exceptionalist, progressive, expansive, prophetic, yet unfinished tones of the Puritan Jeremiad resonate throughout *Star Trek* because it bases its ethos on centuries-old themes and tropes first recognizable in the American continent when the Pilgrims set foot on Plymouth Rock in 1620. When John Winthrop spoke of a "City upon a Hill" he was not only laying out terms for the foundation of a community in New England; he was also unwittingly producing a framework for the continuing progression of American exceptionalist tropes well in the twenty-first century and, as we see in *Star Trek*, into the twenty-fourth [69].

By postulating a future in which war, poverty, sexism, racism, crime, and intolerance, had been overcome, *Star Trek*'s creator Gene Roddenberry envisioned a fictional New Zion in the twenty-fourth century, and used his television series as a vehicle to show his Vietnam-era audience what was needed to reach it. For Roddenberry, and for many of his fans, that future was obtainable, if only the "sins" of the present could be overcome.

Star Trek's ideological message situates *Star Trek* as a City upon a Hill — as a model of and a model for attaining the peaceable Kingdom that lies just outside our current reach. Unlike John Winthrop's City upon a Hill, however, Roddenberry's utopian dream was framed in a secular, humanistic vision of human destiny. As Religious Studies scholar Anne MacKenzie Pearson argues, religion was one of the many "sins" that must be left behind in order to create the new utopia (13–32). And yet, despite this commitment to the emergence of a post-religious world, *Star Trek* was originally and continues to be fully engaged with religious themes and issues, shaped by the American Protestant experience. The difference between *Enterprise* and other *Star Trek* series is that in *Enterprise*, the Utopian dream has yet to be obtained. *Enterprise* becomes the story, therefore, of how the City upon a Hill was built — and of the obstacles strewn along the path to Zion.

"They have their reasons. God knows what they are."

— Henry Archer to his son, Jonathan, "Broken Bow."

When *Enterprise* debuted on September 26, 2001, *Star Trek* fans were introduced to the first *Star Trek* series to have a theme song with lyrics. The original *Star Trek* series theme, written by Alexander Courage, had lyrics added by Gene Roddenberry, but those lyrics were never used (Bond, para. 5). Controversy surrounding the use of lyrics in *Enterprise* erupted among fans, with many arguing strongly that the show should have continued the tradition of instrumental themes ("Star Trek: Enterprise" para 3–6). The theme, variously titled

"Where My Heart Will Take Me," and "Faith of the Heart," is accompanied by images of space flight, including footage of the International Space Station and the Mars Rover ("Where my heart will take me," para. 1). This juxtaposition of space flight images with the lyrics emphasizes what Religious Studies scholar Ian Maher calls the "outward voyage" of *Star Trek*, or the human journey into outer space; the content of the lyrics, however, simultaneously evokes what Maher calls "the inward search"—the theme of spiritual quest and spiritual commitment that runs throughout previous *Star Trek* series and films (65). When Russell Watson sings he has faith, it is easy to imagine that he is speaking for the human species, looking ahead to what fans already know will be the utopian future of Starfleet. The audience is immediately presented with a vision of a valiant humanity, struggling against the forces of physical and psychological oppression, destined to victory but confronted by those determined to limit the human spirit. The first episode of the new series, "Broken Bow," communicates to viewers just who these forces of oppression are—and contrary to first impressions, it is not the Suliban, the gene-twisting, time-shifting, phaser-toting enemy aliens of *Enterprise*'s first season, out to fast-track their way to godhood. Instead, the oppressors of the opening theme are the Vulcans—allies of humanity since making "first contact" over eighty years previously ("Star Trek: First Contact" para. 8). When the lyrics speak of being held down and of attempts to break human destiny, *Enterprise* places the blame squarely on the Vulcan species.

Anti-Catholicism and the Vulcans

Anti-Catholicism in the United States has primarily taken two forms, one theological and the other political. "The first," writes historian Joseph G. Mannard, "derived from the heritage of the Protestant Reformation and the religious wars of the sixteenth century. These writings depicted the Pope as the Anti-Christ, the 'Man of Sin' and the 'Whore of Babylon' described in Revelation, who schemed to deliver the Christian world into the hands of his master, Satan" (1–9). The second emerged in the nineteenth and twentieth century writings of British and American intellectuals, suggesting that Catholicism was antithetical to democracy and science, that adherence to Catholicism automatically meant submission to foreign political power, and that the Catholic Church was plotting to invade the free (protestant) world (McGreevy 97). The treatment of Vulcans in *Enterprise* capitalizes on both of these threads, starting with a largely political critique, and broadening out to the necessity for a full-fledged Vulcan political and spiritual Reformation.

Enterprise establishes the Vulcans as a force of foreign political control in the opening scenes of its pilot episode, where flashbacks from Captain Jonathan Archer's childhood are juxtaposed to scenes of the adult Captain Archer confronting and overcoming the obstructionist behavior of the Vulcan ambassador and his staff. When the child–Archer complains to his father that the Vulcans are holding humans back, his father answers: "They have their reasons. God knows what they are." This invocation of religious language in a *Star Trek* series is startling. With two exceptions ("Bread and Circuses" [1968] and "City on the Edge of Forever" [1967]), the original *Star Trek* series avoided the use of religious language by human beings, and other *Star Trek* series followed suit. The senior Archer's use of this phrase highlights the "retro" feel of the series, where religious language is one of the many archaisms that serve to set the series apart from others in the franchise. It also signifies the utter incomprehensibility of Vulcan behavior. It is not until the fourth season episode "The Forge" (2004) that we learn of at least one motivator for Vulcan obstructionism: fear.

Because *Enterprise* is a prequel series, fans of *Star Trek* already know what humans can and will achieve in the century to come, and that is Gene Roddenberry's utopian dream. That Vulcans should fear the building of *Star Trek*'s City upon a Hill, and seek to oppose it, situates them in a cosmic drama of good versus evil, with Vulcans firmly on the side of darkness. *Enterprise* therefore becomes the story not only of how humans ultimately build *Star Trek*'s new Zion, but of how the Vulcans are redeemed from their fallen ways, to take their rightful place by humanity's side.

Broken Bow

The pilot episode of *Enterprise* tells the story of an injured Klingon courier and the efforts of the crew of the Star Ship Enterprise to return him to his home world, amidst the beginnings of an interstellar war. Although *Star Trek* canon contained no hint of Vulcan political influence in twenty-second century earth history prior to the series *Enterprise*, "Broken Bow" successfully embeds the idea of Vulcan obstructionism into the canon. The Vulcan character of T'Pol, Captain Archer's science officer, acts as the foil through which "authentic" or well-intentioned Vulcan ways are contrasted to the corruption and evils of the Vulcan hierarchy. Establishing the evils of the Vulcan High Command and the threat of Vulcan interference in human affairs early in the pilot episode, Starfleet's human representative, Admiral Forrest, tells Captain Jonathan Archer: "Soval thinks it would be best if we put off your launch until we've cleared this up." Archer responds, "Well, isn't that a surprise. You'd think they'd have come up with something a little more imaginative this time." Vulcan obstructionism has clearly continued since Jonathan Archer first articulated his resentment as a child. Unlike his father, however, Archer is not content to trust that Vulcans "have their reasons."

The opening scenes of "Broken Bow" do more than establish Captain

Archer's resentment of Vulcan political influence; they also serve to establish the suspect motives and questionable morality of Vulcans in the minds of viewers. Discussing the injured Klingon and the hostile alien Suliban who were chasing him, humans and Vulcans engage in a dialogue about sensor logs and the right to know.

Although left unanswered, the question "who gets to decide" is a significant one. Clearly, there is an imbalance of power between the Vulcan embassy and the humans of Starfleet; the Vulcan Ambassador has denied the "right to decide" to humans. However, as the dialogue later suggests, in denying the right to decide to human beings, Vulcans apparently distain the right to decide for themselves also, choosing instead what human ethics suggests is a morally bankrupt choice: the surrender of free thought to the dictates of another.

According to historian John T. McGreevy, one of the central markers of American anti–Catholicism in the twentieth century was the fear that people tired of "doing their own thinking" would be drawn to Catholicism; that Catholicism represented a surrender of the intellectual and moral autonomy necessary for democratic political action (98). Although later *Star Trek* series present the Vulcan philosophy of IDIC — Infinite Diversity in Infinite Combinations — positively, *Enterprise*'s pilot episode equates the Vulcan philosophy with moral bankruptcy — with a surrender of autonomy, and a refusal to decide that is equivalent to murder. Such a treatment echoes American anti–Catholic sentiment that emerged in the 1920s. As McGreevy notes, anti–Catholic writers equated Catholicism with "tired and timid" minds, and suggested that Catholics would abdicate the "responsibility of deciding upon difficult questions (106). The result, anti–Catholics feared, would be a willingness to surrender to fascism and the possibility of an all-out attack on democracy. In keeping with this kind of anti–Catholic rhetoric, *Enterprise* proceeds to chart the fall of Vulcans from venerable aliens and admirable allies as portrayed in every other *Star Trek* series, to fascist warmongers bent on the destruction of spiritual truth, political democracy, and peaceable interstellar relations.

The Andorian Incident, or, the Awful Disclosures of the P'Jem Monastery

One of the most titillating anti–Catholic books of the nineteenth century was Maria Monk's "Awful Disclosures of the Hotel Dieu Nunnery." Filled with lurid details about priestly sexual predators and illegitimate babies murdered and buried in secret tunnels beneath the convent, the book appealed to the prejudices of its predominantly protestant audience. Catholic monasteries and convents have captured the imagination of opponents since the nineteenth century, when a host of anti–Catholic literature was published purporting to reveal their hidden secrets. As social historian Joseph G. Mannard notes, "the primary appeal of anti-Catholic literature rested on its titillating aspects. Books promising to divulge the esoteric rites and rituals of the Catholic Church sold briskly.... Writers pictured nunneries as dens of sex, secrecy, and sedition.... They described the convent system as a subversive network seeking to undermine the institutions of church, family and nation (para. 31).

The *Enterprise* episode "The Andorian Incident" (2001) is short on sex, but when it comes to secrecy and sedition the episode is rife. The episode opens with a scene of four Andorians breaking down the door of what looks very much like a temple or monastery. This is confirmed after the opening credit sequence, when T'Pol refers to the place as "P'Jem ... an ancient spiritual retreat. A remote sanctuary for Kolinahr and peaceful meditation." When Captain Archer expresses an interest in visiting the monastery, T'Pol researches the "protocols" involved in such a visit, and the landing party beams down to find the doors askew and the monastery in disarray. Captured by Andorians, the Vulcans explain the situation to Archer.

Given the status of Vulcans as allies of Starfleet, Captain Archer and the viewing audience assume that the Vulcan monks are truthful and that the Andorians are simply paranoid. When the Andorians torture Captain Archer for information about the purported "sensor-array," there is no suggestion that the Andorians are sympathetic characters or that the Vulcan holy men might be lying. However, as the story unfolds, the Vulcan monks admit to having an ancient transmitter hidden in their "catacombs." Primed to perceive the Catacombs as sacred ground, the viewer is graced with images straight out of a gothic novel, with spider webs, eerily glowing icons, and the mummified remains of monks propped against the walls. Watching these scenes, we might have been reading the pages of an anti-Catholic horror tome, such as Maria Monk's description of the tunnels beneath the Hotel Dieu Nunnery:

> I proceeded down a staircase, with a lamp in my hand. I soon found myself upon the bare earth, in a spacious place, so dark, that I could not at once distinguish its form, or size [...] in a short time I observed before me, a hole dug so deep into the earth that I could perceive no bottom. It immediately occurred to me that [...] this must be the place where the infants were buried, after being murdered. [...] Here then I was, in a place which I had considered as the nearest imitation of heaven to be found on earth, among a society where deeds were constantly perpetrated, which I had believed to be most criminal [36].

Although there are no dead babies in the Vulcan catacombs, Captain Archer does discover the buried secret of P'Jem: it is a front for the previously disavowed long-range sensor array, used to spy on the Andorian home world. If viewers were primed to perceive the Vulcan monastery as an "intimation of heaven to be found on earth," we find instead a hotbed of illicit political activity, a society bent on perpetrating deeds we had believed to be "most criminal."

The symbol of a religious holy place perverted into a place of political espionage echoes the fears of the nineteenth century American Nativists, including Samuel Morse, inventor of the Morse Code: "Let no one be deceived by the Popish apings of Protestant institutions," he wrote. "The Popish seminary has little in common with the Protestant seminary but the name. It is but the sheep's skin that covers the wolf's back; the teeth and the claws are not even well concealed beneath" (89). Just as nineteenth century anti–Catholics were convinced that Jesuits were really at the forefront of a "Papist" army intent on the destruction of America, the Vulcans are shown to be intent on the destruction of the Andorians, disguising their military and political intent behind the walls of a Vulcan monastery. T'Pol's disdainful comment that the Andorians even feared that the Vulcans were planning to invade their homeworld turns out to be prophetic, for the Vulcans do indeed launch such an invasion in the fourth season episode "Kir'Shara" (2004). The depths of the catacombs at P'Jem symbolize the depths of Vulcan duplicity. Only a full-fledged protestant reformation can redeem the Vulcans from their fallen ways.

The Vulcan Reformation

According to Catholic columnist James Martin, the film and television industry is of two minds when it comes to Catholicism: it is fascinated with the visual trappings of Catholicism, the richness and visual impact of "vestments, monstrances, statues, crucifixes — to say nothing of the symbols of the sacraments — [these] are all things that more 'word-oriented' Christian denominations have foregone. The Catholic Church, therefore, lends itself perfectly to the visual media of film and television (para. 28). On the other hand, "the Catholic Church is still seen as profoundly 'other' in modern culture and is therefore an object of continuing fascination ... it is ancient in a culture that celebrates the new, professes truths in a postmodern culture that looks skeptically on any claim to truth and speaks of mystery in a rational, post–Enlightenment world. It is therefore the perfect context for scriptwriters searching for the 'conflict' required in any story" (Martin, para. 28).

What Martin suggests is true for Catholics in contemporary television and film is also true within the *Star Trek* franchise for Vulcans — no other species, with the possible exception of Klingons — is shown to have such a visually rich, exotically "other" religious faith (Pearson 18). Elements of Vulcan ritualism are introduced in the original *Star Trek* series, most notably in the episode "Amok Time" (1967). These elements are elaborated in the film *Star Trek III: The Search for Spock* (1984), where the existence of a Vulcan soul, or katra, is introduced. Meditation, mysticism, belief in the continued existence of the soul after death; communication with the souls of the dead; chanting, incense, icons and candles — these are the things that mark Vulcan spirituality in the *Star Trek* universe. In the original *Star Trek* series and its first three sequels, Vulcan religion is treated with utmost respect. Indeed, as Religious Studies Scholar Gregory Peterson notes, the religions of technologically advanced aliens are the only religions that receive such respect in the *Star Trek* franchise (72). Peterson further suggests that *Star Trek*'s respect for alien faiths falters the closer that faith comes to a Western/Christian model (71–72.) *Enterprise* does not condemn the Christian elements of Vulcan faith, but condemns instead the "corruptions" of that faith in ways that echo anti–Catholic criticisms of Catholicism. In *Enterprise*, the Vulcan faith is redeemed through a Protestant-style reformation, complete with possession by the "holy spirit" and a back-to-the-Bible emphasis to make any Protestant reformer proud.

Back to the Bible, Vulcan Style

According to Protestant reformer Martin Luther, scripture is "queen" over any other source of spiritual knowledge, including tradition. Nothing can supersede the supremacy of the written word, and only the written word carries the true meaning of God's teachings. He writes,

> [It] is an accursed lie that the pope is the arbiter of Scripture or that the church has authority over Scripture.... The pope, Luther, Augustine, Paul, an angel from heaven — these should not be masters, judges or arbiters, but only witnesses, disciples, and confessors of Scripture. Nor should any doctrine be taught or heard in the church except the pure Word of God. Otherwise, let the teachers and the hearers be accursed along with their doctrine [Luther, "Lectures on Galatians" 57–58].

Other Protestant reformers placed equal emphasis on Scripture, and by the nineteenth century in the United States it had become axiomatic that "true" Christians revered the Bible as the sole source of God's word, while Catholics rejected the Bible in favor of extra–Scriptural sources of revelation. Maria Monk, for example, writes "Great dislike to the Bible was shown by those who conversed with me about it [at the Convent], and several have remarked to me, at different times, that if it were not for that book, Catholics would never be led to renounce their own Faith" (21).

The primacy of Scripture, and the anti–Catholic suggestion that access to scripture threatens Catholic faith, emerges in *Enterprise* in the fourth season story-arc of the Vulcan Reformation. Beginning in the episode "The Forge," (2004) and continuing through "Awakening" (2004) and "Kir'Shara" (2004), *Enterprise* tells the story of the discovery of the true writings of Surak, the Vulcan spiritual visionary known as "the Father of Vulcan philosophy." The story arc opens with scenes of the bombing of the Earth embassy on Vulcan. Religious dissidents, known as Syrrannites, are blamed, and evidence implicating them is planted. Convinced at first by the false evidence, Captain Archer and his science officer T'Pol hunt for the Syrrannites in the desert region of Vulcan known as "The Forge," having been given a map of the region by T'Pol's mother, a closet Syrrannite. The importance of text over tradition, and primacy of Scripture, are signaled early in the episode "The Forge" with an exchange between Captain Archer and T'Pol.

Archer's comment, that "with the originals lost, whatever's left is open to interpretation" implies that interpretation is separate from, and inferior to, a reading of the "original text," whose meaning is apparently self-evident. This mirrors Luther's understanding of Scripture, for as Religious Studies and Communications scholar Robert Glenn Howard notes, "For Luther, the Bible has a singular and knowable meaning. Once every potential Christian had the opportunity to experience the Bible and locate this singular meaning for him or herself, the fundamentalist ideology that sees the biblical text as an inerrant conduit of the Holy Spirit became possible" (92). The suggestion that even "original" texts might be open to interpretation did not apparently occur to either Luther or Captain Archer, or to many biblical literalists in our current day. As the story arc unfolds, it becomes clear that only the true text of the teachings of Surak can save the Vulcan people from the forces of darkness. As Archer subsequently tells T'Pol, "There are forces at work on your world right now, trying to undo everything Surak taught your people. If we fail, Vulcan will be consumed by them." It is the word of Surak, as found in the texts, that has the power to save Vulcan, just as Protestants argue that it is the Word of God, as found in the Bible that has saving power. Other religious dimensions, such as Catholic (or Vulcan) ritualism, are powerless to halt the demonic tides.

The Nag Hammadi Kir'Shara?

American anti–Catholic themes are not confined to nineteenth century gothic tales or the writings of early twentieth century intellectuals. Two recent examples of immensely popular fiction that paint the Catholic Church as a "force of darkness" out to destroy spiritual truths are James Redfield's New Age Spirituality classic *The Celestine Prophesy*, and Dan Brown's run-away bestseller *The Da Vinci Code*. Attesting to their popularity, *The Celestine Prophesy* has sold more than twenty million copies, and *The Da Vinci Code* has sold more than sixty million copies worldwide ("The Celestine Prophesy" para. 2, and "The Da Vinci Code" para. 4). Each of these texts belongs within the "conspiracy theory" genre, and draw heavily on the anti–Catholic conviction that individuals duped by the Catholic Church are willing to eradicate anyone or destroy anything that might threaten their religion. According to Religious Studies scholar Philip Jenkins, such novels tap into the long-standing American protestant dream of restoring Christianity to the "true teachings" of "the apostolic age" (para. 14). Discovery of the Nag Hammadi library in 1945, and the subsequent publication of books such as Elaine Pagels' *The Gnostic Gospels*, captured the imagination of the American public, and fed the conviction that "authentic" texts that had been lost for hundreds of years could burst onto the scene and explode the myths of the Catholic Church, to finally reveal the truth of Jesus' teachings.

Enterprise taps into this conspiracy-theory genre with the discovery of the Kir'Shara, a holographic library containing the true writings of Surak. Upon finding the Kir'shara, Archer is convinced that only getting this library of texts to the Vulcan High Command can stop a war and save Vulcan. As the Syrrannite dissident T'Pau states: "The Kir'Shara contains Surak's original writings. It's the only surviving record of his true teachings. It would have an enormous impact on the High Command, and all of Vulcan." Upon hearing about the discovery of the Kir'Shara, however, the leader of the Vulcan High Command, V'Las, is no more willing to accept these documents as authentic than the Pope in an anti–Catholic tome would be willing to accept the "true" teachings of Jesus. Confronted with the knowledge that the Kir'Shara has been found, V'Las at first denies that such a document exists.

In watching the scene, we are reminded of exchanges within *The Celestine Prophesy*, where misguided Church officials seek to suppress the truth of the mysterious Peruvian "manuscript," or sections from *The Da Vinci Code*, where we are told that the Catholic Church has systematically eradicated any suggestion of the "true" nature of Jesus, in order to support its political agenda. In *Enterprise*, this ruthless attempt to stamp out the truth and bolster false faith in support of the political status quo becomes apparent once V'Las's reluctant Vulcan colleague leaves the room and V'Las orders the death of the remaining Syrrannites.

Despite attempts to destroy the religious dissidents and stop the Kir'Shara from being reintroduced to Vulcan society, Captain Archer and his Syrrannite companion T'Pau eventually manage to smuggle the writings of Surak into the headquarters of the Vulcan High Command. They reveal the documents to V'las and the other Vulcans, but V'Las refuses to accept them as genuine.

In their exchange, V'Las's line to T'Pau is perhaps the most telling — "you've spent years trying to subvert me!" — a clear indicator that this Vulcan leader has been exposed to the true teachings of Surak in the past, and has steadfastly closed his mind to the truth. Fortunately, his fellow councilors are not so close-minded. The very existence of the texts is enough to cause them to reconsider a lifetime of false faith. When V'Las attempts to destroy the Kir'Shara to keep its radical truths from the Vulcan populace, a member of his own council renders him unconscious. The war with the Andorians is stopped. Protestantism has saved the day.

The Vulcan Anti-Christ?

If a belief in the inerrancy and singular meaning of sacred texts is the one of the central defining characteristics of Protestantism to be found in *Enterprise*'s Vulcan Reformation story arc, so too is the suggestion that the leader of the Vulcan people can be compared to the anti-Christ. Luther's sixteenth century theological criticism of Catholicism linked the figure of the Pope to the anti-Christ, conceptualized as the exact opposite of everything the true Protestant Christ stood for. In a sixteenth century passional commissioned to illustrate Luther's teachings, for example, the humility of Christ fending off those who would crown him king is contrasted with the anti-Christ, in the figure of the Pope, fending off those who would steal his crown. Images of Christ washing the feet of his followers were juxtaposed against images of the Pope demanding that kings kneel to kiss his feet. Images of Christ driving the moneylenders out of the temple are contrasted with images of the Pope selling indulgences, and so on (Kelly). For Luther, the Pope was the anti-Christ because he embodied the opposite of everything Luther believed Christ stood for.

In *Enterprise*, V'Las's aggressive determination to lead the Vulcan people down the path of interstellar military conquest through deception, oppression, and the suppression of dissent, are contrasted to Surak's calm lamenting that his people have lost their way. Luther's condemnation of the Pope could apply equally well to the actions of the Vulcan High Commander. Having been offered a chance to read the true writings of Surak, V'Las attempts to destroy the Kir'Shara, shouting that the Syrrannites are attempting to subvert him to their heretic creed. Perhaps if one were to ask T'Pau, she might decry, as Luther did of the Pope, that the Vulcan High Commander:

> Cries out that the decrees of the fathers are not to be questioned and decisions made are not to be disputed, otherwise one would have to dance to the tune of every little brother. For this reason the pope, possessed by demons, defends his tyranny with the canon "Si papa." This canon states clearly: if the pope should lead the whole world into the control of hell, he is nevertheless not to be contradicted. It's a terrible thing that on account of the authority of this man we must lose our souls, which Christ redeemed with his precious blood. Christ says, "I will not cast out anybody who comes to me" (John 6:37). On the other hand, the pope says, "As I will it, so I command it; you must perish rather than resist me." Therefore the pope, whom our princes adore, is full of devils. He must be exterminated by the Word and by prayer [Luther, "Table Talk" 330].

The Pope, for Luther, was in league with Satan. *Enterprise*, for all its anti–Catholic parallels, is a predominantly secular show, and Satan, therefore, does not make an appearance. However, *Enterprise* offers the next best thing to account for the evils of the Vulcan High Commander and the decades of obstructionism and duplicity that humans have faced from their Vulcan allies:

V'las is in league, not with devils or Satan, but with Romulans. In the final scenes of the episode "Kir'Shara" (2004), this unholy alliance is made manifest.

As a militaristic, aggressive, politically duplicitous species that fled Vulcan under the winds of change ushered in by Surak's philosophy sixteen hundred years ago, the illicit Romulan alliance suddenly makes sense of years of previously incomprehensible Vulcan policy. The final line, noting eventual reunification, both a promise and a threat, links *Enterprise* to a prominent story arc in the episodes "Unification I and II" (1991) of *Star Trek: The Next Generation*, where the venerable Mr. Spock also attempted to bring about a unification of Vulcans and Romulans. In each case, however, dealing with Romulans turns out to be very much like dealing with the devil.

Gifts of the Spirit—of Surak, That Is

Spirit possession—whether it be possession by the Holy Spirit or possession by demons—is very much a current thread in contemporary evangelical Protestantism. Direct, personal experience of the divine is a hallmark of evangelical Protestant conversion narratives. Controversial American televangelist Oral Roberts, for example, recounts many instances of direct communication with Jesus, including a healing encounter that let him be fully healed of tuberculosis (Harrell 7). Such narratives often situate the communications with Jesus within a call to take up a ministry, to lead people gone astray back to the path of righteousness. According to Oral Roberts, for example, God entered into him and spoke, saying "Son, don't be like other men. Don't be like other preachers.... Be like my son, and bring healing to the people as he did" (Harrell 66).

This call to the ministry via spirit possession is echoed in the Vulcan Reformation story arc. *Enterprise* takes the theme of "possession" by the Holy Spirit and makes it a literal possession of Captain Archer by the spirit of Surak. During the course of their sojourn in the desert in the episode "The Forge" (2004), Captain Archer is given the katra of Surak by the injured leader of the Syrrannite dissidents, via a mind meld. Captain Archer draws upon Surak's memories to lead himself and T'Pol through the desert to the Syrrannite stronghold, where Surak later comes to Archer in a vision. He tells Archer "You don't trust Vulcans, Captain. And, given your experiences with them, I can't say I blame you." When Archer objects that he is not the right man for the job, Surak replies "Open your mind and your heart, and the way will become clear."

Captain Archer is not the first human in the *Star Trek* franchise to have received the katra of a Vulcan—Dr. McCoy receives Spock's Katra in *Star Trek III: The Search for Spock* (1984). Unlike Dr. McCoy, however, who carries Spock's katra unknowingly, Captain Archer is left in no doubt as to the identity of this possessing spirit. Surak comes to Archer in visions, and grants both physical and spiritual gifts. Physically, Archer is able to withstand the heat of the Vulcan sun, apply the Vulcan nerve pinch to enemies, and navigate the tunnels of the Syrrannite complex. Spiritually, he is able to overcome his bitterness towards Vulcans, and find within himself a place of calm previously unknown.

It is the spirit of Surak who moves Archer to find the missing Kir'Shara, the holographic record of his writings lost for sixteen hundred years. Where Vulcans had been searching for the Kir'Shara for over a millennium, and dissident Syrrannites had been searching for it for years, Archer finds it almost immediately, one of many gifts granted by Surak. The coming reformation is therefore no accident — it is Surak's will that the current political regime be overturned, and that a new spiritual path be followed by his people. This path will be the path of reason, logic, and science — a path much more amenable to the scientific worldview of *Star Trek* than the current politically corrupt and morally bankrupt path the Vulcan High Command has been following.

The Liberal Scientific Critique of Catholicism

According to historian John T. McGreevy, one of the most powerful arguments put forward by anti–Catholic intellectuals in the early twentieth century was the argument that Protestantism lent itself to scientific inquiry, while Catholicism limited science. He writes, "Proof that Catholicism hindered science, then, possessed high polemical value. Already by the early 1940s, Horace Kallen viewed Catholics and Nazis as committed to a "spiritual fascism," while "men of science are of a faith more loyal and devout." A *New Republic* writer contrasted a Catholicism prone to censorship of ideas with the "scientific humanism animated by Christian ideals that had become the best by-product of Protestantism." Another analyst offered the view that science depended upon a "moral preference for the dictates of individual conscience rather than for those of organized authority" (McGreevy 117). This suggestion that science and protestant belief go hand in hand meshes seamlessly with *Enterprise*'s treatment of the Vulcan Reformation story arc. The *Star Trek* franchise generally has granted tolerance only to those religions that are in keeping with scientific principles (Peterson 61). Although the dissident Syrrannite religion could very well have been painted as anti-scientific, given its insistence on the existence of and ability to communicate with the souls of dead Vulcans, we are told instead by Surak himself that it is logic and reason that lie at the heart of the faith. Surak tells Archer: "We're paying a heavy price for our foolishness. Logic has not won this day, but this day won't last forever. Logic is at the heart of every Vulcan. Even as the ashes fall, my people are discovering a new way."

The "new way" that the Vulcan people are discovering is the path of logic that integrates Vulcan mysticism with scientific inquiry. Captain Archer attempts to convince his science officer, T'Pol, to give the Syrrannite religion a chance. T'Pol, however, is reluctant, calling the group a "radical faction." Archer, however, persists.

T'Pol's emotional assertion that Syrrannite religion has nothing to do with science reflects her status as an unconverted "Catholic." However, in subsequent episodes we see her studying the Kir'Shara, and undergoing a radical personal and spiritual transformation. As she tells her romantic partner Commander Tucker, "I'm going through something that's very complicated. I'm learning, it seems for the first time, what it truly means to be Vulcan" ("Daedalus" 2005) In a dialogue with the ship's doctor, she speaks to the impact of the Kir'Shara on her sense of self.

T'Pol has served throughout the entire series as the model of the "authentic" Vulcan — the Vulcan closest to those that fans grew to know in the other series in the *Star Trek* franchise. She is a scientist, and now, as a result of the discovery of what Commander Tucker calls "that Bible of yours" ("Daedalus" 2005), she has become a Protestant. With the conversion of T'Pol, she has turned her back on the "backwardness, ignorance and superstition" of the Vulcan (Catholic) hierarchy, and has embraced "material advance, science, and moral improvement" that Protestantism purportedly brings to the righteous (McGreevy 115).

The Moral Supremacy of Dissent

The elevation of a dissident religious group to moral and political supremacy in *Enterprise* is in keeping with the tendency of American pop culture to idealize dissent as an inheritance from the Protestant and Revolutionary heritage of the nation. This elevation of religious dissenters to the moral high ground can be seen as "profoundly anti–Catholic" according to the Catholic League, a Catholic defense organization dedicated to routing anti–Catholic themes in popular culture. In 1997, the Catholic League called for the cancellation of a television series called *Nothing Sacred*, for example, arguing that the show "fed an ugly stereotype: Catholics loyal to the Church were cold-hearted dupes, if not phonies, while those in dissent were enlightened, caring and noble" (Jenkins 163) This image of loyal Catholics as cold-hearted dupes, and those in dissent as enlightened and noble, dominates much of the anti–Catholic literature of the early twentieth century. "Our culture is a Protestant, and not a Catholic, culture," wrote one Harvard professor in the 1930s, "it is a Protestant culture begun in dissent and retaining dissent as its chief characteristic" (Jones 120).

Enterprise continues this tradition of conceptualizing those in dissent as enlightened and those loyal to the religious and political status quo as dupes. The Vulcan Reformation story arc establishes the Syrrannites as religious dissidents early in the episode "The Forge," where T'Pol describes them as "a small group of Vulcans [who] follow a corrupted form of Surak's teachings." The Vulcan High Command blames the Syrrannites for the bombing of the Earth Embassy, and plants evidence implicating them in the crime. The government launches a campaign of suppression aimed at the Syrrannites, rounding them up for arrest and systematically persecuting them for their beliefs. T'Pol's mother is forced to flee, and when T'Pol finds her in hiding with other Syrrannite refuges, she demands to know how her mother could possibly join such a dissident religious group.

The two justifications for her adherence to a dissident religious group state by T'Pol's mother—the listening station at P'Jem, and the suppression of dissent—speak to the cold-hearted corruption of the political and religious status quo. Vulcans working for the High Command have planted false evidence, blown up innocent bystanders, unjustly fired Syrrinites from their jobs, corrupted the sanctuary at P'Jem, attacked the starship Enterprise, and plotted interstellar war. The dissidents, by contrast, are described as pacifists.

This image of the political and religious powers-that-be plotting invasion and war, suppressing dissent, and attacking freedom of conscience echoes Samuel Morse's nineteenth century contrast between Protestantism and Catholicism. As Morse writes, "American Protestantism is of a different school. It needs none of the aids which are indispensable to the crumbling despotisms of Europe; no soldiers, no restrictive enactments, no index expurgatorius, no Inquisition. This war is the war of principles; it is on the open field of free discussion; and the victory is to be won by the exercise of moral energy, by the force of Religious and Political Truth" (66). In *Enterprise*, the majority of the dissident Syrrannites are massacred by the Vulcan High Command, and yet the few who manage to escape hold true to their religious principles, and ultimately manage to defeat the reactionary forces of "crumbling despotisms." It is the dissidents, after all, which had Surak on their side. In keeping with the American tendency to idealize the moral supremacy of dissent, it is the Syrrannites who win the day, and not the combined military/political/religious might of the Vulcan powers that be.

Conclusion: Faith of the Heart

American popular culture has inherited a tradition that elevates individualism, personal experience, reason, democracy, and dissent to the height of the loftiest virtues. It has also inherited a tradition of contrasting these virtues with the perceived vices of Catholicism. As Catholic columnist and editor James Martin writes, "while all religions labor under this postmodern critique, Catholicism has been singled out as a highly visible, seemingly powerful and — therefore — consistently tempting target" (para. 19). The anti–Catholic parallels in *Enterprise* are not aimed at the Catholic Church. They are, instead, directed at the perceived stumbling blocks on the path to *Star Trek*'s utopian future. That these stumbling blocks should accord so closely with accusations made against the Catholic Church by Protestant critics speaks volumes for understanding Roddenberry's utopian vision in Protestant terms. Although Roddenberry attempted to leave behind the influence of his Protestant upbringing, confronting religion time and again in the *Star Trek* series as fraudulent, misguided, and dangerous, the vision he holds up in its stead owes its genesis and nature to the protestant and puritan heritage of the United States.

In the Vulcan story arc, having gotten rid of a corrupt "pope" who was consorting with "demons," having eradicated false teachings based on sixteen hundred years of tradition rather than scripture, having elevated religious dissidents to power, discovered the hidden texts of their founder, having assured that this new faith was in keeping with scientific inquiry rather than reactionary medievalism, and having rescued Surak himself from his tomb in the desert and re-enthroned him in the heart of the Vulcan temple, not only Vulcans but humans are situated to benefit from this Protestant-like reformation. The closing scenes of the episode "Kir'Shara" make this clear.

The City upon a Hill is now ready to be built, on a foundation of ideals drawn from America's puritan heritage. As Luther writes, "That now, I say, upon which you set your heart and put your trust is properly your god" ("Large Catechism," 565). *Enterprise* sets the hearts and minds of *Star Trek* fans firmly on the goals of Roddenberry's Federation. Who knew he was out to make Protestants of us all?

Works Cited

Bond, Jeff. "Star Trek Composer Alexander Courage Dead at 88." Trekmovie.com. 1 October 2008. <http://trekmovie.com/2008/05/28/star-trek-composer-alexander-courage-dead-at-88/>.
Brown, Dan. *The Da Vinci Code*. New York: Doubleday, 2003.
"The Celestine Prophecy." Wikipedia. 12 October 2008, 23:03 UTC. 30 Octpber 2008 <http://en.wikipedia.org/w/index.php?title=The_Celestine_Prophecy&oldid=244867382>.
"The Da Vinci Code." Wikipedia. 29 October 2008, 10:36 UTC. 30 October 2008 <http://en.wikipedia.org/w/index.php?title=The_Da_Vinci_Code&oldid=248379945>.
"*Enterprise* Cast, Producers Answer Questions, Part I." Startrek.com. 26 January 2008. <http://www.startrek.com/startrek/view/series/ENT/news/article/356.html>.
Geraghty, Lincoln. "'For We Must Consider That We Shall Be as a City Upon a Hill, the Eyes of All People Are Upon Us': The American Jeremiad and *Star Trek*'s Puritan Legacy." *Living with Star Trek: American Culture and the* Star Trek *Universe*. Ed. Lincoln Geraghty. London/New York: I.B. Tauris, 2007, 68–85.
Hark, Ina Rae. "Franchise Fatigue? The Marginalization of the Television Series after The Next Generation." In *The Influence of* Star Trek *on Television, Film and Culture*. Ed. Lincoln Geraghty. Jefferson, NC: McFarland, 2008, 41–59.
Harrell, David Edwin, Jr. *Oral Roberts: An American Life*. Bloomington: Indiana University Press, 1985.
Howard, Robert Glenn. "The Double Bind of the Protestant Reformation: The Birth of Fun-

damentalism and the Necessity of Pluralism." *Journal of Church and State* 47(1) January 2005, 91–108.

Jenkins, Philip. "Hidden Gospels." *The Bible and Interpretation*. 1 October 2008. <http://www.bibleinterp.com/articles/hiddengospel.htm>.

Jones, Howard Mumford. "The Drift to Liberalism in the American Eighteenth Century." *Ideas in America*. New York: Russell and Russell, 1965.

Kelly, Annemarie Flynn. "Reformation Visual Aids." *Catholic Answers*. This Rock February 1996. 27 September 2008. < http://www.catholic.com/thisrock/1996/9602feal.asp>.

Luther, Martin. "Against the Roman Papacy, an Institution of the Devil." *Luther's Works: Church and Ministry III*. Vol. 41. Eds Helmut T. Lehman and Eric W. Gritsch. Minneapolis, MN: Augsburg Fortress, 1966.

_____. *Large Catechism*. 1.1–3. Trans F. Bente and W.H.T. Dau. *Triglot Concordia: The Symbolical Books of the Evangelical Lutheran Church*. St. Louis: Concordia, 1921.

_____. "Lectures on Galatians." *Luther's Works*, Vol. 26. Trans Jaroslav Pelikan. St. Louis: Concordia, 1963.

_____. *Luther's Works: Table Talk* 54 No. 441. Eds Theodore G. Tappert and Helmut T. Lehmann. Minneapolis, MN: Augsburg Fortress, 1967.

Maher, Ian. "The Outward Journey and the Inward Search: *Star Trek* Motion Pictures and the Spiritual Quest." In *Star Trek and Sacred Ground: Explorations of Star Trek, Religion and American Culture*. Ed. Jennifer E. Porter and Darcee L. McLaren. Albany: State University of New York Press, 1999, 165–191.

Mannard, Joseph G. "American Anti-Catholicism and its Literature." *Ex Libris* 4 (1) (1981), 1–9. 16 December 2007. <http://www.geocities.com/chiniquy/Literature.html>.

Martin, James. "The Last Acceptable Prejudice." *America: The National Catholic Weekly*, 25 March 2000. 25 September 2008. <http://www.americamagazine.org/content/article.cfm?article_id=606>.

McGreevy, John T. "Thinking on One's Own: Catholicism in the American Intellectual Imagination, 1928–1960." *The Journal of American History* June 1997: 97–131.

Monk, Maria. *Awful Disclosures of the Hotel Dieu Nunnery*. New York: De Witt & Davenport, 1855. Many books.net. 12 September 2007. <http://manybooks.net/titles/monkmarietext058adis10.html>.

Morse, Samuel. *Foreign Conspiracy Against the Liberties of the United States*. The New York Observer, 1835. Google Book Search. 17 December 2007. <http://books.google.com/books?id=J-LChYFcUf8C&printsec=frontcover&dq=samuel+morse+foreign+conspiracy&ei=6fjnSK_RNoy4yAS3kZ2JAQ>.

Pagels, Elaine. *The Gnostic Gospels*. New York: Random House, 1989.

Pearson, Anne MacKenzie. "From Thwarted Gods to Reclaimed Mystery? An Overview of the Depiction of Religion in *Star Trek*." In Star Trek *and Sacred Ground: Explorations of Star Trek, Religion and American Culture*. Ed. Jennifer E. Porter and Darcee L. McLaren. Albany: State University of New York Press, 1999, 13–32.

Peterson, Gregory. "Religion and Science in Star Trek: The Next Generation: God, Q, and Evolutionary Eschatology on the Final Frontier." In Star Trek *and Sacred Ground: Explorations of Star Trek, Religion and American Culture*. Ed. Jennifer E. Porter and Darcee L. McLaren. Albany: State University of New York Press, 61–76.

Redfield, James. *The Celestine Prophesy: An Adventure*. New York: Time Warner, 1993.

"Star Trek: Enterprise." Economic Expert.com. 26 September 2008. <http://www.economicexpert.com/2a/Star:Trek:Enterprise.html>.

"Star Trek: Enterprise." Wikipedia. 22 October 2008, 07:42 UTC. 24 October 2008. <http://en.wikipedia.org/w/index.php?title=Star_Trek:_Enterprise&oldid=246453815>.

"Star Trek: First Contact." Wikipedia. 1 November 2008, 00:24 UTC. 1 November 2008. <http://en.wikipedia.org/w/index.php?title=Star_Trek:_First_Contact&oldid=24891589>.

True Edge. "Why Did *Star Trek: Enterprise* Fail? An In-Depth Look at the Latest *Star Trek* Franchise and Its Shortcomings." Associated Content. 26 January 2008. <http://www.as

sociatedcontent.com/article/542969/why_did_star_trek_enterprise_fail.html?page=2&cat=39>.
"Where My Heart Will Take Me." Memory Alpha. 1 October 2008. <http://memory-alpha.org/en/wiki/Where_My_Heart_Will_Take_Me>.

Star Trek Media Cited

Star Trek *Films*

Star Trek III: The Search for Spock. Dir. Leonard Nimoy. Screenplay Harve Bennett. Paramount Pictures, 1984.
Star Trek: First Contact. Dir. Jonathan Frakes. Screenplay Brannon Braga and Ronald D. Moore. Paramount Pictures, 1996.

Star Trek: The Original Series

"Amok Time." Written by Theodore Sturgeon. 15 September 1967
"Bread and Circuses." Written by Gene Roddenberry and Gene L. Coon. 15 March 1968.
"City on the Edge of Forever." Written by Harlan Ellison. 6 April 1967.

Star Trek: The Next Generation

"Unification, I." Story by Rick Berman and Michael Piller. Teleplay by Jeri Taylor. 4 November 1991.
"Unification, II." Story by Rick Berman and Michael Piller. Teleplay by Michael Piller. 11 November 1991.

Star Trek: Enterprise

"The Andorian Incident." Story by Rick Berman, Brannon Braga and Fred Dekker. Teleplay by Fred Dekker. 31 October 2001.
"Awakening." Written by André Bormanis. 26 November 2004.
"Broken Bow." Written by Brannon Braga and Rick Berman. 26 September 2001.
"Daedalus." Written by Ken LaZebnik and Michael Bryant. 14 January 2005.
"The Forge." Written By Judith Reeves-Stevens and Garfield Reeves-Stevens. 19 November 2004.
"Kir'Shara." Written by Mike Sussman. 3 December 2004.

12

A Vision of a Time and Place

Spiritual Humanism and the Utopian Impulse

BRUCE ISAACS

In the Beginning: A Mainstream Utopian Impulse

> I've been sure from the first that the job of "Star Trek" was to use drama and adventure as a way of portraying humanity in its various guises and beliefs.
> — Gene Roddenberry, creator of Star Trek (Alexander 10)

Much has been made of *Star Trek* since its appearance on American network television in 1966. In the main, commentators have considered its proximity to key historical and political events in recent American history: the Vietnam War, the rise of Feminism, the Civil Rights movement, the contemporaneous development of a Cold War mentality that relied on an essentialist "us-and-them" attitude to the Other. From the beginnings of *Star Trek*, the series offered a vehicle for cultural, social, political, and in its most ambitious incarnation, philosophical engagement. In Gene Roddenberry's words, "Star Trek [was] more than just my political philosophy. It [was] my social philosophy, my racial philosophy, my overview on life and the human condition" (Alexander 14). Roddenberry, later in life to assume the mantle of a bona fide philosopher (Alexander 17), was waxing philosophical from the outset.

Like another grand narrative set in outer space, *Star Wars*, the *Star Trek: The Original Series* (*TOS*) *mythos* fashions a very useful barometer of an American "time," perhaps more than any other TV show of the 1960s. The project to detail a historical time and place is intrinsic to the genre of mainstream American speculative science fiction, and in particular within utopian impulses in speculative fiction. The best of the utopian writing of Ursula Le Guin, which can be distinguished as "critical utopia," is remarkable for the complex rendering of another time and place, but perhaps more significantly, for the depiction of the subtle relationship between a foreign world and the world inhabited by the writer. In *The Dispossessed,* Le Guin's achievement is to challenge the reader with a set of (critical) utopias that offer a fascinatingly vivid expression of anarchist and late capitalist ideology respectively. Without the recognizable "here and now" of a contemporary 1970s America, the novel would be far less interesting as an example utopian literature.

Star Trek's mainstream political gauge obviously reflects also on the (political) science fiction of films such as *The Thing (from Another World)* (1951), Robert Wise's hugely influential take on the escalation of Cold War antagonisms in *The Day the Earth Stood Still* (1951) and Don Siegel's *Invasion of the Body Snatchers* (1956). These films, and episodes of *TOS* (in particular, "A Taste of Armageddon," "The Return of the Archons" (which in broadly thematic terms bears some resemblance to *Invasion of the Body Snatchers*) and "City on the Edge of Forever") reflect an American popular consciousness coming to terms with a historical time and place. These science fiction dramas are context-based, historical and ideologically motivated. From a vantage point forty years in the future, the specific historical and political dramas of *Star Trek* indeed seem a thing of their time.

More recent entries in the *Star Trek* canon — *The Next Generation, Deep Space Nine, Voyager* and *Enterprise* — have increasingly turned to new notions of political and social identity. The worlds depicted in the late 1980s, 1990s and 2000s at least in principle reflect the willingness to engage in dialogue, to express tolerance in the face of cultural and ethnic diversity, and to rework old ideas in new ways. *The Next Generation (TNG)* offers an intriguing reinterpretation of the Prime Directive, to continue to "boldly go where no man has gone before," but to respect the autonomy of other people and cultures; in this sense, *TNG* provides a degree of subjectivity, or authenticity, of the Other that is obviously lacking in the original series (Galdieri 67). We see such an evolution in thinking writ large on one of the best installments in the canon, *Star Trek VI: The Undiscovered Country* (this is, notably, the moment in which "to boldly go where no man has gone before" becomes "to boldly go where no-*one* has gone before," updating the patriarchal bias inherent in the first utterance). In *Star Trek VI,* the *Enterprise,* helmed again by Kirk, must establish that the villain is attempting to obstruct a peace process between the Federation and the Klingons. The conclusion looks forward to a universe that recognizes the differences between species and the very real necessity of establishing a dialogue with the Other, whether human or alien.

In spite of Roddenberry's death in 1991, the *Star Trek mythos* continues to delve into contemporary aspects of the human condition. Kapell, appearing in this volume, reads the representation of the Holocaust in *Deep Space Nine* (*DS9*), arguing that "while the creators, producers, and writers of the series are to be commended for attempting to use their narrative to examine such a bleak and monumental tragedy, their narrative, by virtue of its unique American status, was simply not quite up to the task" (75). This is a fair assessment. *DS9* continues the legacy of speculative science fiction that has been central to *Star Trek*, and without which the show would be merely escapist entertainment. Kapell criticizes the *mode* of representation, distilled as it is from a uniquely American perception of the Holocaust, but the representation itself, the engagement with the "monumental tragedy" of the Holocaust, cannot be denied. Assessment of the *Star Trek* television series (concluding for the time being with *Star Trek: Enterprise*) continues to distinguish it from mainstream television based on its willingness to engage in ideas that are at the forefront of social and political life.

There is thus a context in which the *Star Trek mythos* can be said to be radical merely in the fact that it exists to be re-viewed and recontextualized for new generations of audiences. But it is especially radical, and perhaps even revolutionary, when put alongside mainstream American television in the mid–1960s. Perhaps in the mid–1960s, it was enough merely to interrogate the status quo in a mainstream commercial art form. *TOS* certainly did this. If most television shows were advocating an ideological "right" from "wrong," at least *TOS* was willing to engage dialectically with issues of race, gender and sexuality, national and foreign policy, notions of Self and Other.

In spite of its location of an apparently alternative racial and gender politics in a far-off future, the fact remains that when viewers tuned in to watch the voyages of the Starship *Enterprise*, they were seeing a multicultural cast in a prime-time viewing slot; they were seeing women in positions of authority (alongside the obviously sexist subtext in the original series); they were seeing a negotiation of issues central to American identity that up until the first series of *Star Trek* had received virtually no attention on mainstream television. A black female officer, Uhura, is a remarkable inclusion in an era in which the Civil Rights movement was hardly dinner conversation. Uhura also spoke to the progress made in the new wave of Feminist action that would, to some extent, influence the feminist utopian writing of the 1970s. In Season Two of *TOS*, Pavel Chekhov, a Russian Starfleet Officer and navigator on board the *Enterprise*, is a courageous inclusion in the cast of characters. Chekhov's centrality to the narrative of *Star Trek*, particularly in the feature films between 1979's *Star Trek: The Motion Picture* and 1991's *Star Trek: The Undiscovered Country*, testifies to the show's continued endeavor to challenge existing political and social ideologies. The message of tolerance in the Prime Directive and the Vulcan ethos ("infinite diversity in infinite combinations") is little short of startling in the context of 1960s mainstream American culture.

Star Trek seemed to advocate a respect for all cultures, nationalities and ethnicities in the midst of an America waging war in Vietnam, or in the mid-to-late 1980s, dealing with a reconstructed relationship with the Soviet Union. In this respect, it was indeed a radical enterprise.

Gene Roddenberry: A Humanistic Enterprise

> *It was very clear that the humanists were right. Humanism was right. I've known that for some years.*
> — Gene Roddenberry (Alexander 29)
>
> *It was a hell of a thing when Spock died.*
> — George Costanza, Seinfeld: Season 8, Ep. 135.

His fiancé recently deceased, George Costanza (Jason Alexander) grieves not for Susan, but for Mr. Spock, a fictional character inhabiting the *Star Trek* universe. Spock has died so that others can live, a very Christian thing to do, and George reflects on the importance of this narrative resolution to the absurdity of death in life: "how we deal with death is at least as important as how we deal with life," suggests Kirk in *Star Trek II: The Wrath of Kahn*. With the (admittedly self-periodic) quotation in *Seinfeld*, it is clear that in popular culture circles (among which I include myself as a member) a veritable universe of meaning has been created. Spock's death functions as metanarrative, as a textual quotation, and it is in this sense what Kreitzer calls a "cultural veneer"; a measure of the times.

An intriguing aspect of the textual universe surrounding *Star Trek*, a universe that has evolved over five series, more than ten feature films and a plethora of extra-textual merchandise is, as Atkins argues, the apparent uniformity of its vision (93). More than forty years later, the philosophical foundations of the *Star Trek* canon remain intact. While ideology is, to some extent, refashioned to meet the context of new eras and new political sensibilities, the grand narrative of social and individual progress toward harmony continues to resonate. It is this vision that renders *Star Trek*'s moral and political outlook imminently recognizable to a mainstream (American) audience and it is why, in 2009, *Star Trek* released its next installment in a series of feature films, dealing again with contemporary social and political ideologies, notably the moral and political consequences of genocide. From 1966 to 1969, Kirk and Spock played through, among other things, veiled allegories of the Vietnam War ("A Private Little War") and Cold War antagonisms between America and the Soviet Union ("Errand of Mercy").

The resilience of this single vision, in spite of the collaborative nature of network television production, has much to do with *Star Trek*'s progenitor, Gene Roddenberry. Roddenberry not only created and produced the show but, in its first three seasons, reworked scripts, constructed storylines, and actively helmed its ideological content. He produced a "*Star Trek Guide*, in which he clearly delineated for writers and directors the major premises of the series" (Atkins 93). Roddenberry regulated, to a significant degree, the show's content, impressing upon mainstream American viewers his ideals, moral perspective and abiding interests in the cultural moment. If there is a distinct voice that finds utterance through Kirk's impassioned humanism or Spock's flights of rationality, in *TOS* it is no doubt the voice of Roddenberry.

Examining the nature of this voice, the philosophical foundation of Roddenberry's thinking, is instructive in formulating a "grand narrative," to employ Lyotard's phrase, of the *Star Trek mythos*. My use of Lyotard's reading of the postmodern condition is pointed in this case. Lyotard argues essentially that the grand narratives of Western civilization are outmoded in an age of postmodernity. Postmodernity renders all narratives of progress, utopianism in essence, meaningless. The grand mystical narratives (primarily religion-based) and the rational narratives (Plato's "Theory of Forms" functions as an original expression, but Lyotard focuses primarily on Enlightenment epistemology) have little to offer the postmodern subject; truth has little veracity if history is in a state of constant flux.

And yet in the age of the postmodern condition (the symptoms of which surely stem back as far as the 1960s, if one considers the post-structuralist writings of Barthes or Derrida), in 1966, Roddenberry's epistemological and ethical universe resonated with his mainstream American audience. It continued to resonate in *Star Trek: The Next Generation* (1987–1994), *Star Trek: Deep Space Nine* (1993–1999), *Star Trek: Voyager* (1995–2001) and *Star Trek: Enterprise* (2001–2005), speaking to essential values of self, nation and the unfailing belief in progress. If postmodernity eschewed grand narratives, *Star Trek*, in its overtly utopian voyages, attempted to recuperate the boldest of them all: a faith in an essential *human* being.

This belief system was in no way arbitrarily chosen. In a lengthy interview with *The Humanist* in 1991, Roddenberry expounds on the core philosophy of *Star Trek*. In his description of the *Star Trek* canon as a lead-in to the interview, David Alexander suggests that "*Star Trek* and its successor *Star: The Next Generation*, are solidly based upon humanistic principles and ideas ... the basic message of both *Star Trek* and *The Next Generation* is that human beings are capable of solving their own problems rationally and that, through critical thinking and cooperative effort, humanity will progress and evolve" (Alexander 5). Alexander is correct to stress the essential state of the humanistic self in *progress* toward a new self and society, based on an evolutionary process. It is also significant that he sees Roddenberry's humanism as the philosophical basis of the entire *Star Trek* canon. As such, Alexander acknowledges Roddenberry's vision as central to the development of the philosophical universe of *Star Trek*, from 1966 to 1991, the year the interview was conducted.

Barrett and Barrett recognize that "in *Star Trek* the issue is to humanize as many people as possible. Kirk's insistence at the funeral of his half–Vulcan friend Spock that 'of all the souls I have encountered in my travels, his was the most human' is merely the first in a long line of invitations to alien species to define themselves within the human family" (62). Thus, cultural tolerance, political diversity and ideological difference are expressed *within* a foundational humanistic philosophy. The Human stands in for a "universal (in the literal and figurative spatial sense) subject" and that species of life which resists assimilation to the human form is constituted as Other. Spock's evolution in *TOS* and six feature films is not to achieve the status of a true Vulcan, but to evolve to a point of "wisdom" in which the human half wins out over the (alien) Other. While remaining half–Vulcan, the Vulcan part of the self assimilates to a human imperative to appreciate, among other things, the limits of rational thought. In *Star Trek VI: The Undiscovered Country,* Spock, sounding a lot like Kirk, declares, "logic is the beginning of wisdom, not the end." His character arc in the *Star Trek* canon is thus not only to learn what it is to be human, but to *become* human, a utopian process that resonates within the *Star Trek mythos*. For Roddenberry, humanism offers not only a "message," but in utopian narrative form, the promise to effect an evolutionary change in the alien from Other to assimilated human.

The point I will continue to argue in this essay is that Roddenberry's "human," while superficially inclusive of other species, to a significant degree *excludes* the Other, and opposes more radical alternatives to a humanistic self. I do not dispute that Roddenberry attempted to intervene in the political and ideological practices of what he considered a conservative, deeply flawed society. In response to a question asked about why he almost left television, he replies, "Censorship! Because of the fact that writers and producers are more or less expected, on network television, to perpetuate all the modern myths: the male is vigorous, battle is the true test of a man ... and stereotypes about women and men" (Alexander 10–11). Clearly, Roddenberry attempted to undermine these myths of American identity in the mid–1960s. But what is most intriguing to me, in revisiting *TOS* in preparation for this piece, is the extent to which Roddenberry's humanist philosophy is manifested as an absolutist doctrine in spite of the apparent radicalism of its tolerance of difference. This tension is at play throughout the *Star Trek* canon. In *TOS*, the *Enterprise* "boldly goes where no man has gone before," but under strict guidance of the Prime Directive must respect the difference of other worlds and other species. In "A Taste of Armageddon," however, when Kirk is confronted by a society that wages war perpetually to maintain a veneer of culture, the Prime Directive is put aside — in this instance, Kirk's (and Roddenberry's) humanism triumphs over the sanitized war of Emeniar. A similar fate meets the inhabitants of an artificial utopia in "This Side of Paradise." Kirk, impervious to the seductions of "perfection" reconditions the colonists to appreciate the fallibility of their humanity, which is to say the humanistic essence of their selves. Intriguingly, it is at the end of this episode that Spock laments the fact that, for the briefest moment, he felt "happy," knowing the essence of the human self untainted by his Vulcan rationalism.

It is, paradoxically, Roddenberry's humanism, a modern philosophical discourse, that accounts for a philosophical trajectory that is conservative in spite of its façade of radical political and social ideology. Roddenberry's humanism is a foundation to a traditional mode of American utopian thought that emphasizes the imaginary over the real, and anchors its futuristic vision in a distant *past* rather an attainable future founded upon the established context of a real world. This is essentially the distinction between what I will call the "spiritual utopia" of *Star Trek* and the "critical utopia" of Le Guin in *The Dispossessed*. Underscoring Le Guin's utopian vision is an inherent critique of the possibility of utopia, of the resolution of difference in sameness. But Roddenberry's humanism is nearer to Kirk's faith in the "human condition" than Spock's rational Vulcan mind. Kirk's comment to Spock that "everyone's a little human" establishes the essence of the self as Kirk's human rather than Spock's half Vulcan-half human, or some such expression of a Self-Other symbiosis. In spite of Roddenberry's disavowal of religion in all its manifestations, and his increasingly anti-religious stance in *The Next Generation*, his humanism is in fact a kind of *spiritual*, faith-based philosophy.

Utopia and Difference: The Quest for Political Change

> *[Utopia is] the dream of a just society which seems to haunt the human imagination ineradicably and in all ages.*
> — George Orwell, "Arthur Koestler" (274)

> *Utopia was always an ambiguous ideal, urging some on to desperate and impossible realizations about which it reassured the others that they could never come into being in the first place: so it whipped the passionate and dogmatic into a frenzy while plunging the liberal lukewarm into an immobilizing intellectual comfort.*
> — Frederic Jameson, "Utopianism and Anti-Utopianism" (382)

Utopian thinking is problematic, even for utopian theorists, among whom Jameson is perhaps pre-eminent. Utopian thinking is fraught with inconsistency: while it expresses a vision of a better life and a more just society, it must simultaneously offer the mechanisms of social and political change by which that vision can be made real. The vision of classical utopia is, according to Orwell, a "dream" that is fundamental to the human mind. As a dream, it is essentialist, ahistorical and permanent. But it is not enough for utopia to *show* us a better world; it has to provide the detail of a method of getting there. This duality is inscribed in the word itself: "Utopia is nowhere (*outopia*) and it is also *somewhere* good (*eutopia*). To live in a world that cannot be but where one fervently wishes to be: that is the literal essence of utopia" (Kumar 1).

This is just where utopian thinking is most vulnerable. Projecting a vision of a possible future often precludes the possibility of elucidating a method of getting there. Focusing on an endpoint, the historical aspect of the process is lost. Utopias, from Plato's *Republic* to Thomas More's *Utopia* and most written since are more abstract than concrete in describing alternative societies. Rather, such models are based on a particular mode of thinking; they offer a meditation on what might be rather than a detailed manual on how to effect the change needed to get there. Even Aristotle was critical of Plato's *Republic* in its lack of specificity. More's *Utopia*, like Swift's *Gulliver's Travels*, works successfully as a commentary on the society of the writer. But it also works as *fantasy*; the utopian narrative projects a vision of a society into a distant place that is deliberately cast as fantastical. Gulliver's travels are a journey to another time and place (an aspect of the utopian narrative form) *and* a dream of that journey.

The question posed by this inherent duality is one of agency. How does utopia maintain its imperative to bring about social and political change? If the possibility for change is anchored in a vision in which that change has *already occurred*, how do citizens of a contemporary society effect change to bring about a better and more just society? Much of utopian social and political theory (and indeed modes of utopian representation in literature and film) has been accused of a lack of specificity. Utopia is obviously on one level an abstraction from reality. It must generalize — political theories and social ideologies find their expression in metonymic form. This is also part of utopia's appeal. The fantasy of a better world is what Orwell sees as a fundamental part of human nature; "to deny that would be to miss one of the most powerful sources of its appeal" (Kumar 1).

However, Linda Hutcheon has correctly accused utopian theorists, including Jameson, of failing to adequately address this inconsistency inherent in utopian thinking. She accuses utopian political models of practicing a form of "nostalgia" that, essentially, reflects on what has been lost rather than what can be gained (4). The future is seen in the terms of an outmoded form of social and political organization. An example of such a nostalgized utopianism is evident in a film like *Gattaca*. Ostensibly a dystopic narrative, the hero, rather than subverting the system and forming a mechanism of resistance (and thus of social and political change grounded in a historicized present), assimilates into the dystopic system, projecting his vision literally "into the stars." One could also suggest that the hero's journey could be read as a returning into the womb, the point of origin of the utopian Self.

But where is the account of the *process* of establishing a utopia? Where is the description of how a utopia comes into being? This is, and certainly was for critical utopians, a pressing question. Moylan argues that utopianism, falling upon hard times as a literary mode, reinvented itself in the late 1960s and 1970s: "a central concern in the critical utopia is the awareness of the limitations of the utopian tradition, so that these texts (Moylan notes the work of Le Guin and Samuel Delany as exemplary) reject utopia as blueprint while preserving it as a dream" (10). Essential to the critical utopia was the formation of a blueprint for political change. In *The Dispossessed*, which I would argue is exemplary of the best of the modern utopian tradition, Le Guin casts an imagined world in which utopia and dystopia converge in the form of critical utopia. Her protagonist is Shevek, native inhabitant of the planet moon Annares. The two inhabited worlds of Urras and Anarres, and their divergent political and social histories, offer a way for Le Guin to engage in the political realities of her contemporary American society. Most striking is Le Guin's approach to the form of utopia, and to the utopia as a literary form. Utopia in *The Dispossessed* is problematic — but, Le Guin argues, so it should be. Visions of progress should be fraught with inconsistencies, pluralist rather than singular trajectories, perspectivist rather than linear. The novel thus functions as critique (of a political imaginary and literary mode) as well as social and ideological description. Shevek's repeated attempts to resist orthodoxy and bring about change in Annares occur at the level of community: his daily trials to speak his mind or engage with bureaucracy speak of similar problems in the organization of communities in America in the 1970s. However, in a classical utopian narrative such as *Star Trek*, which I would contrast with Le Guin's critical utopia, utopia on board the *Enterprise*, or in the universe of space, exists in an ahistorical state of perpetuity. For Kirk (and Roddenberry) it is enough simply to be "human"—*contextualizing* the human is another matter entirely.

I argue that the classical utopian narrative, distinguishable from the critical utopian narrative, is founded upon a recuperation of a Self/Other dichotomy. The self is either manifested external to the utopian society (the traveler to other worlds) or as the subject of a utopian society (in which the contemporary society of the writer is cast as Other). The Self is never cast *as* Other. The critical utopian narrative — again I fall back on Le Guin's *The Dispossessed*— deliberately conflates Self and Other, and in the process problematizes the dichotomy. Shevek is at once Self and Other, and as such is a site of difference. Shevek's status as "alien" can be contrasted with Kirk's status as (native) human. Perhaps more significantly, the most authentic alien on board the *Enterprise*, Spock, attains a final authenticity only as a human. It is Le Guin, rather than Roddenberry, who maintains the ambivalence toward the utopian vision, and indeed, to the utopian narrative as a political form of expression.

Star Trek: *A Classical Utopia*

Star Trek manifests itself as a classical utopian narrative in two distinct ways. Utopia exists on board the *Enterprise*, in which the Starship's crew offers a new multiculturalism of a United Federation of Planets, free of the prejudices of race and sexuality, or the religious mysticism emblematic of unenlightened societies. Religious and mystical practices are secondary to the rational imperative within the humanist philosophical doctrine. This is what I would describe as a political utopia. But the *Enterprise* also represents, as several commentators have observed, a technological utopia. Unlike the more fashionable dystopic representations of technology during the 1980s (*Blade Runner* and *The Terminator* come to mind), technology in *Star Trek* is part of the progress toward the perfection of the human. Phasers, communicators, teleporters, and even Bone's miraculous medical kit are tools for personal and social improvement. In *Star Trek III: The Search for Spock,* the Starship *Enterprise* attains a mythic status in which technology and the human (in this case, Kirk) are reunited to complete the quest. Though possibly read also as phallic, the *Enterprise* is often feminized, as in Kirk's instruction to "take her out." In this case, the symbiosis of Starship and Kirk is even more obvious.

The second mode of utopia in *Star Trek* occurs literally *outside* the *Enterprise*. These are the destinations of the voyages of the Starship. Utopia, in one sense, is literally to journey from a point of origin. Utopian narratives are often characterized by a traveler leaving his or her society to discover other worlds. This applies to Raphael in More's *Utopia*, Gulliver in Swift's *Gulliver's Travels* and Shevek in Le Guin's *The Dispossessed*. In *Star Trek: The Original Series,* Kirk encounters the subjects of several utopias: the Emenians in "A Taste of Armageddon," the colonists in "This Side of Paradise," the Organians in "Errand of Mercy." The voyages of the *Enterprise* literally "seek out new worlds."

Star Trek's utopian impulse is, as I've argued, distinctly humanist. The utopian vision is located at an imaginary point within the human subject, whether functioning on board the *Enterprise* or on an alien planet. I contend that both modes of utopia occurring in *Star Trek* emphasize the dream aspect of the utopian vision rather than the imperative for social and political agency. *Star Trek's* utopian vision is, paradoxically, *reflective*, much like *Gattaca's* utopian (in the mist of a dystopic world) vision of a future that reverts to a point of origin of the Self. Kirk's declaration that "everyone's a little human" is to formulate the founding principle of humanism: that all species (human and alien, Self and Other) are conjoined in a point of common origin. Rather than projecting the Self *as* Other, Kirk recuperates the distinction, and in the process assimilates the Other into the social and political ideology of the Self.

"The City on the Edge of Forever": A Static History

In what is widely considered the best episode in *TOS*, Kirk and Spock confront an ancient time portal, personified as a quasi–God figure: recording the process of history, the portal is an omniscient presence. When Bones leaps through the portal, entering an earlier moment in Earth's history, the *Enterprise* vanishes from its orbit. Bones's intervention in the past has erased the *Enterprise* from existence and reconfigured history. The central conflict of the episode then concerns a choice that must be made: to alter history or ensure that it proceeds *as it was always meant to*.

"The City on the Edge of Forever," firmly entrenched in the classical utopian narrative form, inscribes a metaphorical reading of history as linear and unchangeable. The portal presents history as a stream of film images; the crew of the *Enterprise* are able to watch history occurring. The historical turning point, the point of reconfiguration, is Edith Keeler, who in the original version of history is run over while crossing a street. Bones, appearing on the scene, prevents her death, leading to the alteration in a linear history. Keeler, it is learned, will lead a pacifist movement in the United States, influencing the American military establishment to delay entry into the Second World War. This delay enables the Germans to develop the atomic bomb before Oppenheimer succeeds in Los Alamos. If Keeler is allowed to die, as "history" intended, Truman will bring the war to a fruitful end, leading to the promulgation of the democratic ideals of the United States. Kirk chooses to restore history to its original linear trajectory, collapsing the alternative history and returning to the utopian future of the twenty-fourth century in which a United Federation of Planets has continued to foster the American democratic ideal throughout the universe.

The central conflict in "The City on the Edge of Forever" is perhaps the clearest expression of the classical utopian impulse in *Star Trek*. In constructing (American) history as linear, the episode prohibits a reading of history that runs alternate to the orthodoxy. History is utopian in its essential progress from a point of mythic origin to the utopian future of the Federated universe. The promulgation of Keeler's pacifist politics will not only lead to defeat in the Second World War but will evolve into a swelling pacifist movement that can potentially oppose the military establishment of the democratic ideal. While Spock acknowledges that Keeler's pacifism is in some sense "right," he suggests that it was simply not propitious in 1941, when America was considering intervening in the Second World War. Here history is accorded the status of *always already* existing and establishing in the evidence of its existence a "correct" interpretation. What was meant to unfold in the passage of time was in essence *right*. An unchangeable history is equated with a utopian belief in the natural, preordained progress of the humanist self and society.

Regardless of Roddenberry's position on Vietnam, the narrative conflict central to "The City of the Edge of Forever" contrives a uniquely American utopian perspective of history. Surely the rejection of pacifism in a key historical moment reverberates in the context of America's involvement in Vietnam in 1966. While not advocating intervention, the episode reads pacifism as subject to a context that is never elucidated. If, as Spock suggests, pacifism is "right," "The City on the Edge of Forever" avoids elaborating on when or where this might be. All that the screened history tells us is that, at the moment of a possible *re-reading* of an American historical moment, pacifism was wrong. If, through Spock, Roddenberry is implying that pacifism was wrong for 1941 but is now right for 1966, and that America should not involve itself in the Vietnam War, this position is never articulated. The portal merely declares: "time has resumed its shape. Everything is as it was before." The history of America's intervention in the Second World War and its democratic ideal is again accurate.

A linear reading of history eschews alternatives to that reading, or indeed, the possibility of such alternatives existing. This is essentially the challenge Hutcheon levels at utopian theorists: that the utopian dream casts a version of history that cannot be re-interpreted or dialectically challenged. The classical utopian vision is thus to offer a historical reading of the present from a single point of view of the Self that marginalizes the voice of the Other. The Self here is the infallible *human*, the spiritual centre of Roddenberry's epistemological universe.

Returning to Utopia

> *Longing on a large scale is what makes history.*
> — *Don DeLillo*, Underworld *(11)*

The *X-Files* brought postmodernism to prime time America. If its "truth" was out there, neither Mulder nor Scully were ever going to find it. That show's creator, Chris Carter, became increasingly interested in dissembling truth into so many smoke-filled conspiracy theories. Frost was prescient in recognizing America's disinterest in Lyotard's grand narratives. In 1991, America seemed less interested in negotiating a social and political truth than seeing a gargantuan construction of a lie.

Star Trek's utopian narratives appear to have little to do with the postmodern consciousness. If postmodernity de-centered the human subject, essentially displacing the self to the status of Other, *Star Trek* relocated the self at the centre of the universe. I have argued that Roddenberry's humanism was nearer to a kind of spirituality, an essence of self that was uncontaminated by the context of alien species or alternative histories. In spite of the barrage of postmodern narratives in popular American culture, *Star Trek* continued to flourish with *Deep Space Nine, Voyager, Enterprise* and numerous feature films. Utopian humanism was prevalent in spite of a pervasive lack of faith in narratives of progress. In response to Rothstein's question — "is there even widespread conviction now that there is such a thing as progress?" (15) — *Star Trek*'s continuing voyages seem to answer "yes."

The legacy of *Star Trek* is, as I have suggested, the creation of a popular culture universe. This legacy is apparent in perhaps the most sophisticated example of a popular critical utopian narrative, the refashioned *Battlestar Galactica*. But while *Battlestar Gallactica* establishes some degree of continuity with the *Star Trek mythos,* the critical utopian epistemology of *Battlestar Galactica* is immediately distinguishable from *Star Trek*'s classical utopianism. *Star Trek*'s spiritual humanism is founded upon a recuperation of the essential self that locates the alien species as Other. Romulans, Klingons, even Vulcans, are projections of a human self. In *Battlestar Galactica,* the human self exists only in relation to the artificial and alien Cylons. Indeed, several narrative arcs of the show are founded upon a symbiosis of human and Cylon. In Season Two, a child is born of a human–Cylon union that the President of the Colonies describes as the future of human–Cylon relations. In spite of *Battlestar Galactica*'s mainstream television audience, the ontology of the self as human–Cylon is nearer to Deckard's replicant in the postmodern archetypal *Blade Runner* than *Star Trek*'s humanism. The utopianian (critical) imaginary of *Battlestar Gallactica* seems indeed far removed from Roddenberry's earlier form of humanism. As Silvio and Johnson persuasively argue of *Battlestar Gallactica,* "the relationship between the utopian and the hegemonic — utopia's role as bribe — is intentionally made explicit so that the viewer might see — and begin to ask questions about — the ideological function utopian narratives serve" (50). This critical awareness of the fallibility of the utopian narrative form seems at best a vague disturbance in the *Star Trek mythos.*

Perhaps what resonates in the spiritual humanism of *Star Trek* is its optimism in the future of a world beset by political and social turmoil. If postmodernism's ethos seeks out the detritus of a utopian vision, *Star Trek*'s recuperation of the ideal, the unfailing belief in one's Self and society, is certainly more appealing. It is, as DeLillo suggests in his examination of the American dream, about *longing.* In the rejection of the critical utopian spirit, and in the apparent absence of a real model of social and political change, the longing for a past ideal is all the more resonant. For Roddenberry, and DeLillo, there is something profoundly human about this.

Works Cited

Alexander, David. "Gene Roddenberry: Writer, Producer, Philosopher, Humanist." *The Humanist* 51.2 (1991): 5–30.

Atkins, Dorothy. "*Star Trek:* A Philosophical Interpretation." In *The Intersection of Science Fiction and Philosophy.* Ed. Robert E. Myers. Westport, CT: Greenwood, 1983. 93–108.

Barrett, Michele, and Duncan Barrett. *Star Trek: The Human Frontier.* Cambridge, UK: Polity, 2001.

DeLillo, Don. *Underworld*. London: Picador, 1997.
Galdieri, Christopher J. "Alexis de Tocqueville's *Democracy in America* and the American Enterprise." *Extrapolation* 42.1 (2001): 65–74.
George Orwell. Vol. 3. Ed. S. Orwell and I. Angus. Harmondsworth, UK: Penguin, 1970.
Hutcheon, Linda. *Irony, Nostalgia, and the Postmodern*. 14 February 2008
Jameson, Fredric. "Utopianism and Anti-Utopianism." *The Jameson Reader*. Ed. Michael Hardt and Kathi Weeks. Oxford: Blackwell, 2000. 382–392.
Kapell, Matthew Wilhelm. "Speakers for the Dead: *Star Trek*, the Holocaust and the Representation of Atrocity." *Extrapolation* 41.2 (2000): 104–114. [Reprinted this volume as Chapter 5.]
Kreitzer, Larry. "The Cultural Veneer of *Star Trek*." *Journal of Popular Culture* 30.2 (1996): 1–28.
Kumar, Krishan. *Utopianism*. Minneapolis: University of Minnesota Press, 1991.
Le Guin, Ursula. *The Dispossessed: An Ambiguous Utopia*. New York: HarperCollins, 1974.
Lyotard, Jean-Francois. *The Postmodern Condition: A Report on Knowledge*. Trans. Geoff Bennington and Brian Massumi. Minneapolis: University of Minnesota Press, 1993.
More, Thomas. "Utopia." *Ideal Commonwealths*. Ed. Henry Morley. London: Routledge, 1885.
Moylan, Tom. *Demand the Impossible: Science Fiction and the Utopian Imagination*. New York: Methuen, 1986.
Orwell, George. "Arthur Koestler." *The Collected Essays, Journalism and Letters of*
Plato. *Republic*. Ed. Benjamin Jowett. 3d ed. Oxford: Clarendon, 1888.
Rothstein, Edward. "Utopia and its Discontents." *Visions of Utopia*. Ed. Edward Rothstein, Herbert Muschamp and Martin E. Marty. New York: Oxford University Press, 2003. 1–28.
Swift, Jonathan. *Gulliver's Travels*. New York: Norton, 1970.

Films Cited

Blade Runner. Dir. Ridley Scott. Screenplay Hampton Fancher and David Webb Peoples. Warner Bros., 1982 (Director's Cut, 1991).
Day the Earth Stood Still, The. Dir. Robert Wise. Screenplay Edmund H. North and Harry Bates. Twentieth Century–Fox, 1951.
Gattaca. Dir. Andrew Niccol. Screenplay Andrew Niccol. Columbia, 1997.
Invasion of the Bodysnatchers. Dir. Don Siegel. Screenplay Daniel Mainwaring. Allied Artists, 1956.
The Terminator. Dir. James Cameron. Screenplay James Cameron and Gale Anne Hurd. Orion Pictures, 1984.
The Thing (from Another World). Dir. Christian Nyby. Screenplay Charles Lederer. RKO Radio Pictures, 1951.

Television Cited

Battlestar Galactica. Developed by Ronald D. Moore. 2003–2009.
Seinfeld. Created by Larry David and Jerry Seinfeld. 1989–1998.
X-Files. Created by Chris Carter. 1991–1997.

Star Trek *Media Cited*

Star Trek *Films*

Star Trek: The Motion Picture. Directed by Robert Wise. Screenplay by Harold Livingston. Paramount Pictures, 1979.

Star Trek II: The Wrath of Khan. Directed by Nicholas Meyer. Screenplay by Jack B. Sowards. Paramount Pictures, 1982.

Star Trek III: The Search for Spock. Directed by Leonard Nimoy. Screenplay by Harve Bennett. Paramount Pictures, 1984.

Star Trek VI: The Undiscovered Country. Directed by Nicholas Meyer. Screenplay by Nicholas Meyer and Denny Martin Flinn. Paramount Pictures, 1991.

Star Trek: The Original Series

"City on the Edge of Forever." Written by Harlan Ellison. 6 April 1967.

"Errand of Mercy." Written by Gene L. Coon. 23 March 1967.

"A Private Little War." Written by Gene Roddenberry. 23 August 1968.

"Return of the Archons." Written by Boris Sobelman. Story by Gene Roddenberry. 9 February 1967.

"A Taste of Armageddon." Written by Gene Roddenberry and Gene L. Coon. 23 February 1967.

"This Side of Paradise." Written by D.C. Fontana and Nathan Butler. 2 March 1967.

13

The Kirk Doctrine

The Care and Repair of Archetypal Heroic Leadership in J.J. Abrams' *Star Trek*

STEPHEN MCVEIGH

In 2009 Captain James T. Kirk and the crew of the USS *Enterprise* returned, rebooted and ready to continue their ongoing mission. The nature of their return is timely and provocative. The crew's last appearance in *Star Trek VI: The Undiscovered Country* in 1991 ended with the *Enterprise* setting course for a fairy tale ending. The return begs the question: why now? This new incarnation is not a re-run of the crews' greatest adventures, it is no simple remake or rehash. Yet, crucially, neither is it a complete re-imagining of the original *Star Trek* universe; this is not a new departure from the original material that maintains only a passing relationship to the 1960s television series and subsequent motion pictures. The film's political and mythological tendency, rather, lies between these poles. And this *is* a political film, performing the same kind of maintenance of and reflection upon American heroism and leadership as did the TV series during the aftermath of the Kennedy era.

The Kennedy style was indisputably a refrain throughout Roddenberry's original and a key element of Kirk's persona. In 2009, this political dimension is similarly front and center. The film-makers cite Barack Obama as the political impetus for the reboot. Zachary Quinto, the new Spock, said in an interview for *Entertainment Weekly*, "this is a franchise that offers a hope for unity — and so does Barack Obama. When this movie comes out, and Obama is president, hopefully there will be some parallels." J.J. Abrams, the director and creative force behind the reboot, in the same article, stated that the thing that had attracted him to *Star Trek* was its "unabashed idealism": "I think a movie that shows people of various races working together and surviving hundreds of years from now is not a bad message to put out right now." He goes on to put it even more succinctly: "it was important to me that optimism be cool again" (Jensen). Clearly the filmmakers are keen to tap into the rhetoric of hope and change that was so central to the message of Obama's presidential campaign. However, the extent to which the film is optimistic and idealistic is arguable. This is a universe clearly changed from that with which audiences are familiar. Far from a frontier of unexplored possibilities, it is closer to McCoy's observation to Kirk upon their first meeting: "space is disease and danger wrapped up in darkness and silence." The opening moments of the film reveal not a starscape of idealistic opportunity but of threat and menace, of pain and massive violence. By the movie's end, it is a galaxy that witnesses the destruction of two entire worlds, and the near extinction of two civilizations, one through natural disaster, the other out of vengeful genocide. It is consequently a space where "a peace keeping and humanitarian armada" is transformed into a more overtly military operation, and a United Nations like Federation of Planets is recast into a more NATO like organization on the cusp of a new era of galactic belligerence. In this context, claiming a connection to Obama's rhetoric is disingenuous, a canny marketing device perhaps intended to play into the zeitgeist but it actually bears little relationship to the security context and the type of leadership the film portrays. It is in fact, however surprisingly, the presidential style and leadership of George W. Bush that forms the film's political underpinnings.

The reboot is predicated on a well-worn yet subtly handled time-travel concept. The new *Star Trek* and the original *Star Trek* are both legitimate, connected and co-exist. The new iteration does not cancel out the original. Rather, in the opening sequence of the movie, the Romulan vessel, the *Narada*, captained by Nero, attacks the USS *Kelvin*, and in so doing marks the point at which the timeline bifurcates and the characters and the universe of *Star Trek* spin off on a simultaneously familiar and different course. This concept is rigorously built into the film's narrative. An exchange between the characters on the bridge is illustrative. Kirk suggests that acting unpredictably and not following pre-established arrangements might offer the *Enterprise* an advantage over Nero.

The presence of Leonard Nimoy as Spock authenticates the reboot and acts as the bridge between these parallel timelines. The future Spock, or Spock Prime as he is named in the credits, has had all of the adventures and experiences that the audience has shared over the past 40 years, and acts now as *deus ex machina*, offering context, solutions and the manipulation of vital elements of the new timeline, not least his orchestration of Kirk's friendship with Spock, something not guaranteed without his intervention. This narrative device has the dual capacity to offer new adventures with a notionally new crew (of actors at least) while building in the possibility of future entanglements of old and new, of history and nostalgia. It also forces the audience to ring in the changes, and not all of those changes belong to the twenty-third century. In the movie's terms, the parallelization occurs because of time travel. In reality is occurs because the film is the product of America's passage through the late twentieth and early twenty-first century. This new generation is one and the same as the old generation, but it has absorbed the implications of the recent American past.

The election of Barack Obama over John McCain represents a movement away from Bush's type of nonintellectual, instinctive leadership toward a more reflective, cerebral and thoughtful sort. Obama's victory to some extent dramatizes an urge to re-establish links to a better America, a more inclusive, more intellectual, less belligerent version than that identified with Bush, one that can perhaps wipe the negative connotations of Bush's presidency from the collective memory. And yet Bush's legacy is in many ways a contradictory one. In the immediate aftermath of 9/11, a president without a clear mandate was transformed into a war president and enjoyed some of the highest approval ratings of any chief executive. Amidst even the more discontented assessments of Bush's presidency, one meme recurs: "he kept us safe." The logic seems to be that in the seven years following the attacks on the World Trade Center and the Pentagon, there were no further attacks on American soil. The maintenance of American security was the overriding priority for President Bush after 9/11 and it was a "mission accomplished." The United States was not attacked after the events of September 11, 2001, and that, it seems to be generally accepted, was because Bush did something right.

On a number of levels, *Star Trek* deals with this legacy and is concerned with processing the type of heroic leadership projected by Bush, absorbing the positive qualities and removing the negative. The election of Obama can certainly be understood as a statement, given Bush and Obama are clearly such opposites (Obama's qualities as an intellectual, articulate, cautious, diplomatic Democrat are almost a photo negative of Bush's own). *Star Trek*'s response is more sophisticated though because it seeks not to dismiss or erase Bush, but to absorb him and the qualities he displayed as Commander-in-chief after 9/11, into the archetype of American heroic leadership. In this way, the James Kirk of 2009 can be read as an attempt to rehabilitate Bush and as such Kirk's narrative arc of rebellious youth to starship captain comes into focus as a version of Bush's own journey.

The Warping of Federation Space-Time

The opening moments of the film are a blur as the camera sweeps over the undulating form of the USS *Kelvin*. Accompanying the images is an instantly familiar soundscape of beeps and whirrs from *Star Trek*'s imagined technology. However, this familiarity is shattered as the *Narada*, captained by Nero, a "particularly troubled Romulan" emerges from a black hole and begins a vicious attack upon the *Kelvin*. This unforeseen, inexplicable event will change everything that comes after it. Indeed, it is illustrative to identify what has changed as a consequence of the attack upon the USS *Kelvin*, the event that originates the new timeline. On a macro level, the representation of Earth is immediately striking. No longer is the planet dominated by a benign, global military system, a post-capitalist, post-nation sterile utopia. Earth, bar some architectural detail, seems not so very different from today's reality. The 1960s vision of humanity's future, where all work in the service of a planet wide military bureaucracy was linked very closely to its immediate and pervasive Cold War context. The *Enterprise* and her crew were essentially an advance party, explorers to be sure, but also scouts, looking to identify the direction of the next attack or manipulate the shape of the next conflict. At the beginning of this new *Star Trek*, that function is strikingly different. The crew of the *Enterprise*, Starfleet and the Federation are no longer active combatants in a galactic Cold War of threat and standoff but rather operate as, in the words of Captain Christopher Pike, "a peacekeeping and humanitarian armada." Earth is still visibly at the head of these organizations, but they are now organizations charged with intervening and alleviating suffering throughout the galaxy. Indeed, much of the action revolves around the exploitation of these functions and the *Enterprise* being subsequently drawn into conflict under the banner of relief and rescue missions.[1]

Such a context seems to resonate more convincingly with the state of American identity and mission in the 1990s than at the beginning of the twenty-first century. The collapse of the Soviet Union and the end of the Cold War created an environment wherein social scientist Francis Fukuyama could formulate a thesis heralding "the end of history," a situation where the United States and more specifically its underpinning systems of democracy and capitalism, had emerged victorious over other social and political models, most notably Communism. It was also a period when, because there seemed to be no substantial external threat to American security, the concept of heroic leadership became almost irrelevant. George H. W. Bush's "victory" in Desert Storm in 1991 was forgotten by the election of 1992, and Bill Clinton, his successor, is remembered as the "postmodern president": "Clinton has transcended the classic polarities of politics. Clinton is both left and right. He is the first postmodern President, the first to turn 'anything goes' into a political creed" (Jaffe).

The original crew grappled with just such a context in the *Star Trek VI: The Undiscovered Country*, released in 1991. The film, which explicitly deals with the implications of glasnost, changing historical and political currents and the role of cold warriors once the war is over, ends on a deliberately whimsical note, for all intents and purposes, a fairy tale ending. The reference to *Peter Pan* and the directions to Neverland imply that all is safe, the ending happy. This sense of security, of an unassailable American dominance in foreign affairs is a key feature of the 1990s. A good deal of the power of the new *Star Trek* emerges from its juxtaposition of the course of American history as it was expected to continue in 1991 and the radical change of course it experienced on September 11, 2001. The traumatic effect it had on the United States' (and *Star Trek*'s narrative) is inestimable. In his Address to a Joint Session of Congress following the 9/11 attacks, which was delivered on the 20th September 2001, Bush vividly portrays the implications of this new direction:

> Some speak of an age of terror. I know there are struggles ahead, and dangers to face. But this country will define our times, not be defined by them. As long as the United States of America is determined and strong, this will not be an age of terror; this will be an age of liberty, here and across the world. Great harm has been done to us. We have suffered great loss. And in our grief and anger we have found our mission and our moment. Freedom and fear are at war. The advance of human freedom, the great achievement of our time, and the great hope of every time, now depends on us. Our nation, this generation will lift a dark threat of violence from our people and our future. We will rally the world to this cause by our efforts, by our courage. We will not tire, we will not falter, and we will not fail [Bush "Address"].

Star Trek's narrative hook then is one that resonates with post–9/11 America, with the implications of processing an unforeseen event, without warning or precedent and after which nothing could be as it once was. Just as the Romulan ship emerges quite literally out of nowhere and through an act of unprecedented terror fundamentally changes everything, so too did 9/11. The attacks on the World Trade Center and the Pentagon served notice of a new global situation and established the context of a new war, very different from the last one. This is a war without borders, without geographical and state identities, a clash of civilizations, to borrow Samuel Huntingdon's phrase. In this way, *Star Trek* is an allegory that charts the impact of 9/11 and the onset of the War on Terror. Equally importantly however, just as the galactic context is one that reflects the post–9/11 global situation so Kirk's captaincy is modeled on the Bush character and foreign policy style that emerged from it.

The End of (Federation) History and the New Kirk

James T. Kirk as portrayed by Christopher Pine alludes to and resonates with the forty-third president on a number of levels: biographically, characteristically as well as ideologically and performatively. In so doing it underpins the role with an entirely different model of heroic leadership than that which informed William Shatner's Kirk. Where John F. Kennedy provided the model in the 1960s, the new Kirk is an encapsulation or more precisely a distillation of the life and career of George W. Bush. The emulation is not merely a reflection, but rather, the reconfigured Kirk seeks to make virtues of Bush's leadership style and qualities, to replay his greatest achievements, specifically those which manifested themselves in the days, weeks and months after 9/11, and to incorporate them into the norms of American heroic leadership.

Much has changed within and between all of the characters in *Star Trek*. A great deal of effort has gone into casting actors who are physically identifiable as younger versions of the originals casts' selves. However, beneath the surface verisimilitude, their presentation and interactions have undergone some interesting and revealing shifts. The most important modification occurs in the relationship between Spock, McCoy and Kirk. In *TOS* and the subsequent movies, Spock and McCoy were presented as different elements of Kirk's psyche. To best discharge his duties as Captain, Kirk would invariably seek counsel and opinion from the two men before deciding upon a course of action. Spock provided a cool, scientific, logical, rational perspective, devoid of emotional bias that clouds judgment. Spock's advice frequently considered an issue at the macro level, and his counsel articulated the "big picture." This approach is most famously illustrated by the scene in *Star Trek II: The Wrath of Kahn* (1982) where, moments before he is overcome by radiation in a suicidal attempt to repair the *Enterprise*'s warp drive, he explains why he has sacrificed his own life: "the needs of the many outweigh the needs of the few. Or the one." McCoy's character, a physician (so also a man of science), is in many ways the opposite of Spock. McCoy is often presented as being highly strung, prone to emotional outbursts and keen to point out the things that make humans human. This last element means that McCoy's perspective is often concerned at the micro level, displaying a concern with the individual, regardless of the wider context. It is fitting then that in *Star Trek III: The Search for Spock*, it is McCoy's actions that invert Spock's dying observation (even if it is Kirk who delivers the inversion), leading the entire crew into danger in the quest for their shipmate. An episode from *TOS* illustrates this interplay of characters even more vividly. In "A Private Little War," one of the most obviously allegorical and political episodes in the show's run, Kirk returns to an Edenic planet, Neural, that he had surveyed as a junior officer. At that time it was populated by a tribal but peaceful people. Now, however, the crew finds that one group, the villagers, have been armed with sophisticated weaponry by the Klingons, and are being incited to war against another, the hill people. In this allegory of Cold War hegemony, Kirk's dilemma is how to create a "balance of power" while working within the conventions of the Prime Directive. Running along side the contemporary political context, the fact that in this episode Kirk's actions and dialogue bring him closer to Lyndon Johnson than John Kennedy, the interaction of Kirk, Spock and McCoy is fascinating. In the teaser, Spock is injured by one of the Klingon-supplied weapons, a flintlock rifle, and is consequently removed from the episode, his logical perspective is unavailable to Kirk. As Worland writes, "perhaps Spock's usual role as the outsider who can comment objectively on human foibles might have made him dangerous here. Would the Vulcan have perceived instantly the illogic of the whole situation and denounced the Neural/Vietnam War?" (Worland 115). While the Spock-side of his psyche sleeps, McCoy performs his function as Kirk's emotional aspect and points up the human cost of intervention. Upon finding Kirk training the Hill men in the use of the flintlock rifle captured from the Villagers, McCoy registers his dismay.

The exchange about balance of power externalizes the angst and doubts Kirk has. For a character that repeatedly states his refusal to accept such a thing as a no-win scenario, the problem posed in this episode comes very close to being just that. It is worth noting that "A Private Little War" ends on a downbeat note, not the usual relaxed banter on the bridge that suggests resolution and balance. The tension that exists within Kirk between the coolly rational and the highly emotional and the way that tension is articulated in his relationship with Spock and McCoy is vital to Kirk's character.

In 2009 however, Kirk is a man alone. McCoy is little more than a grumpy, vaguely foul mouthed comic relief. He still has the fiery emotion of DeForest Kelly's McCoy, but is often depicted talking to himself; Kirk is not listening. Spock too has undergone a modification. The authority roles between Spock and Kirk have changed; Spock is captain for the majority of the movie, so he is issuing orders, not proffering advice. This does not mean the Kirk follows those orders and, when he repeatedly rejects Spock's orders to rendezvous with Starfleet, is in fact ejected from the *Enterprise* for his refusal to do so. Immediately before his removal from the ship, the two argue over the strategic value of adhering to the order to rendezvous rather than pursuing Nero and rescuing Captain Pike. This exchange is instructive insofar as it reminds the audience that the old Kirk never needed to be told to follow orders and further delineates what is new about the new Kirk. For the majority of the film, Kirk and Spock clash, each suspicious of the others legitimacy and motives, and even once the inevitable rapprochement occurs, they remain clearly individual, their conception of themselves and their roles remain very different.

Kirk, the film suggests, does not need to court opinion, to seek the advice and support of those around him. This stands in contrast to the original Kirk. In *TOS* episode "Arena," Kirk is driven to exact revenge upon the perpetrators of a massacre on a Federation outpost. The *Enterprise* pursues the aggressor's vessel, Kirk pushing the ship's engines to dangerous levels so as to catch up to the vessel and destroy it. In an exchange that conveys single-mindedness akin to the new Kirk, Spock offers his opinion on the Captain's actions. In the exchange, Kirk clearly rejects his logical side and acts out of emotion. As the episode progresses, it becomes apparent that they themselves may be the invaders, the Federation having located a base within the aliens' territory. It is the case that Kirk's instincts are not infallible, even if his actions ultimately redeem him.

In the new film, Kirk's instincts are central to his heroic and leadership credentials. In his first meeting with Pike, the Starfleet veteran neatly articulates this aspect of Kirk's character, saying: "That instinct, to leap without looking ... in my opinion it is something Starfleet's lost." The privileging of the instinctive means Kirk comes to resemble one of the most influential early and lasting portraits of Bush in the immediate aftermath of 9/11. In Bob Woodward's *Bush at War* (2002), the journalist sketches Bush as a man of action who relies on instinct over intellect:

> the president spoke a dozen times about his "instincts" or his "instinctive" reactions, including his statement, "I'm not a textbook player, I'm a gut player." It's pretty clear that Bush's role as a politician, president and commander in chief is driven by a secular faith in his instincts— his natural and spontaneous conclusions and judgments [Woodward 342].

This portrayal of Bush is prevalent: Carolyn B. Thompson and James W. Ware in *The Leadership Genius of George W. Bush* argue that "Much of Bush's success as a leader is explained by his willingness to trust his gut" (250). "[He] has an uncanny instinct for when to fight, when to concede, when to run, when to wait out, when to start a venture." (254). Such observations of Bush's anti-intellectualism is certainly not intended to be a criticism. Indeed it is actually an endorsement and connects Bush to the archetypal American mythological system of the frontier. Bush had engaged frontier/western imagery from the very beginning of the crisis, talking of smoking out the perpetrators and alluding to wanted posters as an illustration of the kind of justice he was seeking for the atrocity. Crucially, the invocation of this language and imagery played incredibly well with the American public, offering an accessible script with which to detail Bush's plans to prosecute the War on Terror. In this there is another matrix of connections tying *Star Trek*, Kirk and Bush together. The original *Star Trek*'s relationship to the frontier is strong and influential, from the opening voice over and its reference to the "Final Frontier" to Gene Roddenberry's initial pitch for the series as "Wagon Train to the Stars." In 2009 this constellation of connections is still incredibly potent. Indeed, it is important to note that the Western is a genre that has made an unexpected and revealing comeback in the political climate of the War on Terror. However, there are differences. If the original was a pioneer tale depicting the adventures of people who embody the skills of the frontiersman, lighting out for new territory, the new *Star Trek* takes its inspiration more directly from the popular western, with the lone gunfighter at the forefront.

A new James Kirk is quite literally born in the opening moments of *Star Trek*. His birth coincides almost precisely to the onset of a new historical context. In keeping with the western image system, Kirk is presented from the very beginning as the ultimate frontiersman: he is born simultaneously at Frederick Jackson Turner's "meeting point of savagery and civilization" in spatial terms and John Kennedy's "New Frontier" in a temporal sense. The original series was able to tap into the rhetoric of Kennedy's "New Frontier," a political metaphor that evoked the uncertainty of the future on the threshold of the 1960s. The type of frontier narrative at the core of the 1960s incarnation of *Star Trek* was that of the pioneer experience, heading for new territory, mapping and charting, opening passages and blazing trails for those that would follow, laying the way for settlement and civilization. This is reconfigured in 2009. The frontier narrative moves away from the wagon train and toward the Western, in its literary and cinematic modes. Bush's similarly central and prolific use of the frontier is more identifiably pop-cultural and nostalgic, evoking the form's binary morality and triumphalism. *Star Trek* reflects this by depicting an impressive collection of Western tropes: the Midwestern landscape of Kirk's early years, bar brawls, shootouts with "guns" (not phasers), half breeds, promises broken to a minority group of homeless wanderers, who were once miners, moving through the galaxy in a ship shaped like tumbleweed, massacres, revenge, a clear good guys/bad guys moral structure, regenerative violence, individualist morality.

At the center of this is Kirk, retooled from an able organization man to a rebellious outsider, yet possessing the skills and temperament, the sheer will for leadership. These he has acquired not through a formative period consisting of hard work and education, as Spock's early years are presented in the film, but rather these qualities are innate, notionally inherited from his father. This is another dimension to the Kirk/Bush connection. Both have to live up to the legacy of their respective fathers. In the film, Kirk receives a beating at the hands of a number of Starfleet cadets which is broken up by Captain Pike.

However, the Kirk-Pike exchange that follows implies that there is a sense of shame or embarrassment, that somehow Kirk's father is a failure, something Pike corrects and which can be seen as a sort of epiphany for the young Kirk, allowing him to begin his ascendancy to starship captain.

This recalls Bush's relationship to his father's legacy, living in his shadow, and proud of his achievements, but somehow feeling he did not go far enough, especially in his handling of the latter stages of the Gulf War, by not taking Baghdad and removing Saddam Hussein. Bush's repetition of his father's rhetoric in his statement upon receiving news of the second plane hitting the World Trade Center is illustrative of this vexed relationship:

> "Terrorism against our nation will not stand," he said, echoing the famous "This will not stand" formulation his father had used 11 years earlier when he faced his greatest challenge after Iraq invaded Kuwait in August 1990. Bush felt his father's declaration of resolve on the White House lawn several days after the invasion was among his finest moments as president. "Why I came up with those specific words, maybe it was an echo of the past," the president said later. "I don't know why.... I'll tell you this, we

didn't sit around massaging the words. I got up there and just spoke.... What you saw was my gut reaction coming out" [Woodward 16].

Both characters react to these imposing father figures in a similar manner, both rebel, destroys cars, gets drunk, and brawl in bars, and it is interesting to see how similar the representation of the young Bush is to Kirk in Oliver Stone's biopic, *W.*, the first cinematic treatment of Bush's life.

This, then, is a very different Kirk, with his difference predicated on the changed context he is born into and his difference seems to changes those around him as a consequence. Old Kirk may have been impetuous and unorthodox but he was clearly part of the system. In *TOS* episode, "The Galileo Seven," while en route to deliver medical supplies, Kirk orders a shuttle with seven crew members to investigate a strange anomaly. The craft is pulled off course and crashes on the surface of a barren planet populated by a violent, primitive race. While on the planet surface the crew work to repair the shuttle, on board the *Enterprise*, Kirk is unable to do anything, the anomaly having disrupted the sensors' abilities. The drama of the episode is compounded by the presence of High Commissioner Ferris, who is traveling with the *Enterprise* to make sure that the medical supplies arrive in time. He gives Kirk a deadline by which they must stop searching and leave behind the shuttle's crew if necessary. What is surprising is that Kirk accepts the deadline and adheres to it with only the slightest resistance. In contrast, the new Kirk, while clearly of the system, stands outside of it, a position evidenced in the subversion of the Kobayashi Maru test most obviously, but also in such details as his uniform, which for much of the movie is different from everyone else's and his disregard for the Starfleet practice of informing them of the *Enterprise*'s location or plans.

In terms of character then there is much in the new *Star Trek* to connect Kirk with aspects of Bush. But they do not stop at such biographical and characteristic convergences. An even richer vein of similarities and references presents itself when one considers the ideology of the two men.

The Kirk Doctrine

The differences between the Kirk of *TOS* and in J.J. Abrams' film are profound and reflective of America's changing role in the world. Where the original Kirk was essentially reactive and operated within the Cold War paradigms of containment and deterrence, the new Kirk exists in a post-state context where containment is impossible and the enemies' motivations so fanatical that deterrence or negotiation are meaningless. This contrast offers perhaps the most illuminating dimension to the Bush analogy: Kirk's actions are a twenty-third century enactment of the Bush doctrine, an essential component of the War on Terror.

The National Security Strategy of the United States (2002) constructed the foundational character of the Bush doctrine. The document's opening lines establish its principles: "The United States possesses unprecedented, and unequalled, strength and influence in the world. Sustained by faith in the principles of liberty, and the values of a free society, this position comes with unparalleled responsibilities, obligations and opportunities." From this starting point, which is makes a neat summation of the principles that might underlie a "peacekeeping and humanitarian armada," the NSS proceeded to elaborate new and controversial directions for American foreign policy: pre-emption, unilateralism, forceful interdiction, the export of American democracy and the War on Terror.

Historians have elaborated upon the revolutionary nature of the Bush foreign policy, the way it fundamentally altered America's conduct of international relations. Former Vice-President Al Gore commenting upon the NSS in a speech entitled "Iraq and the War on Terrorism" in 2002 said it outlined "one of the most fateful decisions in history: a decision to abandon what we have thought was America's mission in the world." (Gore). Kirk's doctrine too has changed in the post–*Kelvin* universe in which he lives and his promotion to Captain at the end of the movie suggests it will be adopted to deal with the new galactic context. A comparison of their doctrines further unlocks *Star Trek*'s importance in re-shaping archetypal images of American heroic leadership.

Daalder and Lindsay in *America Unbound: The Bush Revolution in Foreign Policy* (2003) delineate what was revolutionary about the Bush doctrine. They identify that it was not the goals that had changed but the means of achieving them:

> In his first thirty months in office, he discarded or refined many of the key principles governing the way the United States acted overseas. He relied on the unilateral exercise of American power rather than on international law and institutions to get his way. He championed a proactive doctrine of pre-emption and deemphasized the reactive strategies of deterrence and containment. He promoted forceful interdiction, preemptive strikes and missile defenses as means to counter the proliferation of weapons of mass destruction.... He preferred regime change to direct negotiations with countries and leaders that he loathed.... And he tried to unite the great powers in the common cause of fighting terrorism and rejected a policy that had sought to balance one power against another [3–4].

This description is readily mapped onto the thoughts and actions of Kirk in the new film. When the Nero demands Captain Pike shuttle across to the *Narada*, elements of all these issues can be detected in the advice offered by Kirk and Spock.

Pike is clearly representative of the traditions of Starfleet, and is being advised that the old ways are no longer viable. This is because the nature of the threat represented by Nero is new. This is no longer a standoff between the superpower binary of the Federation and the Klingons. Nero is a fanatic and he has declared something akin to jihad on those he perceives allowed his home world to be destroyed. It is crucial to note that he has not come back in time simply to prevent or mitigate the effects of the natural disaster that has vaporized Romulus in the future. He also wants to destroy the Federation, one planet at a time. The annihilation of every civilization that constitutes the Federation is, he believes, the only way to secure his own. The implications of Nero's statement of destruction echo the Bush administration's interpretation of the aims of the enemy in the War on Terror: nothing less that the eradication of an entire way of life. This is the enemy Bush detailed in speeches throughout his presidency. In the same speech where Bush identified 9/11 as establishing his and America's "mission and moment," he told America and the world that "this is civilization's fight." More recently, in a speech delivered at the Veterans of Foreign Wars national convention in Kansas City, on August 22, 2007, Bush describes a conflict which fits precisely the war Nero is waging:

> I stand before you as a wartime President. I wish I didn't have to say that, but an enemy that attacked us on September the 11th, 2001, declared war on the United States of America. And war is what we're engaged in. The struggle has been called a clash of civilizations. In truth, it's a struggle for civilization. We fight for a free way of life against a new barbarism — an ideology whose followers have killed thousands on American soil, and seek to kill again on even a greater scale [Bush, "Veterans"].

Just as the events and aftermath of 9/11 had precipitated a new foreign policy direction for Bush, Nero's attack also necessitates the adoption of a new strategy. However, the requisite shift in strategic thinking is resisted. Kirk and Spock argue at length about the best course of action to deal with Nero and rescue Pike. Kirk's suggestion is a clear articulation of an element of the Bush doctrine: "What we need to do is catch up to that ship, disable it, take it over and get Pike back."

However, Spock is against this strategy of forceful interdiction and prefers to return to the fleet, to regroup and discuss how best to proceed. Spock, in an effort to maintain his authority, incapacitates Kirk and jettisons him from the ship. A subsequent exchange between Spock and McCoy succinctly articulates *Star Trek's* approach to redeeming the positive qualities of a controversial and problematic presidency. The dialogue about a logical choice vs. the right choice contains the essence of the film's absorption of Bush into the model of heroic leadership: imperfect, impulsive *but necessary*. Following guidance from Spock Prime whom he meets on the ice planet, once back on the ship, Kirk manipulates Spock into admitting that he is emotionally compromised and thus not fit to captain the *Enterprise*. As Pike made Kirk First Officer before he left for the *Narada*, this admits Kirk to the captain's chair. Once there he articulates his doctrine: "I know you were all expecting to regroup with the fleet but I am ordering a pursuit course of the enemy ship to Earth. I want all departments to battle stations.... Either we're going down or they are."

This then lays bare how *Star Trek* is working to incorporate Bush, by celebrating the pro-active vision while not allowing, in their telling of the tale, the negative outcomes to intrude. It accomplishes this very simply: Kirk's instincts are always right, from when to leap from a car careening off a cliff, to the recognition of the repetition of conditions surrounding the *Narada*'s first attack to running in the correct direction, away from the ice monsters but towards Spock Prime. And once in command, he orchestrates Nero's defeat. A key feature of Kirk's success using Bush's methods is to witness Spock endorse them. At the end of the movie, Kirk and Spock have thwarted Nero's genocidal plans and all but destroyed the *Narada*. In what seems to be an act of compassion redolent of his 1960s incarnation, Kirk offers to take aboard the stricken Romulans, who earlier had destroyed Vulcan. While this could be seen as Kirk beginning to think and act like his original incarnation, or is perhaps an example of an Obama-like urge to diplomacy, it is also a test for Spock. Kirk is not making a genuine offer of assistance. In the earlier scene between McCoy and Spock in which the two discuss whether sending Kirk away was the right thing to do, McCoy invokes an old Earth saying: "If you're going to race in the Kentucky Derby, you don't leave your prize stallion in the stable." Spock observes that the analogy is interesting because a stallion must first be broken, suggesting that is precisely what he has accomplished with Kirk. However, once Spock signals his wish not to bring the Romulans aboard, to go against the clear logic Kirk expounds, it is Spock who is "broken," who has altered his thinking and converted to the Kirk doctrine. Fortunately for all concerned, the offer is unequivocally refused by Nero. Even if the original Kirk would not have accepted the answer and brought them aboard anyway, this response guiltlessly and without tarnishing his heroic credentials, allows Kirk to cathartically and spectacularly blow the ship out of existence, avenging his father and establishing his style of heroic leadership in monumental fashion.

Conclusion

Describing what they call "The New Heroic Paradigm" Lawrence and Jewett write in terms that illuminate this new Kirk. They argue that the American archetypal hero is of "pure motivations" [on] "a redemptive task [and with] extraordinary powers." They continue:

> He originates outside the community he is called to save, and in those exceptional instances when he resides therein, the superhero plays the role of idealistic loner ... his desire for revenge is purified.... When he is threat-

ened by violent adversaries, he finds an answer in vigilantism, restoring justice and thus lifting the siege of paradise" [47].

This is not the type of heroism displayed by Kirk in the original series, a heroism predicated upon duty and responsibility to his ship and all the souls aboard her. Kirk, the Cold Warrior, finds his will constrained by the military structures he is bound by, and his personality mediated between the extremes of logic and emotion represented by Spock and McCoy. In J.J. Abrams' reworking of Kirk, however, he is removed from such constraints, unbound, and is able to act instinctively, from the gut and without interference. And like the generations of frontiersmen before him, who endure because of their innate abilities, Kirk's gut reactions are *always* right, an approach to leadership and crisis management Bush, "the decider," frequently projected and claimed for himself.

The newest *Star Trek*, then, is not simply another reboot, another TV franchise dusted off and freshened up by a Hollywood that has run out of original ideas. Rather, the film reengages one of the most important and influential popular cultural artifacts of the twentieth century. When the *Enterprise* headed for Neverland at the end of *Star Trek VI: The Undiscovered Country*, she did so because the kinds of big questions that *Star Trek* had always dealt with had been resolved. Perhaps inevitably, such triumphalism was short-lived and the events of 9/11 once again opened up an entire galaxy of military conflict, intercultural clashes and moral dilemmas. And so the original crew of the USS *Enterprise* has returned, with modifications informed by the narratives and characters dealing with the aftermath of that traumatic day.

In some ways this first *Star Trek* of the new franchise is an origins picture, detailing how the crew came together, how certain individual characters were formed. Having established the context, the ground zero for the franchise and adopted a heroic style for the archetypal man who will lead them, it will be interesting to see the threats and challenges the crew will meet in the future and the strategies they employ to meet them while continuing to push the boundaries of the Final Frontier.

Notes

1. This shift in perspective can be detected in the *Star Wars* prequels. In *The Phantom Menace* (1999), Lucas creates a Jedi Order that fulfils the role of a peace-keeping organisation at a time before Bush stole an election and terrorists felled the World Trade Center. That role changes in *The Attack of the Clones* (2002) wherein the Jedi have become generals of the Army, clearly no longer standing apart from conflict.

Works Cited

Bush, George W. Address to a Joint Session of Congress following the 9/11 Attacks, 20 September 2001. *www.americanrhetoric.com/speeches/gwbush9lljointsessionspeech.htm* (Accessed 14 July 2009).

_____. Remarks to the Veterans of Foreign Wars national convention in Kansas City, 22 August 2007. *www.nytimes.com/2007/08/22/washington/w23policytext.html* (Accessed 11 July 2009.)
Daalder, Ivo H., and Lindsay, James M. *American Unbound: The Bush Revolution in Foreign Policy*. Washington, D.C.: Brookings Institution, 2003.
Franklin, H. Bruce. "*Star Trek* in the Vietnam Era." *Film and History* 24:1–2 (1994: February/May): 36–46.
Fukuyama, Francis. *The End of History and the Last Man*. New York: Free, 1992.
Gore, Al. "Iraq and the War on Terrorism." Speech to the Commonwealth Club, San Francisco. 23 September 2002. *www.smh.com.au/articles/2002/09/24/1032734162294.html* (Accessed 12 July 2009.)
Hellman, John. *American Myth and the Legacy of Vietnam*. New York: Columbia University Press, 1986.
Huntington, Samuel P. *The Clash of Civilizations and the Remaking of World Order*. London: Simon and Schuster, 1997.
Jensen, Jeff. "*Star Trek*: New Movie, New Vision." *Entertainment Weekly* 24 October 2008. *www.ew.com/ew/article/0,,20233502,00.html* (Accessed 1 July 2009.)
Joffe, Josef. "The First Postmodern President: Bill Clinton Uses Both Sides of the Road and That's Why He'll Win a Second Term." *Time International Magazine* 7 October 1996, 148:15. *www.time.com/time/international/1996/961007/essay.html* (Accessed 13 July 2009.)
Lawrence, John Shelton, and Robert Jewett. *The Myth of the American Superhero*. Grand Rapids, MI: William B. Eerdmans, 2002.
McNeill, William, "The Care and Repair of Public Myth." *Foreign Affairs*, Vol. 61, No. 1 (Fall 1982), pp. 1–13.
National Security Strategy of the United States 2002. *www.au.af.mil/au/awc/awcgate/nss/nss_sep2002.pdf* (Accessed 3 July 2009.)
Neumann, I. B. "Grab a Phaser, Ambassador": Diplomacy in *Star Trek*. *Millennium: Journal of International Studies*, Vol. 30, No. 3. (1 December 2001), 603–624.
Thompson, Carolyn B., and Ware, James W. *The Leadership Genius of George W. Bush: 10 Common Sense Lessons from the Commander-in-Chief*. New York, Wiley, 2003.
Woodward, Bob. *Bush at War*. New York: Simon & Schuster, 2002.
_____. *Plan of Attack*. New York: Simon & Schuster, 2004.
Worland, Rick. "Captain Kirk: Cold Warrior." *Journal of Popular Film and Television*, 16. 3 (Fall 1988): 109–117.
_____. "From the New Frontier to the Final Frontier: *Star Trek* from Kennedy to Gorbachev." *Film and History* 24:1–2 (1994: February/May): 19–35.

Films Cited

Star Wars Episode I: The Phantom Menace. Directed by George Lucas. Screenplay by George Lucas. Lucasfilm, 1999.
Star Wars Episode II: The Clone Wars. Directed by George Lucas. Screenplay by George Lucas and Jonathan Hales. Lucasfilm, 2002.
W. Directed by Oliver Stone. Screenplay by Stanley Weiser. Lions Gate, 2008.

Star Trek *Media Cited*

Star Trek *Films*

Star Trek. Directed by J.J. Abrams. Screenplay Roberto Orci and Alex Kurtzman. Paramount Pictures, 2009.

Star Trek II: The Wrath of Khan. Directed by Nicholas Meyer. Screenplay by Jack B. Sowards. Paramount Pictures, 1982.

Star Trek III: The Search for Spock. Directed by Leonard Nimoy. Screenplay by Harve Bennett. Paramount Pictures, 1984.

Star Trek VI: The Undiscovered Country. Directed by Nicholas Meyer. Screenplay by Nicholas Meyer and Denny Martin Flinn. Paramount Pictures, 1991.

Star Trek: The Original Series

"Arena." Story by Frederick Brown. Teleplay by Gene L. Coon. 19 January 1967.

"The Galileo Seven." Story by Oliver Crawford. Teleplay by Oliver Crawford and S. Bar-David. 5 January 1967.

"A Private Little War." Story by Jud Crucis. Teleplay by Gene Roddenberry. 2 Feb 1968.

14

Conclusion

The Hero with a Thousand Red Shirts

MATTHEW WILHELM KAPELL

My very first *Star Trek* book was given to me as a gift in 1993. It was *Star Trek: The Next Generation Technical Manual*. Not exactly an exorbitant gift, but the young lady who presented it to me joked that it was worth "at least a dime" and proceeded to spend many more days poking fun at my "*Star Trek* dime novel." At the time I didn't know precisely what a "dime novel" was, but today I remain impressed by her insightful analysis of the book — and by implication the entire *Trek* franchise — by way of a joke.

Why insightful? Because it was through the dime novel that the *mythos* of the American West was created — in much the same way that my "dime novel gift" of *Star Trek: The Next Generation Technical Manual* helped create another kind of *mythos*. And while dime novels do not represent an actual American West any more than the content of my *Star Trek* manual represents a "real" technical manual, both aid enormously in an understanding of the production and consumption of such media.

The Technical Manual has detailed schematics of *The Next Generation*'s entire USS *Enterprise-D*, virtually deck by deck, as well as additional information about the *Star Trek* universe. I had watched *Star Trek* prior to receiving my "dime novel gift," but through exploring the manual, was offered an entrée into an entire universe, rich with information and history of our cultural universe and the "history" of *Star Trek* as well. My gift-giver was right: in a very real sense *The Technical Manual*, like other books before and since, is a kind of postmodern dime novel. Thus, these books — many actual novels, many "technical manuals" — along with other material made by both professionals and fans of the *Star Trek* franchise, much like dime novels themselves, have created a continuing and ever-evolving *mythos*. And, like the relationship between the dime novel and the historical American West, the relationship between *Star Trek* and the associated "other" media products is key to understanding its success culturally and — as this book attempts to assess — mythologically.

Dime Novels and the Mythography of Star Trek

The dime novel was key to the process of making the myth of the American West and, perhaps more importantly, in making the West "American." As the original "pulp fiction" in America, the Beadle & Adams "Dime Novel" series that was first published in 1860 gave name to a type of literature that already existed, and helped create a *mythos* of the American frontier. The small, brief novels introduced American culture to heroes of Western expansion and so-called American Exceptionalism — some based on real people, some about wholly fictional characters. Printed in large numbers, claiming authenticity despite a less than correlative relationship to anything resembling the facts, dime novels were, first and foremost — as their name indicates! — *cheap*. The dime novel was part of what Kent Steckmesser called the "typical cycle" of legend-making about the American West, from "biographies, histories, novels, juveniles, movies, and television plays" (247) making it necessary, in any understanding of the cultural significance of the American West, to take into account, "a study in history, fiction, and folklore" (xii). Thus, to understand how Americans conceive the concept of the frontier one must examine the "fantasy West," as contributor to this volume Stephen McVeigh noted in his *The American Western*, by looking to "dime fiction, Wild West re-enactments, literary fiction and film" (13). While the frontier experience for Americans might have been an historical process, how Americans understood that process involved much more than simply history — and was usually wholly contradictory to history.

Star Trek has followed a very similar path to its perennial popularity. An original series of limited success became, after the first *Star Trek* convention in 1972, a cultural construct unlike any other. The folklore of *Trek* conventions, the contemporary "dime novel" manifestations of the hundreds of inexpensive mass-market paperback novels, the fan fiction written by uncounted numbers of individuals and groups, all contribute to the *mythos* of *Star Trek*. This mythic cycle is neither new, nor surprising.

An example of such mythmaking serves to illustrate exactly how such "myths and legends" are created. Steckmesser, in his cultural examination of *The Western Hero in History and Legend*, traces the story of "Wild Bill" Hickok and his legendary gunfight with the (allegedly) train-robbing "McCanles Gang." The historical veracity of Hickok's gunfight, in which some members of the outlaw gang were supposedly killed, cannot be verified — we still don't know if it happened as has been repeatedly reported! However, the culturally heroic version that depicts "Wild Bill" confronting the McCanles Gang can be followed through various forms of literature, something Steckmesser does with great care. He notes that "by 1931 [the McCanles gunfight] had appeared in an autobiography (1879), a biography (1880), a dime novel (1882), a popular anthology (1907), a novel (1923), a movie (1923), a *Saturday Evening Post* article (1926) and countless newspapers" (247).

Of course the fictional character of James T. Kirk has no relationship with any kind of factual history at all. However, by 2009 it is possible to trace the character through the original *Star Trek* (1966–9) series, seven films (1979–1994), and William Shatner's autobiographies of his time on the original series: *Star Trek Memories* (1993), of the films, *Star Trek Movie Memories* (1994), and his quasi-ethnographic examination of his fellow actors and *Trek* fans, *Get a Life!* (1999). William Shatner has even added to the *mythos* of James T. Kirk by co-writing many of his own, non-canonical *Trek* novels, including *The Return* (1996) in which a post–*Star Trek: Generations* Kirk is resurrected by the evil Borg. There are countless other novels such as Diane Carey's story of the young Jim Kirk's second trip into space, *Best Destiny* (1992), and multiple award-winning writer Vonda McIntyre's version of the very first mission of the entire crew, *Enterprise: The First Adventure* (1986). Add to this the countless contributions of fan fiction from the late 1960s onward, including the "slash" fiction positing a romantic relationship between Kirk and Spock, of which Diane Marchant's "A Fragment out of Time" (1974) is generally cited as the first. There is also the fan-produced "second five-year mission" of the *Enterprise* in *Star Trek: Phase II* (2003–present) with James Cawley as Kirk, and the newest *Star Trek* (2009) with Chris Pine as Kirk. In short, there is as much material for James T. Kirk as there ever was for "Wild Bill" Hickok. And, like Hickok, the information available is frequently contradictory, always open for debate among those who care, and is continually evolving. And while "James T. Kirk" might not be an historical personage, the "historical" Hickok wasn't particularly related to the mythic "Hickok" referenced in the "history" of the American West, either!

Thus, both Kirk and Hickok are very much mythical constructs. Tracing the myth-making tendencies of the countless creative forces behind *Star Trek* is about as easy as doing so for Hickok in the American West. And if, at times, it seems as though the future history of the United Federation of Planets is, to paraphrase nineteenth century historian and proponent of heroes in history Thomas Carlyle, the biography of the Great Men who were Captain of the *Enterprise* (or *Defiant*, or *Voyager*) then that, too, is an indication of the *mythos* of *Star Trek*. To undertake an examination of *Star Trek* is to take part in a study of myths and symbols, both terms open to far too many definitions to be easy to work with. Henry Nash Smith, in his classic 1950 book on myth and symbol of the American West, *Virgin Land*, begins with a famous apology, one easily as applicable to this volume. "The terms 'myth' and 'symbol' occur so often in the following pages," he writes, that the reader deserves some warning about them. I use the words to designate larger or smaller units of the same kind of thing, namely an intellectual construction that fuses concept and emotion into an image. The myths and symbols with which I deal have the further characteristic of being collective representations rather than the work of a single mind [v].

It is the contention of this book that, like Smith's *Virgin Land*, or Steckmesser's *The Western Hero*, *Star Trek*'s mythic images, ideas, contentions and pretensions are the most important part of the franchise. Where Smith and Steckmesser had to contend with myths and symbols that bear some relationship to the thing we have come to call "history" *Star Trek*, quite obviously, does not.

That difference, however, really does not matter at all.

From the perspective of understanding the cultures that produced such stories, "Wild Bill" Hickok's gunfight with the McCanles gang has as much bearing on reality as James T. Kirk's reprogramming of the simulator to "win" the Kobayashi Maru test. Both are equally important for an understanding of the originary culture, regardless of the "truth" of either story. It is the fact that the story is told, over and over again, in different ways and at different times and with different details, that makes it mythical. And, it is in the retelling of the tale that the viewer (or reader, or listener) is really experiencing a story about themselves and their society — which is precisely what *Star Trek* provides us.

In organizing the various contributions to this volume I've taken religious scholar Darcee L. McLaren at her word when she notes that "if ... *Star Trek* is a modern myth, then it will have multiple meanings, it will be interpreted differently by the same people at different times and by different people at the same time" (233). This is why, in organizing a book containing roughly half reprints, an effort has been made to allow those scholars whose work reappears here to add a contemporary statement. The astute reader will note that while their opinions have stayed the same in many ways, they have also been altered by changes in both contemporary culture and in the *Star Trek mythos* itself.

Thus, I am sure that, in twenty years' time, returning to those scholars who have here original essays and eliciting a re-statement, we would also find that for them the *mythos* of *Star Trek* has continued to evolve — as has their understanding of the idea of "myth" itself.

Star Trek*'s Eternal Return*

Each contributor to this volume, then, operates with their own working definition of myth, and of the *mythos* of *Star Trek* specifically. As a result, each essay captures a moment in time of both *Trek* and of each contributor's fluid perception of how myth functions within that narrative. But even more than this, each contributor produces — in an admittedly very specialized and analytical way — a narrative about understanding *Star Trek*. Each essay is a narrative examination of what continues to be an important form of myth-making in the contemporary world. The myth scholar Bruce Lincoln notes in his *Theorizing Myth*, quite rightly I think, that students and scholars of myth tend to be, "particularly given to producing mythic, that is ideological, narratives, perhaps because the stories they tell about storytelling reflect back on them as storytellers themselves" (209). This is especially true of the contributions here: each analysis of the *mythos*—what Lincoln calls, the "ideology in narrative form" (207)—of *Star Trek* also does much to suggest the perspective of the writer. Each contributor tells their own "story" of what *Star Trek* means and why it is important.

Yet each contributor to this book, regardless of how critical they are in their analysis of *Star Trek*'s use or abuse of various mythic structures, do seem to agree on the importance of such mythic analysis—and on the importance of *Star Trek* as a contemporary form of myth. And, in each case, each scholar is able to show that such an analysis gives *Star Trek* the ability to shed light on those stories humans tell each other, time and again. It is in the telling of such stories that humans—all humans, across time, from the African savannah two million years ago to *Trek* fans in their living rooms today—are attempting to understand the world and their place in it. And it is in the retelling of such stories that we affirm what we consider to be important for each person living a life.

It is in the retelling of such stories that J.J. Abrams' 2009 *Star Trek* film finds itself. The producers call it a "reboot" of the franchise, but in reality it is yet another retelling. It is the modus operandi of myth to tell similar stories in a multitude of ways, after all. So, while the details differ, the mythic themes in Abrams' *Star Trek* are both subtly different and, strangely constant. Both fans and scholars will debate (as McVeigh does here) how the differences change the film's overall meaning, but at its heart the newest *Star Trek* remains a mythic journey. And as with all myth, truth remains unimportant—the fact that the voyages of the Starship *Enterprise* are really all fantasy is important only because it is through that fantasy that *Star Trek* adds to our understanding of the human condition. As myth scholar William G. Doty has noted, part of the purpose of myth—and also a key to understanding the mythic significance of *Star Trek*—is that "myths do not attempt to replace empirical explanations but *to add to their lot*" (446, emphasis in original).

Star Trek's *mythos* allows it to take viewers beyond simple logic, science and quantifiable knowledge. In a contemporary world increasingly dominated by the *logos* of computers and work schedules, technological and pharmaceutical fixes to age-old problems, the stories *Star Trek* tells are more than the simple technological solutions we have come to expect. *Star Trek*, instead, adds to the mythic basis of contemporary society by retelling stories as old as our species in ways understandable to the modern and postmodern viewer.

Growth and change are keys to both personal and cultural evolution, and the creators, characters and fans of *Star Trek* know this. In *Star Trek: The Motion Picture* a mysterious cloud enshrouding a space probe approaches Earth and, once again, the crew of the *Enterprise* is called upon to both comprehend it and save the planet. When it becomes obvious that the probe, V'Ger, is on a quest of growth beyond its machine self Spock tells Kirk that, "logic and knowledge are not enough." Kirk replies that, "what V'Ger needs in order to evolve is a human quality ... our ability to leap beyond logic." That leap beyond the logical mundane everyday life is, fundamentally, the purpose of myth in general and a journey *Star Trek* continually allows its viewers to experience. *Star Trek* is a much more serious undertaking than starships and phasers, humanoid aliens with ridged foreheads, and violations of the laws of physics might suggest.

James T. Kirk is also not the only Kirk to understand this need to surpass the obvious, empirical and logical part of existence. It was a different Kirk—British classical myth scholar Geoffrey S. Kirk—who might have made this most clear. "Myths," he wrote, "often have some serious underlying purpose beyond the telling of a story" (41). And thus, in many different ways—yet in the spirit of both Kirks—each contributor to this volume has unearthed some of those many serious underlying purposes that, together, make up the collective *mythos* of *Star Trek*.

Works Cited

Carlyle, Thomas. *On Heroes, Hero-Worship, and the Heroic in History*. Lincoln: University of Nebraska Press, 1966.

Doty, William G. *Mythography: The Study of Myths and Rituals*. 2d ed. Tuscaloosa: University of Alabama Press, 2000.

Kirk, G. S. *Myth: Its Meaning and Functions in Ancient and Other Cultures*. Cambridge: Cambridge University Press, 1970.

Lincoln, Bruce. *Theorizing Myth: Narrative, Ideology, and Scholarship*. Chicago: University of Chicago Press, 1999.

McLaren, Darcee L. "On the Edge of Forever: Understanding the *Star Trek* Phenomenon as Myth." Star Trek *and Sacred Ground: Explorations of* Star Trek, *Religion, and American Culture*. Ed. Jennifer E. Porter and Darcee L. McLaren. Albany: State University of New York Press. 231–244.

McVeigh, Stephen. *The American Western*. Edinburgh: Edinburgh University Press, 2007.

Smith, Henry Nash. *Virgin Land: the American West as Symbol and Myth*. Cambridge: Harvard University Press, 1971.

Steckmesser, Kent Ladd. *The Western Hero in History and Legend*. Norman: University of Oklahoma Press, 1997.

Sternbach, Rick, and Michael Okuda. *Star Trek, the Next Generation: Technical Manual*. New York: Pocket, 1991.

Star Trek Media Cited

Star Trek *Films and Web Series*

Star Trek. Directed by J.J. Abrams. Screenplay Roberto Orci and Alex Kurtzman. Paramount Pictures, 2009.

Star Trek: The Motion Picture. Directed by Robert Wise. Screenplay by Harold Livingston. Paramount Pictures, 1979.
Star Trek: Phase II. Various Writers. Fan Produced Web Series, 2003–present. *http://www.startreknewvoyages.com/*.

Star Trek *Written Sources*

Carey, Diane. *Star Trek: Best Destiny*. New York: Pocket, 1992.
Marchant, Diane. "A Fragment Out of Time." *Grup* #3, 1974.
McIntyre, Vonda N. *Enterprise: The First Adventure*. New York: Pocket, 1986.
Shatner, William. *Star Trek Memories*. New York: HarperCollins, 1993.
_____. *Star Trek Movie Memories*. New York: HarperCollins, 1994.
_____, Judith Reeves-Stevens and Garfield Reeves-Stevens. *The Return*. New York: Pocket, 1997.

About the Contributors

Djoymi Baker is a lecturer in cinema studies and cinema management at the University of Melbourne, Australia. Her dissertation "Broadcast Space: TV Culture, Myth and *Star Trek*" won the Chancellor's Prize for Excellence. Her work on *Star Trek* fandom has been published in the online journal *Refractory*; on *Star Trek* as cosmology in Kate Daw and Vikki McInnes' 2008 book *Bureau*; and on the relationship between stardom and the mythic heroes from *Doctor Who* and *Star Trek* in an anthology edited by John Perlich and David Whitt (McFarland, 2010). Recent work on the epic genre — a not entirely unrelated passion — can be found online in *Senses of Cinema*.

Peter J. Claus is a professor emeritus of anthropology and Asian studies at California State University East Bay, Hayward. His primary field is southern India, and he has published several books and numerous articles on folklore and oral traditions of this region, including *South Asian Folklore, an Encyclopedia* (jointly edited with Margaret Mills and Sarah Diamond; Routledge, 2004) and *Oral Epics in India* (jointly edited with Stuart Blackburn, Susan Wadley and Joyce Flueckiger; University of California Press, 1989).

Bruce Isaacs has a Ph.D. from the University of Sydney where he teaches film, literature and other aspects of popular culture. His 2008 book *Toward a New Film Aesthetic* (Continuum) is a work ostensibly about his love of all things filmic. That love has also resulted in chapters in Kapell and Doty's *Jacking In to the Matrix Franchise* (2004) and Kapell and Lawrence's *Finding the Force of the Star Wars Franchise* (2006), among other publications.

Richard R. Jones is a professor of anthropology at Lee University in Cleveland, Tennessee. Recent publications include articles on chant, Coptic monasticism, religion and anthropology, and Joseph Greenberg in the *Encyclopedia of Anthropology* (Sage, 2006), and essays on kinship systems and values in anthropology in *21st Century Anthropology: A Reference Handbook* (forthcoming). He also contributed "Religion, Community, and Revitalization: Why Cinematic Myth Resonates" for Kapell and Doty's *Jacking In to the Matrix Franchise* (2004).

Matthew Wilhelm Kapell edited, with John Shelton Lawrence, *Finding the Force of the Star Wars Franchise* (2006) and, with William G. Doty, *Jacking In to the Matrix Franchise* (2004). With training in biological anthropology and American history, he has published on human biology and genetics, the utopian fiction of Mack Reynolds, media studies, and Christian romance novels. He is in the Department of Political and Cultural Studies at Swansea University in Wales, working in the American studies and war and society programs.

Roger Kaufman is a founding member of the Institute for Contemporary Uranian Psychoanalysis, the first organization devoted to gay-centered psychoanalytic theory and practice. He is also an adjunct faculty member for the master's degree in clinical psychology program at Antioch University Los Angeles, where he received his M.A. in 1999 following a B.A. from Brown University in 1983. His writings on gay-centered archetypal psychology and film have been published in several books and periodicals, including Kapell and Lawrence's *Finding the Force of the* Star Wars *Franchise*, the *Jung Journal*, the *Journal of Analytical Psychology*, the *Los Angeles Times*, *White Crane Journal*, and the *Gay & Lesbian Review Worldwide*.

Jeffery S. Lamp holds a Ph.D. from the Trinity Evangelical Divinity School in Deerfield, Illinois, and is a professor of the New Testament at Oral Roberts University, Tulsa, Oklahoma. The author of *First Corinthians 1–4 in Light of Jewish Wisdom Traditions* (Edwin Mellen), he has contributed to several dictionaries, journals, and collections of essays (this is his third essay contribution related to *Star Trek* and religion), and is co-editor of the Studies in Bible and Early Christianity Series (Edwin Mellen). He is an elder in the Mid-America Conference of the Free Methodist Church of North America.

John Shelton Lawrence is an emeritus professor of philosophy at Morningside College. With Robert Jewett he has coauthored *Captain America and the Crusade against Evil* (2003) and *The Myth of the American Superhero* (2002; American Culture Association "best book"). He has written for *Hollywood's White House* (2003), *Hollywood's West* (2005), and *Why We Fought* (2008). With Matthew Wilhelm Kapell he co-edited *Finding the Force of the* Star Wars *Franchise: Fans, Merchandise, and Critics* (2006). He has recently written articles on comics and popular culture for the British magazine *Philosophy Now*. He wrote about *Star Trek* for the first time in his book, with Robert Jewett, *The American Monomyth* (1977).

C. Scott Littleton is a professor of anthropology, emeritus, at Occidental College in Los Angeles. Littleton received a Ph.D. in anthropology from UCLA in 1965 and taught at Occidental till 2002. He is a specialist in Japanese religion, the legends of King Arthur and the Holy Grail, and comparative Indo-European mythology, and has written *The New Comparative Mythology* (1982), *From Scythia to Camelot* (with Linda A. Malcor, 2000), and *Shinto* (2002). He published a memoir, *2500 Strand: Growing Up in Hermosa Beach, California, During World War II* (2008), and a science fiction novel, *Phase Two* (2009).

Stephen McVeigh is director of the War and Society Program at Swansea University in Wales. His teaching and research explores American political culture and military history in literature and film. He is the author of *The American Western* (Edinburgh University Press, 2007) and his essays have appeared in Engel's *Clint Eastwood: Actor and Director* (University of Utah Press, 2007) and Kapell and

Lawrence's *Finding the Force of the Star Wars Franchise* (Peter Lang, 2006). He is writing a book on the Second World War propaganda movies of several key Hollywood directors, an essay exploring the mythic dimension of 1980s American cinema and an article on the Spanish Civil War.

Ace G. Pilkington has a D.Phil. in Shakespeare, history, and film from Oxford University and is a professor of English and history at Dixie State College. He is the author of *Screening Shakespeare from Richard II to Henry V*, a book about *Star Trek*'s best screenwriter. Pilkington is an active member of the Science Fiction and Fantasy Writers of America, and his work has appeared in *Astounding, Asimov's, Weird Tales*, and *Serve It Forth!* (Anne McCaffrey's collection of sf recipes). His essays about *Star Trek* have appeared in *Literature/Film Quarterly* and he wrote "Galaxy Quest" for Robert Kahn's *Movies: The Ultimate Insider's Guide*.

Jennifer E. Porter is co-editor, with Darcee L. McLaren, of *Star Trek and Sacred Ground: Explorations of Star Trek, Religion and American Culture* (SUNY Press, 1999) and an associate professor of religion and popular culture at Memorial University of Newfoundland. Her research and teaching interests include the religious elements of such popular franchises as *Star Trek, Harry Potter, Buffy the Vampire Slayer*, and *Star Wars*, the latter leading to an essay on fandom and religion in Kapell and Lawrence's *Finding the Force of the Star Wars Franchise*. She is currently exploring the religious dimensions of Disney films, theme parks, and fan communities.

Wm. Blake Tyrell is a distinguished professor of classics at Michigan State University. His most recent book is *Word Power: Building a Medical Vocabulary* (3rd ed., Focus Press, 2009). His first book was *A Legal and Historical Commentary to Cicero's Oratio pro Rabirio perduellionis reo* (Hakkert, 1978). Five years later came *Amazons: A Study in Athenian Mythmaking* (Johns Hopkins University Press, 1984). The inaugural issue of a new journal, *Psychocultural Review*, included his "Dionysus in Sendak's Night Kitchen." He has also written books on Sophocles' *Antigone*, Greek mythmaking, Greek athletics, and the life of Sophocles.

Index

Abrams, J.J. 28, 79, 90, 197–210, 217
"Accession" (*DS9*) 115, 116, 120, 126
Alien film series 148
aliens 13, 20, 23, 46, 49, 54, 56, 58–60, 67, 71, 82, 85, 86–87, 93, 104, 108, 115–116, 119, 125, 129, 132, 133–134, 141, 152, 153–154, 164, 168, 171, 183, 187, 190–191, 193, 194, 218
"All Good Things..." (*TNG*) 14, 96, 106, 108
allegory 201, 202
American Exceptionalism 214
American Monomyth 12, 93–111
"Amok Time" (*TOS*) 57, 170
"The Andorian Incident" (*ENT*) 168–170
Andorians (fictional species) 168–170, 173
anima 145
anthropology 11, 29, 50n, 76n
Apollo (Greek god) 44, 81–82, 99–101
Apollo Program (NASA) 4–6, 93
"The Apple" (*TOS*) 21, 23
Archer, Captain Jonathan (character) 52, 53, 138, 166–168, 169, 171–173, 175–176
archetype 11, 13–14, 68, 93, 94–95, 145–146, 149, 199
"Arena" 47, 203
Argonauts 46
Armageddon 95
Armstrong, Karen 6–7
astronauts 5, 6, 12, 93
"Awakening" (*ENT*) 171

Bajorans (fictional species) 67–68, 72–75, 112–113, 115–122, 124, 125–126
"Balance of Terror" (*TOS*) 55
Barthes, Roland 186
Bashir, Dr. Julian (character) 74, 83
Battlestar Galactica (television series) 194

Bellamy, Edward 69
Beowulf 82
Berman, Rick 68, 74, 164
Bible 29, 82, 113–126, 171, 172
"The Big Goodbye" (*TNG*) 133
Bladerunner (film) 191, 194
Borg (fictional species) 64, 96, 156–7, 158, 215
Borg Queen (character) 63, 64, 96, 157, 158, 159
"Bread and Circuses" (*TOS*) 167
"Broken Bow" (*ENT*) 165, 166, 167–168
Bush, George H.W. 200
Bush, George W. 13–14, 198–210
"The Cage" (*TOS*) 49, 131

Campbell, Joseph 65, 94, 100–101
Cardassians (fictional species) 67, 72–75, 96, 120, 123, 126
Catholic Church 13, 163–174, 179
Catholicism 72, 170, 171, 174–176, 177–178
Celestial Temple 115, 118, 119, 124, 126
Celestine Prophecy, The (Redfield) 172, 173
"Chain of Command (parts I and II)" (*TNG*) 73
Chakotay, Commander (character) 104, 105, 158
Chapel, Nurse Christine (character) 102
Chekov, Lieutenant Pavel (character) 58, 99
Chomsky, Noam 135
Circe 46, 86–87
"The City on the Edge of Forever" (*TOS*) 97, 167, 183, 192–193
Cold War 95, 98, 182, 183, 185, 200, 202, 206, 210
Coon, Gene 26n6, 45
Crusher, Dr. Beverly (character) 102

"Daedalus" (*ENT*) 177
Daniels, Marc 45, 81
"Darmok" (*TNG*) 133, 140
Data, Commander (character) 52, 104
"Datalore" (*TNG*) 133, 139
The Da Vinci Code (Brown) 172, 173
Dax (character) 83; Jadzia Dax 119; Ezri Dax 122
"The Day of the Dove" (*TOS*) 56
Deep Space and Sacred Time (Wagner and Lundeen) 5, 149
USS *Defiant* 215
DeLillo, Don 193, 194
Derrida, Jacques 186
de Saussure, Ferdinand 134–135
"Destiny" (*DS9*) 116, 119, 120, 122
"The Devil in the Dark" (*TOS*) 55, 133
"Devil's Due" (*TNG*) 99
Diaspora 67, 73
Dime Novels 69, 213, 214–6
"Divergence" (*ENT*) 89
"The Dogs of War" (*DS9*) 119
"The Doomsday Machine" (*TOS*) 57, 78
Doty, William 2, 156, 217
"Duet" (*DS9*) 74
Dukat, Gul (character) 118, 122, 124

ego 86, 109, 146, 150, 151
"Elaan of Troyius" (*TOS*) 82, 101, 108
Eliade, Mircea 21, 47
"Emissary" (*DS9*) 74, 115, 116
"The Enemy Within" (*TOS*) 55, 59
"Ensign Ro" (*TNG*) 73
USS *Enterprise* 1, 4, 6, 7, 10, 19, 20, 21–23, 25, 26, 37, 38, 40, 44, 45–49, 55, 56, 57, 58, 60, 68, 77, 79, 82, 84, 87, 90, 93, 95, 96, 98, 99–103, 106, 108, 109, 123, 140, 141, 178, 184, 190, 191–192, 197, 191, 197, 198, 200, 202–203, 206, 208, 210, 215, 217, 218; USS *Enterprise-D* 213; NASA Shuttle *Enterprise* 4
"The Enterprise Incident" (*TOS*) 55
Epic of Gilgamesh 14, 46, 47
"Errand of Mercy" (*TOS*) 20, 56, 132, 185, 191,
"Evolution" (*TNG*) 133
"Ex Post Facto" (*VOY*) 88–89
"Extreme Measures" (*DS9*) 74

"Favor the Bold" (*DS9*) 117, 120
Ferengi (fictional species) 132
Fern, Yvonne 103, 109
first contact 140, 164, 166,
The Fisher King 46–47
Fontana, D.C. 26n6, 27n15, 45

"For the World Is Hollow and I Have Touched the Sky" (*TOS*) 21
"The Forge" (*ENT*) 167, 171, 172, 175, 177
Franklin, H. Bruce 97, 98
"Friday's Child" (*TOS*) 56
Frye, Northrop 20, 26n7

"The Galileo Seven" (*TOS*) 206
Gattaca (film) 189, 191
Genocide 12, 73–75, 77–78
Geraghty, Lincoln 164
Gerrold, David 54, 57, 96, 97, 99, 105
"The Gift" (*VOY*) 64, 154, 156,
The Gnostic Gospels (Pagels) 173
Golvin, Sandra Lee 145–147, 154
Greenwald, Jeff 103, 109
Gulf War 205
Gulliver's Travels (Swift) 189, 191

Hassler, Donald M. "Mack" 67
Hercules (television series) 81
The Hero with a Thousand Faces (Campbell) see Campbell, Joseph
"Heroes and Demons" (*VOY*) 89n15
Holocaust 12, 56, 67–79, 184
holodeck 107
"The Homecoming" (*DS9*) 115

IDIC 130, 131; defined 168
Iliad (Homer) 48, 69, 80, 82
"Image in the Sand" (*DS9*) 118, 119, 122
Imperialism 22, 70; American Imperialism 65
"In the Cards" (*DS9*) 124
"In the Hands of the Prophets" (*DS9*) 119, 122
"The Inner Light" (*TNG*) 101
Inside Star Trek: *The Real Story* (Solow and Justman) 4

Jameson, Frederic 188, 189
Janeway, Captain Kathryn (character) 53, 63–64, 85, 87, 103, 108, 138, 144, 148–149, 150–160
Jesus Christ 105, 112–113, 114, 173, 175; as Messiah figure 116–126
"Journey to Babel" (*TOS*) 57, 58
Jung, Carl Gustav 13, 145–146, 148–149, 152
Justman, Robert 4, 97; see also *Inside* Star Trek: *The Real Story*

Kennedy, John F. 4, 9, 197, 201, 202, 205
Kes (character) 63, 149, 151, 152–156

Kim, Ensign Harry (character) 85, 86, 151, 152
King, Martin Luther, Jr. 58, 108
Kira, Major Nerys (character) 74, 117
Kirk, Geoffrey S. 1, 3, 14, 218
Kirk, Captain James T. (character) 1, 6, 9, 10, 14, 21, 22–24, 25, 28, 37, 38, 40, 45–46, 47–48, 49, 52–53, 54, 55–58, 59, 63–64, 78, 82, 83, 94, 95–97, 98- 101, 102–104, 105, 108–109, 138, 140, 185–188, 190–193, 197–210, 215–216, 218
"Kir'Shara" (*ENT*) 170, 171, 172–175, 176, 177, 179
Kitses, Jim 20
Klingons (fictional species) 20, 55–56, 83, 89–90, 96, 97, 103, 129–130, 132, 140, 170, 183, 194, 202, 208
Kobayashi Maru test 109, 206, 216
Korea 93
Kottak, Conrad Philip 10

Langer, Lawrence 71, 72, 79
Leach, Edmund 23, 27n17, 29, 36, 41n1
Le Guin, Ursula 183, 188, 190–191
"Let That Be Your Last Battlefield" (*TOS*) 58
Lévi-Strauss, Claude 12, 29–41, 42–43, 47, 81
Limerick, Patricia Nelson 8
Lincoln, Bruce 3, 5, 217
Logos 3, 4–6, 7–8, 217
The Lord of the Rings (film series) 148, 157
"The Lorelei Signal" (*TAS*) 88
Lucas, George 2, 94, 210n1
Luther, Martin 13, 163, 171–172, 174, 179
Lyotard, Jean-Francois 186, 193

MacArthur, Douglas 75
The Making of Star Trek (Whitfield and Roddenberry) 9, 19, 26n1, 49, 54, 58, 68, 100, 101, 131, 132
Manifest Destiny 8; *see also* American Exceptionalism
McCoy, Leonard (character) 10, 21, 22, 23, 24, 47, 52, 55, 56, 59, 60, 97, 99, 175, 198, 202, 203, 208, 209, 210
"Menage a Troi" (*TNG*) 104
"The Menagerie" (*TOS*) 27n11, 51n36
Messiah 13, 112–126
"Metamorphosis" (*TOS*) 27n12, 57, 139,
"Mirror, Mirror" (*TOS*) 56
Moby Dick (Melville) 82

Mogen, David 10
Monomyth 12, 93, 94; *see also* American Monomyth
More, Thomas 189
Mulgrew, Kate 103, 144
myth (defined) 2–4, 20, 21–22, 30–31, 45, 80–82, 93, 130–131, 164–165, 184, 214
Myth of the American Superhero (Lawrence and Jewett) 12
Mythos 1–8, 11–15, 20, 70, 77–80, 82, 99, 149, 182, 183–184, 186, 187, 194, 213–214, 216–218
Mythscape 93

Narrative 2–3, 5–8, 10, 12, 14, 19–21, 30–33, 45, 53, 68, 70–72, 75, 78–82, 84, 88, 93, 100–5, 112–114, 118, 120–121, 124–126, 164, 175, 182, 184, 185, 186, 189, 190–191, 192–194, 198, 201, 205, 210, 216–217
NASA 4–7, 12, 166
Native Americans 9, 20, 56, 57, 94
NATO 198
Nazi Germany 55, 72, 73, 176
"The Next Phase" (*TNG*) 74
Nichols, Nichelle 58
Nimoy, Leonard 21, 52, 96, 106, 198

Obama, Barack 14, 65, 197–199, 209
O'Brien, Miles (character) 74, 83
The Occupation 67, 68, 72–74, 75
Odo, Constable (character) 83
Odyssey (Homer) 14, 46, 63, 69, 85–88
Okrand, Marc 132, 141n3
"Omega Glory" 98
"11001001" (*TNG*) 133
"Operation: Annihilate!" (*TOS*) 60
Osiris (Egyptian God) 48–49

paradise 21, 23, 25
"The Paradise Syndrome" (*TOS*) 27n12, 57
Paris, Tom (character) 64
"Past Prologue" (*DS9*) 74
"Patterns of Force" (*TOS*) 57, 59
"Penumbra" (*DS9*) 119
Picard, Captain Jean-Luc (character) 1, 14, 52, 53, 63, 73, 99, 102–103, 104, 106, 107, 108, 133, 138, 140
Pike, Captain Christopher (character) 200, 203, 205, 207–208
Piller, Michael 68, 74
Plato 3, 95, 104, 148, 186, 189
"Plato's Stepchildren" (*TOS*) 47, 58

postmodernism 11, 12, 146, 147, 170, 178, 186, 193, 194, 200, 213, 217
post-structuralism 12, 186
"Prey" (*VOY*) 64
The Prime Directive 70, 106, 164, 183, 184, 187, 202
"A Private Little War" (*TOS*) 56, 59, 97, 185, 202, 203

Q (character) 14, 107, 109

race 12, 37, 38, 49, 58, 81, 87, 96, 122, 164, 184, 191, 197, 206
The *Ramayana* 46
"Rapture" (*DS9*) 117, 119, 120, 125
"The Reckoning" (*DS9*) 117, 119, 122
The Reformation 13, 166, 170–171, 174, 176–179
"Return of the Archons" (*TOS*) 183
Riker, Commander William T. (character) 52, 104
Ro, Ensign Laren (character) 73, 74
Roddenberry, Gene 1, 2, 4, 7, 9–10, 14, 19, 21, 24, 28, 45, 49, 52, 57, 58, 68, 95, 96, 98, 100, 101, 103, 104, 109, 131–132, 165, 167, 179, 182, 183, 185–188, 190, 192–194, 197, 204
Romulans (fictional species) 20, 55, 96, 101, 132, 175, 194, 209
Roosevelt, Theodore 8
Rosenfeld, Alvin 71, 73, 76n

"Sacrifice of Angels" (*DS9*) 117, 119, 120
Sato, Ensign Hoshi (character) 139
Schindler's List (film) 68, 72, 75
Scott, Commander Montgomery "Scotty" (character) 56, 99
Seinfeld (television series) 185
Seven of Nine (character) 63, 64–65, 148, 149–150, 155–159
sex 13, 20–21, 23–24, 35, 85, 87, 100–105, 130, 144, 145–159, 165, 168, 169, 184, 191
"Shadows and Symbols" (*DS9*) 117, 119, 120
Shakespeare, William 12, 82
Shatner, William 21, 54, 55, 201, 215
Singh, Kahn Noonian (character) 28
Sinuhe the Wanderer 46
Sirens 85–88, 101
Sisko, Captain Benjamin (character) 13, 53, 103, 138; as Bajoran Emissary 112–126
"Skin of Evil" (*TNG*) 133
slash fiction 13, 148, 215

Slotkin, Richard 98
Smith, Henry Nash 215
Soviet Union 185, 200
Space: 1999 (television series) 20
"Spectre of the Gun" (*TOS*) 56
Spock (character) 21–22, 23–25, 27, 38, 40, 46, 47–49, 52, 55, 57, 58–60, 65, 77, 83, 93, 96, 97–99, 100, 102–104, 106, 109, 132, 164, 175, 185, 187–188, 190, 192, 193, 197, 198, 202–203, 205, 207, 208, 209–210, 215, 218
Star Trek (2009) 52–53, 65, 77, 90, 101, 109, 185, 197–210, 215, 217
Star Trek and Sacred Ground (Porter and McLaren) 13
Star Trek: The Animated Series (1973–1974) (*TAS*) 69, 80, 88
Star Trek: Deep Space Nine (1993–1999) (*DS9*) 12, 13, 27, 52, 53, 67–76, 78, 83–84, 90, 93, 96, 103, 112–126, 131, 183, 184, 186, 193
Star Trek: Enterprise (2001–2005) (*ENT*) 13, 52, 78, 89, 131, 139, 163–179, 184, 186
Star Trek: First Contact (1996) 52, 107
Star Trek: Generations (1994) 52, 103, 215
Star Trek: Insurrection (1998) 52, 104
Star Trek Lives! (Lichtenberg, Marshak, Winston) 21, 96, 97, 101, 102, 106
Star Trek: The Motion Picture (1979) 50n1, 80, 184, 194, 218
Star Trek: Nemesis (2002) 52
Star Trek: The Next Generation (1987–1994) (*TNG*) 14, 27, 52, 69–70, 72, 73 84, 87, 90, 93, 96, 99, 101, 104, 106–107, 110, 112, 131, 133, 139, 140, 175, 183, 186, 188, 213
Star Trek: The Original Series (1966–1969) (*TOS*) 10, 28, 52, 69, 78, 80, 82–83, 84, 87–88, 93, 95–98, 100, 105–106, 131, 132–133, 139, 140, 182, 184, 186–187, 191, 192, 202, 203, 205, 206, 210, 215
Star Trek: Phase II (fan series) 215
Star Trek: Voyager (1995–2001) (*VOY*) 52, 82, 85, 90, 93, 94, 104, 112, 131, 144–161, 163, 186
Star Trek II: The Wrath of Kahn (1982) 57, 78, 185, 202
Star Trek III: The Search for Spock (1984) 48, 170, 175, 191, 202
Star Trek IV: The Voyage Home (1986) 55, 59, 107
Star Trek V: The Final Frontier (1989) 52, 60, 104
Star Trek VI: The Undiscovered Country

(1991) 52, 55, 58, 107, 183, 187, 197, 200, 210
Star Wars (film franchise) 2, 28, 78, 94, 108, 148, 149–150, 157, 182
Starfleet 57, 58, 60, 63, 67, 69, 83, 88, 104, 108, 112, 114, 117, 122, 125, 126, 138, 141, 153, 166, 167, 200, 203, 204, 205, 206, 207
"Strange Bedfellows" (*DS9*) 122
Structuralism 1, 3, 11, 29–40, 42–43, 47, 81, 135, 137; *see also* Levi-Strauss, Claude
Sulu, Captain Hikaru (character) 10, 49, 58
Surak (character) 171–176, 178, 179
Sybok (character) 60, 104
symbol 5, 8–10, 20, 29, 34, 60, 94, 96, 98, 101, 102, 120, 121, 123, 130, 138, 144, 145, 146, 152–153, 155, 170, 215, 216

"A Taste of Armageddon" 56, 57, 183, 191
"Tattoo" (*VOY*) 104
"Tears of the Prophets" (*DS9*) 119, 120, 122
Terminator (film series) 191
"This Side of Paradise" (*TOS*) 22, 23, 59, 187, 191
"Ties of Blood and Water" (*DS9*) 115
"Till Death Do Us Part" (*DS9*) 122
"Time's Arrow (Parts I and II)" (*TNG*) 111
Torres, Lieutenant B'Ellana (character) 63, 96, 151
T'Pau (character) 173, 174
T'Pol, Subcommander (character) 167, 169, 170, 172, 175, 176–177, 178
"Trials and Tribble-ations" (*DS9*) 83–84
trickster imagery 47–48, 49, 52
Troi, Councillor Deanna (character) 103, 104, 107
trope 10, 68–70, 72, 75, 165, 205
"The Trouble with Tribbles" (*TOS*) 56, 57, 83, 97, 140
Tucker, Commander Charles Tripp III (character) 177
"Turnabout Intruder" (*TOS*) 4
Turner, Frederick Jackson 7–10, 20, 204
Tuvok, Lieutenant (character) 64, 152
Twain, Mark 69, 82, 107

Uhura, Lieutenant (character) 10, 49, 58, 184
"Unification (parts I and II)" (*TNG*) 175
United Federation of Planets 10, 55, 56–57, 63, 68, 69, 74, 78, 93, 95–97, 104, 107, 112, 114, 115–117, 121, 123, 125–126, 130, 138, 140, 179, 183, 191–192, 198, 199–200, 203, 208, 215
United Nations 68, 93, 198
"Up the Long Ladder" (*TNG*) 89n14
utopia 10, 13, 59, 68–70, 107, 114, 126, 130, 164, 165–167, 179, 182–194, 200

Vietnam 22, 93, 97, 98, 165, 182, 185, 192, 193, 203
USS *Voyager* 13, 27, 53, 63, 64, 85, 86, 90, 150, 151, 152, 154, 155, 157, 158, 160, 215
Vulcans (fiction species) 24, 38, 48, 52, 58, 59, 65, 77–79, 96, 106, 132, 136, 140, 141, 163–179, 184, 187, 188, 194, 202, 209

Wagner, Richard 2
"*Wagon Train* to the stars" 9, 10, 19, 54, 68, 69, 100, 204
Walker, Mitch 145–146, 147, 148–149, 150–158, 160
War on Terror 201, 204, 206–208
Westerns (narrative) 19–21, 30, 56–57, 69, 205, 214
"What You Leave Behind" (*DS9*) 75, 118, 119, 122
"When the Bough Breaks" (*TNG*) 89n14
"Who Mourns for Adonais?" (*TOS*) 27n12, 44, 81, 82, 88, 98, 100
"Who Watches the Watchers?" (*TNG*) 106
Worf, Lieutenant (character) 83, 84, 94
Worland, Rick 69, 98, 202–203
The World of Star Trek (Gerrold) 54
World War Two 1, 55, 67–68, 74, 75, 97, 192, 193

X-Files (television series) 81, 193
Xena (television series) 81
Xindi (fictional species) 78

"Year of Hell (parts I and II)" (*VOY*) 64
"Yesteryear" (*TAS*) 61n8

www.ingramcontent.com/pod-product-compliance
Lightning Source LLC
Chambersburg PA
CBHW032049300426
44116CB00007B/668